IN SEARCH OF HUMANITY

IN SEARCH OF HUMANITY

The Role of the Enlightenment
in Modern History

by

ALFRED COBBAN

GEORGE BRAZILLER
New York   —   1960

Library of Congress Catalog Card Number: 60-13305

Printed in the United States of America

First Printing

Contents

Preface

THE term 'Enlightenment' is hardly naturalized in English. This is curious, because the intellectual and moral revolution which it describes perhaps obtained its most widespread acceptance and exercised its most lasting influence in Great Britain and the English-speaking world. But although the word is not familiar, and is open to some objection, other possible titles are even less happy. Why, for example, should we describe as the 'Aufklärung' a movement which had, or so I believe, only a superficial and transient influence on the German mind? Again, we can legitimately concentrate on the eighteenth century as 'le siècle des lumières' and give the En-lightenment that title; but at the risk of forgetting that practically all its essential ideas were inherited from the previous century. If we go back to that flowering-time of genius we shall find that it already has a name in the text-books: it is the Age of Reason. And its philosophic rationalism, while in some respects the ally, was also the enemy of the empiricism which was one of the dominant elements in the Enlightenment.

The ambiguities of the term 'reason', and the conflict between empiricism and rationalism, is a second source of confusion about the Enlightenment and one of the reasons why it has been the subject of such different and even contrary interpretations. I do not pretend to be in agreement with all my predecessors on this subject. If Hazard's classic *La crise de la conscience européenne* would fit in very well with my theme, Taine's *L'ancien régime*, Carl Becker's brilliant *Heavenly City of the Eighteenth-century Philosophers*, or Professor Talmon's influential *Origins of Totalitarian Democracy* represent a fundamentally opposed view; and Cassirer's 'Aufklärung', beginning in Leibniz and culminating in Kant, may seem to trace the history of quite another intellectual development, as indeed it largely does. These differing interpretations partly stem from con-centration of interest on the intellectual history of separate countries, and partly from a tendency to exclude, or at least to regard as some-how not part of the general European movement, the development of ideas in Great Britain. It seems to me, on the contrary, that such

7

thinkers as Bacon, Newton, Locke, Hume and Bentham, occupy key positions in the whole evolution of 'enlightened' Europe.

This study of the ideas of the Enlightenment does not, of course, claim to discuss the thought of the seventeenth and eighteenth centuries as a whole. Some of the greatest names in the history of philosophy — Hobbes, Spinoza, Leibniz, Vico, Berkeley, Kant — are omitted, because they do not seem to me to belong to my subject. Again, much of the religious thought of the period has no place here: Law, Butler, Wesley, Malebranche, Lamy, Fénelon, Zinzendorf and many others are alien to the story. Even in respect of the Enlightenment proper it has been necessary to concentrate attention mainly on England and France, and on their greater, or more influential, thinkers. It would have been easy to be less selective and to crowd this study with a thick growth of minor writers and forgotten books, but only at the risk of losing the wood for the trees. My object has been to mark out in its main lines what seems to me a dominant, but often misunderstood, feature in the landscape of modern history, not to itemize every stone or blade of grass composing it.

Nor can I pretend that this is history 'for its own sake', whatever that may mean. I would not have written it if I had not thought that the subject was important, both for the understanding of the historical development of the modern world and in a particular sense for us today. On the contemporary issues that are involved, impartiality is impossible, and if possible would be undesirable. The major part of the book, however, is an historical study of the ideas of the Enlightenment. A short piece I wrote earlier on the Enlightenment produced the criticism that it seemed cool to this great movement and conscious of its weaknesses. This may be true, and I do not apologize for it. Even if the historian is committed in the present, he need not allow that commitment to blunt his faculties in dealing with the past, particularly with a movement which contributed so much to the creation of critical history.

Although the subject of this book is one which has been in my mind for many years, it was an invitation to lecture at Harvard University in 1958 which gave me the stimulus and opportunity to write it. I must express my gratitude to the Harvard History School for the invitation, to the students of Harvard and Radcliffe, who provided such an enjoyable and easy audience, and to Professor David Owen, the Master, and the Fellows of Winthrop House, in whose hospitable walls the first draft of the book was written.

I am indebted to Dr Winifred Edington for her assistance in the task of verifying my references, and to the editors of the *Political Science Quarterly*, *The Review of Politics*, *The Hibbert Journal*, *Encounter* and *History* for permission to use in a revised form some material that has appeared in articles in their pages. Except where otherwise indicated, translations are by myself.

ALFRED COBBAN

University College London. 1959

I

The Problem of the Twentieth Century

EACH age has many problems, but among them one or another seems in turn to take precedence and to present the major threat to society, or to civilized life, if it is not eliminated. In fact – and this is encouraging – such problems seldom are solved: most often they are transmuted by time, fade into the general mass of difficulties that beset every generation, and under the influence of some obsessive new threat are seen to be no longer as fundamental as was once thought. Boom and slump, inflation and deflation, mass unemployment, over-production and under-production, economic crisis in all its forms, presented the basic problem of the 'twenties and 'thirties of this century. In the 'thirties the economic problem became also a political problem, assuming the menacing shape of totalitarianism. This in turn merged into total war, which in the period since the Second World War has mushroomed into the ultimate threat of the atomic or hydrogen cloud. As we look back on these several crises they melt into one another and are seen to be less separable than we may have thought at the time, as well as less novel. Economic distress, political tyranny, war – though now on a larger scale than ever before – are not new. Basic to them all are not the changing though calculable objective facts but the changeless and incalculable human behaviour that can at any moment give urgency to a perennial danger.

To admit so much is to perform the opening gambit in the familiar manœuvre which begins with a platitude and ends with Original Sin, the most convenient, indubitable and compendious of explanations for all human evils. It has many advantages. Since it came about once for all, and so long ago, we ourselves need not feel more than a vicarious responsibility for it. At the same time, since it is now an integral part of human nature, we can hardly be expected to change it, at least in other people, who make up the majority of the human race. Original Sin, as such or secularized as simple human nature, is the perfect scapegoat for all the ills of society.

If, however, we concentrate our attention on human behaviour rather than human nature, the whole argument changes, for human behaviour has frequently been altered in the past and therefore presumably can be altered again. Thinking in terms of behaviour, and forgetting that elusive thing human nature, we may be less willing to seek salvation only by plunging into those mystic depths in which all remedial action is sunk without trace, and more prepared to conceive the possibility of positive effort to counter current evils. It is not unreasonable to approach our problems from this direction. Economic crises, totalitarianism, war, may or may not be the inevitable consequences of human nature. They may be the product of good or bad, noble or ignoble motives. They may be calculated, or unintended, results of our actions. But at any rate they are all aspects of human behaviour, and we deplore them not because of their varying and suppositious motivation, but because of the effects that flow from them. From this point of view they can fairly be considered together, for not only are they bound together historically but their results are fundamentally the same. Economic crisis meant declining standards of life, destitution, and a kind of suspended animation for masses of the people; totalitarianism meant inter alia the murder, torture, exile, or use as slave labour, of incalculable numbers of human beings; and we should have a fair idea what total war in the form of the hydrogen bomb means. All these add up to the deliberate infliction of pain or death on such a colossal scale that it numbs the imagination. Yet it is only the monstrous proportions that prevent us from recognizing what we dislike in all this as a very simple and common thing. On a smaller scale it would be called cruelty. There may be other reasons for objecting to economic distress, totalitarianism and war, but the major reason why we regard them as such great evils is, I suggest, because they are inseparable from the infliction on a colossal scale of otherwise avoidable pain, suffering and death. This may be a mere emotional reaction, but it is a widespread and influential one and it is probably the determining factor in the identification of our major problems; because if we did not have this reaction we should not necessarily have found these forms of behaviour objectionable, or not objectionable in the particular way in which we do. It may be said that such a supposition is inconceivable; but it would only be so if the feeling of revulsion against cruelty is as much to be taken for granted as we are apt to suppose.

That this assumption needs further consideration could easily be demonstrated from the contemporary world. It was brought to my mind during a short pleasure trip along one of London's canals, when the helmsman pointed out a family of ducks – a mother and six or seven ducklings scuttling through the water in the prettiest way. There were nine or ten to begin with, he said, and she will be lucky if she rears two of them. He added, apart from those that will die from cold nights and natural enemies, the boys kill them by stoning. It seemed a pity, but for one's mind to veer to Belsen and Buchenwald was perhaps rather inconsequent. Between killing a baby duckling for pleasure and the murder of six, eight or ten million human beings, the difference is so great that it seems almost indecent to mention them in the same breath. Yet boys, or men and women, have done, or do, both; and one has only to look at popular fiction or films to suspect that many people, even those who would not easily bring themselves to do cruel things, enjoy reading about them or seeing them represented.

The liking for cruelty has come to be regarded as particularly a sexual perversion more or less by historical accident, because it is associated with the name of the marquis de Sade. He enticed young women into his house for the purpose of making scientific experiments, including near-poisoning and flagellation. His was a very mild case and only really notable because he wrote a book to prove that this method of expressing a natural tendency was a good thing. Other books have subsequently been written to show that he was a great if misunderstood moralist. He was undoubtedly rather mad. But the regrettable marquis did not invent sadism, he merely provided it with a name. The Nazi regime in Germany was an exhibition of sadism on a colossal scale, but the scale, not the thing, was new. Cruelty, it must be confessed, is an ingredient in human nature and is to be found in all peoples and at all times.

It is often believed that, say, the Germans, Japanese and Russians, during the last generation, have committed, or acquiesced in, cruelties of such an extensive nature that no other nation could have, or has, been guilty of their like. Yet if, as I have just suggested, a taste for cruelty is so common, why should they be different from the rest of us? The evidence scarcely suggests that they have any monopoly of cruel proclivities. The Nazis had no difficulty in recruiting their torture gangs from the natives of conquered countries. In France the Darnand militia was more feared than the German secret police. The Balts are alleged to have been particularly useful in the extermination camps. The Rumanians outdid the Germans in atrocity when they invaded Russia. The Poles were less efficient in their persecution of the Jews, but they had done their best in the past with slower and more old-fashioned methods. We know about the German concentration camps and the Gestapo. We do not know the death-rate in the forced transfers of population in the Soviet Empire or the number of the victims of the Russian secret police. On the other side of the world, Japanese atrocities during the Second World War are well known: did the Chinese Nationalists and Communists commit none on a comparable scale? Or are atrocities only atrocities when they are committed by the enemy?

But why should this inquiry be confined to the present day? If we go back two or three centuries, the tortures and massacres which have astounded and shocked us so much in recent years would have seemed much more normal and presumably therefore less shocking. Nor need we go to Germany or Eastern Europe, Russia or Asia, for examples. The tortures and massacres in France during the Religious Wars, the still admired proceedings of the Spanish Inquisition, the burning of hosts of unfortunate old women – and sometimes, which was perhaps even more pleasing, young ones – as witches in most Western countries, the ordinary processes of judicial torture – such things, if those involved at any one time were fewer than the victims of the Nazis or Communists, went on much longer and were more a part of normal everyday life. The French Revolution witnessed some tolerably bloody massacres and countermassacres, quite apart from the harvest of the guillotine. What are we to say of Cromwell and his troops in Ireland? Were the Englishmen of those days a different breed from us, with a different nature? It would be a nice question to what extent the use of forced labour in the Soviet Union has exceeded in atrocity or fallen below the English and French exploitation of the slave trade in the past. The only clear distinction I can discover is that the British abandoned the slave trade a century and a half ago, though the Arabs still continue it; the massacres in Ireland took place in the seventeenth century, and the massacres of the Jews and the Russian labour camps in the twentieth.

It is tempting to suggest that this change in behaviour, so far as it has occurred, must be the result of progress in civilization. I hardly think that this view can be maintained in the ordinary sense of the word. For centuries Rome spelt civilization, not by our ideas a very humane one. China, some three centuries ago, might well have been considered the greatest civilization in the world, and the Chinese were famed, rightly or wrongly, as specialists in the art of torture. More recently the Germans, who invented Nazism, reckoned themselves the most civilized of European nations. The United States is technically the most advanced community that the world has ever seen, but the cult of violence is not absent from American life or popular art. In British prison camps in Africa it seems possible that civilization may have been inculcated by beating prisoners to death. If it was ever seriously believed that progress in material civilization necessarily meant a decline in cruelty, that illusion should have been shattered by now.

There may be a suspicion in the mind of the reader that my argument is leading up to some sort of apology for totalitarian excesses. This does not follow from what I have said. What does follow, I think, is that the significant fact that requires explanation is not that all nations have perpetrated cruelties on the grand scale at some time or other, but that some nations have on the whole stopped torturing and massacring people, whereas others apparently have not.

The most profitable line of approach to this problem is to examine a few specific cases to see how and why some national patterns of behaviour have been changed in this respect. For example, why did we stop burning witches? To say that it was because we became more humane is mere tautology: to stop burning witches and doing a lot of other cruel things is to become more humane. The real answer may perhaps be found by asking why we burnt witches in the first place. They were burnt simply because they were, or were believed to be, witches, who by an unholy communion with the Devil had acquired all sorts of dangerous powers. They could make little manikins of their enemies and by mutilating these inflict pains and ills on the persons they represented and ultimately achieve their death. From a distance, by their devilish arts, they could cast diseases on animals, burn down houses, cause children to be stillborn, produce blindness or madness. They stole babies and murdered them for their magical practices. They desecrated all holy things and their covens were conspiracies for the overthrow of all religion and morality.

Various painful devices were the only way of detecting a witch and burning the only safe method of disposing of her. I dare say some, especially the professional witch-hunters, rather enjoyed, as well as profited from, the proceedings; but given the generally accepted facts, the customary methods of dealing with witches, however unpleasant, were logical and necessary. Only when the accepted facts were examined empirically in a scientific spirit and shown to be no facts at all, or misinterpretations of phenomena which had other and more reasonable explanations, did the whole institution of witch-burning break down.

To take another example: French law, like many other legal systems, assumed that the way to discover the truth about a crime, and above all to secure a confession, which was regarded as the only certain proof of guilt, was by torture. This belief in the importance of securing a confession obviously survived in the twentieth century in Russia and Eastern Europe. English law in general did not subject the accused person to torture, but it had an appalling list of capital offences, because it was held that only by savage punishments could crime be prevented. Humane men often lamented the sad fate of criminals or suspected criminals, but alas they knew there was nothing that could be done about it. And nothing *was* done about it until the eighteenth century, when a great school of law reformers ceased lamenting and challenged the assumptions on which the criminal laws were based. Writers like Beccaria and Bentham simply said: your facts are wrong, this is not the best way of detecting and preventing crime. And when their views were put into practice in reformed legal systems they were proved to be correct.

It is not quite so easy to explain why people stopped burning one another for the sake of the true religion, but at least part of the explanation is to be found in a change of opinion about the facts involved in religious persecution. In the sixteenth century, and largely in the seventeenth also, it was practically a universal opinion that two religions could not exist side by side in the same State without tearing society to pieces. Given the experience of many States this was a reasonable opinion. It was held with such axiomatic conviction that it was only really put to the test when, in France, the Politiques, wearied of incessant bloody civil strife, concluded that even such a risky experiment might be worth making. In due course, after a certain number of false starts, it turned out that it was in fact possible for more than one religion to survive, comparatively peaceably, in the same State. In other words, the facts which were assumed in the theory of religious intolerance were at least in this respect wrong.

In each of the examples I have given, a major step in the direction of increased humanity and a notable decrease in man's inhumanity to man was the result, in part, of a more correct appreciation of the relevant facts. But of course this new appreciation would not have been found if it had not been sought, and the fact that it was sought suggests that there may be, as well as an inclination towards cruelty, also a tendency in human nature to condemn whatever is regarded as *unnecessary* cruelty. There is also the implication that, by and large, this tendency is the stronger. This is a reasonable supposition, for if it were not so we should all of us be living all our time in a society no better than Hobbes's State of Nature, and life would be permanently even more nasty, brutish and short than it is.

Moral and humane tendencies presumably provided the motive force for ethical advance in the seventeenth and eighteenth centuries; but they were only released when the empirical investigation of the facts assumed by systems of organized cruelty eliminated their appearance of rational justification. The consequent great reappraisal of social institutions, which brought down many Molochs of cruelty, was largely the work of the empirical and utilitarian thinkers of Western Europe. They did not discover, as is sometimes implied, that men liked what they liked and disliked what they disliked, and that pain fell into the latter category: this was already known. But they concentrated attention on the newly discovered fact that pain is in itself a bad thing. The systematic theory they erected on this basis had its flaws and limitations; but at least it led men to consider whether all the pain which resulted from the normal processes of society was actually necessary in the interests of some higher end. It was soon concluded that it was not.

This was part of the movement known to historians as the Enlightenment. It brought with it a great change, not in human nature but in judgments about human behaviour. In other words, it effected an ethical revolution. This would hardly have been possible unless, in spite of the sadistic elements in man, there were also a disposition to feel disapproval in some circumstances of acts of cruelty, and to express this disapproval in the form of ethical judgments. Now the peculiar character of these is that they are not, in the last resort, susceptible of proof. If I tell you that it is wrong to drive your car all over the road, you may reasonably ask why. To the answer, because this will involve the risk of injuring or killing harmless passers-by, which would be wrong, you may also ask why it would be wrong, but without any reasonable expectation of an answer except in terms of a restatement in fuller terms of the same judgment.

Ethical judgments, it has been suggested, cannot be proved or disproved, because they are data given by experience and not conclusions. Yet they differ from other facts of experience in one important respect. Every sane person knows that if he puts his hand in the fire he will burn it: there is less general agreement, it seems, on ethical matters. This does not necessarily invalidate the ethical judgment, but it means that the problem of differences in ethical judgment cannot be ignored. How was it that English and French, as well as most other nations in the past, and millions of Germans more recently, could regard as good, actions and policies which now seem to us atrociously wicked? To attempt an answer by hypothesizing great differences in human nature is fanciful as well as unnecessary. What we have to explain, as I have said, is not human nature but human behaviour. Obviously there are those who act under the influence of a more or less insane sadism; but when a whole society appears to be thus perverted, some further explanation is required. Exhibitions of cruelty for purposes for public entertainment have been common but are usually of limited scope. Wanton cruelty, by which I mean cruelty purely for pleasure, though it exists, is normally restricted in the interests of the more important ends of social life, which could not be achieved if the tendency to cruelty were allowed unrestricted play. It may, or may not, have been true in the past, but at least in more recent times social and political mesures which involved cruelty of an atrocious nature and on a nation-wide scale have had to be provided with the appearance of a rational justification to enable them to win general acceptance.

This is why organized cruelties, when they are part of the *mores* of a society, are commonly justified on the ground that they are necessary in the interests of some higher end. An apparently rational theory, or better still a religious or pseudo-religious doctrine, is needed for their justification. In the past, religious and judicial systems were perhaps the chief patrons of organized cruelty. In our time this function has largely been taken over by politics. The contemporary problem of cruelty, since it is largely concerned – at least in the forms which have been mentioned in this chapter – with aspects of collective behaviour which are under political control, or subject to political motivation, is therefore a political as well as an ethical one. It presents itself to us only because we pass moral judgments on political behaviour. Now the systematic discussion of such judgments is the function of political theory, and it is therefore to this field that we must look in the first place for a discussion of the problem.

II

The Decline of Political Theory

POLITICAL theory is not a progressive science. At least, anyone who puts, say, Aristotle's *Politics* beside the political writings of the twentieth century could be excused if he thought that progress in the subject is imperceptible. A cynic might even argue that everything that is worth saying on political theory has already been said ad nauseam, and draw the conclusion that it is time we gave up such wearisome reiteration. But this view would be false, because the conditions of social life alter, sometimes more slowly and sometimes more rapidly, in the last few centuries at an increasingly dizzy pace; and as they alter, the words we use, and the ideas they convey, lose old meanings and acquire new ones. For this reason a continual restatement of political principles is both necessary and inevitable — as long, that is, as the tradition of political thinking, which is one of the peculiar characters of Western civilization, remains alive.

It is a tradition with a history of some two and a half millennia, though with one considerable break. Century after century the political ideas of the Western world have undergone progressive modification. The interplay of ideas with institutions has changed now one and now the other, and the flow has been punctuated at intervals by the synthesis created by a great political thinker. No such synthesis has appeared in our own day or for some time past, but this is not surprising. Great political thinkers cannot be produced to order, and we need not wail and beat our breasts because there is no contemporary Burke or Bentham. If a general tendency to cease thinking about society in terms of political theory were to be observable, that would be a matter of greater significance than the mere fact that there are no intellectual giants in the field of political theory today. I propose to suggest that there *is* such a tendency. It has been very evident, for example, in the historical writing of the last generation.

The view that our cherished political ideas may be capable of dying will naturally meet with opposition, yet there is nothing impossible in such a development. Political ideas, like institutions, are not immortal, however we try to identify them with eternal values. Conscious of our own mortality, we cling all the more to the belief that there must be something presiding over our destinies which is eternal. There may be, but it is not likely to be the little gods of our own creation, whether we call them Imperial Rome, or the Divine Right of Kings, or even Democracy. Ideas grow and decay, change into new forms and are reborn. It would be a cause for amazement if the process of continuous transformation were to come to an end while political thinking, as it has existed since fifth-century Athens, still survives.

But does it survive? Conceivably political theory at the present day may *not* be undergoing one of its many metamorphoses, passing through a chrysalis stage before emerging in a new form. It may just be coming to an end. This has happened in the past. Once before in the history of Western civilization a great age of political thought came to an end. The development of Greek political ideas reached its climax in the writings of Plato and Aristotle. In the Hellenistic age attention began to turn away from political theory and into other fields. For a time, with the rise of the Natural Law school of thought and the elaboration of juristic conceptions by the Roman lawyers, it might have been possible to regard the process as still one of growth and development. But in the Roman Empire politics turned into the struggle of court factions and military dicatators, and political thinking as the Greeks understood it ceased.

The experience of the Greco-Roman world is not without relevance to our own time. Some at least of the conditions which accompanied this earlier decline and fall of political theory are repeated today. It is a commonplace that State activity is irresistibly expanding. More and more of the functions of society are falling under the control of bureaucracy and therefore to some extent outside political control. Great scientific military machines are being created, to the support of which more and more of the wealth of society has to be diverted. These are as yet, it is true, the servants and not the masters of the civil power but so were the legions in Rome for a long time, This is an age of revolutions, like the age of Marius and Sulla and Caesar, and revolutions are apt to end in military dictators; in more than a few countries they begin with them as well. The knowledge of this tendency is perhaps one reason why it has hitherto failed to operate in Soviet Russia. In Nazi Germany also the Army was never able to challenge the Party successfully.

Possibly in the new form of party organization a technique has been found for averting military dictatorship and the rule of praetorian guards to which the Roman Empire degenerated. But the substitution of the party machine for the military machine is not necessarily much improvement. It means the rule of a small oligarchy, with political life concentrated in the internal struggles of its factions. Both bureaucracy and party seem also in practice to involve the emergence of a super-bureaucrat or party chief, or both rolled in one, in whom ultimate power is concentrated, and who is himself semi-deified as the incarnation of the State, like the Roman emperors. Since the majority of the population are naturally outside the chosen circle of bureaucracy or party there is also a need, as long as a degree of political consciousness survives in any part of this excluded majority, for a machinery of repression, a system of delation and espionage, political police, concentration camps or prisons, and the rule of universal suspicion – such as Tacitus described in dreadful detail in his imaginative account of the last years of Tiberius, and Camille Desmoulins borrowed for a description of France under the Terror.

It may be said that this picture represents only half of the world, but are these tendencies completely absent anywhere? Contemporaries naturally notice differences. Historians, looking back on an age, are often more struck by similarities. The most fundamental trends in any period are those which exist at the same time in the most diverse and apparently opposed camps. Asked what are the deepest underlying tendencies of our age, we should look for something which communist Russia and capitalist America have in common. At bottom, it seems to me that there are more similarities than either side would be very pleased to admit, and they are sufficient to make the parallel with the ancient world a fair one, though obviously it must not be pushed too far.

The parallel is also noticeable with respect to the decline of political theory. In the period when Caesarism was rising, the ideas associated with the old Roman conception of *libertas* were falling. The connection between new conditions of society and the decline of political thinking may be obscure, but it would be dangerous to suggest that there is none. The rule of 'senatus populusque romanus' led to anarchy when an empire had to be governed instead of a city. Rome was faced with the choice of abandoning the political principles by which it had achieved greatness, or seeing the Roman world degenerate into a chaos of warring States. Its solution was the empire, in which, however, the classic political theories of the city state could find no place, any more than the institutions by which they had achieved some measure of realization. For political theory to exist, it seems to me, there must be an active political life. One does not expect to find it flourishing among Australian aboriginal tribes, in the Russia of Ivan or Peter, the Paraguay of the Jesuits or the empire of the Caesars.

Are there signs — I do not say more — that our own political ideas may be coming to their end as those of the ancient city states did? It would be absurd to suppose that a continual stream of new political ideas, or old ones new-fashioned, is possible or desirable; but there has been rather a long interval since there was last any original political thinking. It is necessary to go back to the eighteenth century to find it. This, I admit, is a sweeping statement, which it would require considerable space to attempt to justify.

But let me present one consideration. The dominant political idea in the modern world is democracy. Most of the contradictions of contemporary politics find their place under the democratic umbrella, but broad as that is they jostle one another, and moreover the umbrella seems to be leaking badly. And where are the political theorists of democracy today? Instead of a rational theory it has become a sort of incantation. It is the open sesame of political treasure hunters everywhere. The world is full of would-be Aladdins chanting 'Democracy'. The masses, at least in those countries which have no experience of democracy, are waiting in a state of mystic faith on the revelation that the word is to produce. Where the idea has been known longer expectations are not so high. Is it unfair to suggest that there is even a certain degree of disillusionment, a feeling that the traditional conceptions of democracy do not answer our greatest problems?

The world of practice is apt to be a generation, sometimes a century, behind the world of original thought. Liberal democratic principles, evolved in the seventeenth and eighteenth centuries, dominated the nineteenth century, which however failed to refashion and think out anew, for the benefit of its successors, the ideas that it was living on. It provided, admittedly, an intellectual ancestry for nationalism and fascism and communism, but that is another story. Meanwhile democracy, for lack of thought, ceased to be a living political idea. It became a shibboleth, and is now not even serviceable as such. A password is no good when all the hostile camps use it indiscriminately. For the most part the democratic idea has ceased to be discussed seriously and in relation to the concrete problems of practical politics. It has become a meaningless phrase. Politicians, like the princess in the fairy-tale condemned to the oracular utterance of frogs, seem scarcely able to open their mouths without some platitude about democracy flopping out, wet and flabby and slightly repulsive, but is this political theory? If it is, no wonder that practical men prefer to ignore it. Coins can remain valid currency even when they are worn quite smooth. Political ideas need periodical recoining if they are to retain their value.

It may be said that this is not a fair argument, that practical politics has always been conducted on the basis of platitudes, and that this is just as well. A Burke was the exception, his fellow member for Bristol, whose political principles were summed up, according to the legend, in 'I say ditto to Mr Burke', the norm; but at least he had a Burke to say ditto to, and besides Burke there existed a great body of informed and serious public discussion on the rights and wrongs of political behaviour. Where will we find a discussion of theoretical questions on the same level today?

Of course, there have been those in the last few decades who have had something significant to say about the contemporary political situation, but the same conclusion about the decline of political theory seems to emerge from a study of their work.[1] The thing that impresses them most about political life is the State as power. They envisage power as a kind of electric force, now diffused and now concentrated, which not merely runs through society but is its very essence. 'The laws of social dynamism', says Lord Russell, 'are only capable of being stated in terms of power.' The wretched individual atoms of which society is composed are massed together, hurled violently about, disintegrated, by power which they did not create and cannot control.

Traditional political theory, in so far as it has failed to recognize this fact, is regarded as no more than a beautiful fairy-tale. To quote Reinhold Niebuhr:

> It may be possible, though it is never easy, to establish just relations between individuals within a group purely by moral and rational suasion and accommodation. In inter-group relations

[1] I am thinking of such writers as Ferrero, Russell, Bertrand de Jouvenal, E. H. Carr, Reinhold Niebuhr, Lasswell, Hans Morgenthau and others.

this is practically an impossibility. The relations between groups must therefore always be predominantly political rather than ethical, that is, they will be determined by the proportion of power which each group possesses at least as much as by any rational and moral appraisal of the comparative needs and claims of each group.[1]

According to Niebuhr the tragedy of the human spirit lies in 'its inability to conform its collective life to its individual ideals'. This is the reason why men 'invent romantic and moral interpretations of the real facts, preferring to obscure rather than reveal the true character of their collective behaviour'. In other words, it is the dilemma of 'moral man and immoral society'. Man, when he became a social and political animal, sacrificed his individual morality to the egoism that is the accompaniment of social life. The complaint is not a new one: it was the theme of Rousseau's *Discourse on Inequality*. But for the modern thinker, unlike Rousseau, there is no resolution to the tragedy of society. Humanity is caught in a cul-de-sac. In such a situation absolute pessimism is unavoidable. There is no possibility of creating, as Rousseau set out to do in the opening chapter of the *Contrat social*, a society in which justice can be allied with utility and authority with freedom, no hope of establishing rational or ethical control.

In a different way the same conclusion was reached by Ortega y Gasset. He wrote:

> We live at a time when man believes himself fabulously capable of creation, but he does not know what to create. Lord of all things, he is not lord of himself. He feels lost amid his own abundance. With more means at his disposal, more knowledge, more technique than ever, it turns out that the world today goes the same way as the worst of worlds that have been; it simply drifts.[2]

All this is degrees of pessimism below Machiavelli. The author of the *Prince* saw society at the mercy of arbitrary power, but believed that somehow evil could be used to achieve good; the tyrant would serve social ends that a better ruler might not be able to fulfil. We have lost the innocence of a Machiavelli now and do not look for

---

[1] *Moral Man and Immoral Society*, 1931, pp. xxii-iii.
[2] *The Revolt of the Masses*, 1932, p. 47.

moral good to be born of political evil. Political pessimism is deeper than it has been since St Augustine wrote the *De Civitate Dei*.

The decline of political theory is not irrelevant to the problem raised in our first chapter. It may be regarded as a reflection of the feeling that ethical values have no place in the field of social dynamics and power politics. This, I believe, is the real significance of 'the revolt of the masses': it means the rise to control of those who live their lives without theory, to whatever class they may happen to belong. Another term for it is the rule of the expert, I mean the technician, the 'Fachmann', to use the German word. Twenty years ago Ortega y Gasset explained what it meant:

> Anyone who wishes can observe the stupidity of thought, judgment and action shown today in politics, art, religion and the general problems of life and the world by the 'men of science', and·of course, behind them, the doctors, engineers, financiers, teachers and so on.[1]

The politician who merely repeats platitudes is no worse than his own experts; and how can he be held responsible for failing to translate political theory into practice if there is no theory to be translated?

There is another way of looking at the decline of political thought. Professor Toynbee sees our civilization going the way of previous civilizations, and consoles himself with the idea that the death of a civilization may be the birth of a religion. Ferrero put it differently: mysticism, he said, is a form of escapism from the horror of illegitimate power. Such was the purport of the early Christian invocation: 'The poet has said, "O lovely city of Cecrops", wilt thou not say, "O lovely city of God"?' And a modern poet echoes the cry:

> Man, frustrated and sleep-forsaken,
> Gloom-regarding from inward sight,
> Sees the city of God unshaken
> Steeply stand in unworlded white;
> Sees, adrift from his faith-lost learning,
> Sun-remote from terrestrial thought,
> Power, envisioned by earth's discerning,
> Peace, by mortal aspiring wrought.[2]

[1] *The Revolt of the Masses*, p. 124.
[2] Siegfried Sassoon, 'Ode' in *Vigils*, 1935.

It is a nobly phrased restatement of an ideal that appeared to men in a former time of troubles, but it is one that belongs to a non-political age. Religious revival *may* be a way out, but it is not a political way, and the religious approach to political problems is not without its dangers. The Nazi Revolution of Destruction gained greatly by being able to drape its horrors in the robes of chiliastic aspiration.

In this analysis – though that is to dignify a brief indication of some contemporary tendencies with too ambitious a title – I may seem to be bent on a pessimistic interpretation of the trend of the modern world; but what I have said so far is only a one-sided view of the current situation. To take it as the whole truth would be to despair prematurely. If it is true that political theory has ceased to develop, is this a sign that political life is in fact coming to an end and that we are entering a non-political age, as the ancient world did. Here one must appeal to a broader view of the facts. The differences are far greater than the similarities. There is little evidence that the world is moving in the direction of universal empire. Bureaucracy is not yet the major reality of government, nor are praetorian guards or political parties yet the masters rather than the servants in any Western country. If there has been a decline of political theory there seems no reason to believe that this is the result of the appearance of a social and political situation in which it no longer has any valid raison d'être. It is rather a symptom of general intellectual malaise, related to the ethical problem which I have taken as the starting-point of this inquiry.

In another age than the present, or society than our own, it might be unjustifiable to pick on the decline of political theory as the major symptom in a diagnosis of its ills. But Western civilization is essentially political, and politics has been its vital centre throughout the modern period, even though the last great age of fundamental political thinking was the eighteenth century. It might seem then that, if this is so, the solution to our problem is not far to seek. To restore ethical values means to revive political theory, and to achieve this what is needed is a return to the ideas of the eighteenth century, to pick up the threads where they were then dropped or broken off.

This solution is too simple. The political ideas of the eighteenth century were part of a world of ideas with its own inner coherence, in which what was political cannot be understood in isolation from the rest. Moreover, this world of ideas was not static but had developed and was continuing to develop. The ideas of the eighteenth century were derived from and depended so intimately on those of the previous century that a line cannot be drawn between them.

A further difficulty lies in the assumption, already implied, that through the two centuries can be traced a single and consistent system of thought. Obviously this should not be read as an assertion that there were no contrary streams of thought or opposing ideas in seventeenth- and eighteenth-century Europe. Without artificial simplification, however, it may perhaps be taken as generally agreed that this period was marked by an important and continuous trend of thought which effected a revolutionary change in the outlook of the educated classes in Europe. If it is true that this was the last great creative age in moral and political thought, and if there is any justification for seeing the problem of the twentieth century as essentially a problem of political morality, then there is evidently a case for a reconsideration of what seems to be relevant among the ideas of the seventeenth and eighteenth centuries. This does not mean only a study of their political thinking, but the identification, discovery and repossession of a whole pattern of thought.

PART TWO

THE FOUNDATIONS OF THE
ENLIGHTENMENT

III

The Rise of Modern Science

CONTEMPORARIES at the time, and historians since, have agreed in characterizing the intellectual developments of the seventeenth and eighteenth centuries by such terms as the Enlightenment, the 'Aufklärung', the Age of Reason or 'le siècle des lumières'. Such descriptions by themselves imply a principle of selection and the exclusion of currents of thought which are not consistent with them. This is obviously necessary. But many of those who have written on what, for the sake of brevity, I will call the Enlightenment seem to me to start not only with such a pre-supposition but also with a judgment framed on the basis of a con-temporary scale of values, which in effect predetermines what they will accept as representative of the Enlightenment and what they will tacitly ignore. Some principle of selection is, of course, inevitable, otherwise we might find ourselves including anything and every-thing in the history of the Enlightenment; but the principle must not be merely a disguised and preconceived verdict.

To say that the seventeenth and eighteenth centuries were marked by great changes in ideas is probably as near as we can come to a neutral statement. It allows us to include in our survey any intellectual developments that can be identified as new. It also provides us with — what is bound to be a somewhat arbitrary choice — a point at which to break into this world of ideas. If we ask what was the most original, and in the long run the most influential new intellectual development of the early modern period in Europe, it is difficult, even considering the rival claims of new forces in religion, literature and art, and allowing for medieval origins or anticipations, to deny that the answer must be the rise of modern science.[1]

[1] Two excellent general histories, which have helped me greatly in this section, are H. Butterfield, *The Origins of Modern Science 1300–1800*, 1949, and A. R. Hall, *The Scientific Revolution 1500–1800: the Formation of the Modern Scientific Attitude* (American edition, 1956).

It would be absurd to suggest that science began in the sixteenth century. Classical Greece and Rome possessed extensive knowledge of natural phenomena. Systematized above all by Aristotle, it was inherited by the men of the Middle Ages, who themselves were not lacking in the desire to add to their stock of knowledge, especially knowledge of what seemed to them the secrets, the arcana of nature. Already, however, one limiting factor on medieval science has been suggested, in the very tendency to systematization, which could degenerate into the cult of compendia or text-books, the ultimately fatal disease that affects all large-scale educational enter- prise, and the mortal enemy of intellectual progress. A more funda- mental obstacle to the development of science consisted in the attitudes which dominated the classical and the medieval approach. Both were basically rational. The object was to discover and establish first principles or universal truths. It would be unfair to charge ancient scientists with ignoring facts. The Greeks began with observed and generally accepted natural phenomena, to account for which they constructed what seemed to them rational explanations or theories. Once the theory had been accepted, however, further experimental data was not sought to test it. New facts, if any appeared, were simply fitted, with such success as was possible, into the accepted theory: if they did not fit in, so much the worse for them.

Medieval scientists, regarding with natural awe the achievements of the ancient world, accepted Greek scientific doctrines almost without question; and since they did not contemplate the possibility that any new factual discoveries could overthrow them, naturally they found none that did. Moreover, there was an element in medieval thought which provided a reasonable and easy explanation for any aberrant data, in the form of a spiritual or animistic world- view. Although the greater gods had deserted Olympus and the vast proletariat of lesser deities their mountain, wood or stream, Christianity replaced them with its own hierarchy of angels and ministers of grace, cherubim and seraphim, and all the spirits that move corporeal bodies. It was a spiritual world. Balanced against the grosser elements of earth and water were the more spiritual ones, aspiring upwards like Cleopatra, when she stretched her slender length and cried she was all air and fire.[1] Above the world of mundane elements, in the concentric circles of the Ptolemaic

[1] Cf. E. M. W. Tillyard, *The Elizabethan World Picture*, 1943, p. 55.

heavens, swung the crystalline spheres, incorruptible and changeless, circling the earth, set with stars like jewels and sounding a hymn of praise to their Creator. Beneath the night sky a lover could not but cry to his mistress:

> Sit, Jessica. Look how the floor of heav'n
> Is thick inlaid with patines of bright gold;
> There's not the smallest orb which thou behold'st
> But in his motion like an angel sings,
> Still quiring to the young-ey'd Cherubims;
> Such harmony is in immortal souls;
> But whilst this muddy vesture of decay
> Doth grossly close it in, we cannot hear it.

These lesser spirits of the empyrean, under the greater superintendence of their Master, exercised a subordinate sway over human destinies, to which their motions afforded a clue that was the subject of intense, and, given its presuppositions, scientific investigation.

It used to be believed that the Renaissance brought such ideas to an end, that it 'freed the human mind from medieval superstition' and inaugurated the scientific age. This was hardly a plausible consequence of a movement that is now seen as still so much one with the Middle Ages. And was a revival of pagan antiquity likely to have done other than intensify the outlook imbibed by the Middle Ages from classical science, or bring back the shades of Apollo and Venus, Pan and all his troop to their ancient haunts? We need only look, for the transmutation of the ideas of medieval science into the pure gold of poetic vision, to Shakespeare. When Caesar boasted that the fault why men were underlings lay not in their stars but in themselves, to the Renaissance mind he was inviting retribution from the celestial powers that controlled human destiny. In the sixteenth century alchemy and astrology flourished as never before. Paracelsus was the Renaissance model of a scientist, not lacking in novelties and even experimentalism in his medical practice, but still holding to the transmutation of elements, seeking for the philosopher's stone, supporting his medicinal treatments with incantations, and continuing all the esoteric devices of alchemy. To medieval traditions was added a reborn Platonic mysticism; and religion remained the bulwark of science, for the Catholic Church had integrated the Aristotelian and Ptolemaic systems so thoroughly in its teaching, that any questioning of them was almost bound to be interpreted as heresy. The Protestant schism was even more firmly attached to the medieval picture of the natural world. Finally, it should not be forgotten that the age of Renaissance and Reformation was also the great age of witchcraft and witch-burning.

A change was soon to come about and modern science was to be born. No single source of this new development can be found or should be looked for. Great revolutions, of any kind, arise not out of the operation of one decisive force but from the critical flowing together and fusion of many factors, which acquire their power of transformation from their confluence and mutual interaction. Only a few of these can be mentioned here. Geographical discoveries upset some accepted ideas, and the recovery of lost classical sources, which did not always agree with the standard authors, others. The rise of naturalism in art heightened men's appreciation of, and interest in, the physical world. Printing facilitated communication and speeded up, or even made possible, the mutual stimulation, interpenetration and fecundity of new ideas. This brief enumeration obviously comes nowhere near exhausting the list of new influences that were brought to bear on a medieval system of thought which was already hesitating on the verge of new ideas.

The name that must always be associated with the scientific revolution of the sixteenth century is that of Copernicus. True, he was inspired by a mystical Renaissance belief that such a noble orb as the sun should rightly be in the centre of the universe, and merely replaced the earth by the sun as the fixed point round which the heavens moved; so that it has been said that the one idea on which both Ptolemy and Copernicus were fundamentally wrong – that there must be such a fixed centre – was the one point in which they were agreed. When Copernicus gave the world *De Revolutionibus Orbium Coelestium* in 1543, however, he did something more than work out a newer kind of mysticism. His profoundest motives, perhaps, were two which lie close to the heart of the scientific revolution. He was worried by the existence, here and there, of isolated facts, known to medieval astronomers, which stubbornly refused to fit into the neat Ptolemaic pattern of the heavens. It may be said that in a concrete form Copernicus had already grasped the significance of Bacon's negative examples. And secondly, the Ptolemaic system, even though it could not account for all celestial phenomena, for the great number which it did explain had to assume the existence of an extraordinarily involved system of sphere upon sphere moving round the earth, which seemed to Copernicus intolerably complicated. In the true spirit of modern science he sought for an explanation which should be both more comprehensive and simpler. To conceive the idea of revolving the earth, instead of the whole heavens with their eighty crystal spheres, every twenty-four hours, was the kind of simplification that is the mark of a scientist rather than a mystic, and it required a masterly recalculation of astronomical data to fit all the known facts into the new pattern.

Although there was much of the mystic in Copernicus, then, he had set astronomers on the task of simplifying explanations and removing anomalies. The heavens themselves seemed determined to assist the work that then was going on. When a *nova* flared up in 1572 and disappeared in 1574, what was happening to the change-lessness and incorruptibility of the crystal spheres? When, in 1577, a comet appeared, cutting a swathe across the sky, scything its way through the same spheres, the affront to the Ptolemaic system was blatant. Though the ideas of Copernicus spread only slowly, astronomers were becoming aware that something would have to be done about all this. But what? Tycho Brahe collected a mass of new astronomical observations. His assistant, Johan Kepler, inter-preted them in mathematical terms, and formulated his three laws. Early in the seventeenth century, reports of the telescope, invented in Holland, reached Galileo at Padua. He constructed a simple telescope for himself and at once worlds without end swam into his ken, and physical astronomy became both necessary and possible. New theories could now be backed by an army of facts, and the Ptolemaic system was engulfed for ever in the immensity of the new-found universe.

If a date has to be given when modern science sprang in arms and militant from the brain of the scientist it could only be when Galileo published his *Dialogues on the Two Principal World Systems* in 1632. Written in Italian, and in the polemical style that the dialogue form permits, this work was an appeal to the educated public in favour of a new interpretation of the empirical discoveries of astronomy. Galileo's mathematical analysis may have been helped in the first place by the work of the fifteenth-century mathematicians of Oxford and their successors at Paris. In these speculations, wafted from Merton and the Sorbonne over the space of two centuries to Padua, and finding there in the mind of Galileo soil ready prepared for their reception, is to be found, it seems, if anywhere, the first seed of modern science. Stimulated by his need to reduce the vast body of new astronomical observations to some kind of coherence, and by the challenge of the fifteenth-century scientists to the long authoritative Aristotelian explanation of motion; adding his own observations of the movement of little balls on inclined planes; Galileo achieved the statement of the principle of inertia. Instead of the Aristotelian world of common sense, in which all things, from the fixed stars in heaven to the atoms of dust on the ground, stayed where they were unless some force, inspired by a principle or spirit or will, intervened to set them in motion, and in which they ceased to move as soon as the force or spirit ceased to move them, Galileo made the crucial leap to a hypothetical conception of the world as a vacuum in which the continuation of any existing motion in a straight line was the norm and only changes in rate and direction of motion required explanation. It was a revolution in the conception of nature of a far more fundamental nature than that made by Copernicus. The foundations of the cosmos were shaken and they have never since regained the stability with which appearances and Aristotle had formerly endowed them. The classical ideal of immutability was dethroned and an age in which change was no longer equated with degeneration was inaugurated. The result was not anarchy but a new kind of order and a more comprehensive one, because it formalized empirical data in terms of abstract laws of nature, which could in turn be tested by specific observation or experiment.

Galileo not only set the investigation of the physical universe on a new path, he taught its explorers what language they would have to use to interpret their findings. That he was fully conscious himself of what he was doing can be shown by his own words:

Philosophy is written in that vast book which stands forever open before our eyes, I mean the universe; but it cannot be read until we have learnt the language and become familiar with the characters in which it is written. It is written in mathematical language, and the letters are triangles, circles and other geometrical figures, without which means it is humanly impossible to understand a single word.[1]

Galileo would have been less great, and the scientific advance with which his name is associated impossible of achievement, if he had not been able thus to combine physical observation with mathematical

[1] Quoted in *The Age of Reason*, ed. Stuart Hampshire, 1956, p. 33.

theory. There was a time when the theoretical element in scientific discovery was underestimated. Because of this we must not fall into the opposite error of attributing everything to theory and disregarding the contribution that was made to the creation of modern science by the intense interest that developed in factual discovery, in other words, observation and experiment. After all, this was the new thing. Francis Bacon, more clearly than anyone else, put into words the shift from the metaphysical or spiritual to the empirical approach to the natural world: 'It cannot be [he wrote] that axioms established by argumentation should avail for the discovery of new works; since the subtlety of nature is greater many times over than the subtlety of argument.'[1] Though Bacon hardly appreciated the importance of scientific theory, his appeal to the facts is not to be dismissed as the mere interest in a jackdaw collecting of miscellaneous data. The true nature of scientific empiricism is to be clearly seen in what he says of experiment.

> Not only is a greater abundance of experiments to be sought for and procured, and that too of a different kind from those hitherto tried; an entirely different method, order, and process for carrying on and advancing experience must also be introduced. For experience, when it wanders in its own track, is, as I have already remarked, mere groping in the dark, and confounds men rather than instructs them. But when it shall proceed in accordance with a fixed law, in regular order, and without interruption, then may better things be hoped of knowledge.[2]

It cannot be claimed that, apart from his enunciation of principles, Bacon made any serious contribution to science himself. He lacked the necessary mathematical knowledge, and failed to appreciate the significance of mathematical analysis. But his rejection of the Copernican theory should not be held against him, for it was on the ground of its failure to account for all the relevant phenomena. He was on the side of future scientific advance in insisting that the facts of observation should never be disregarded or trimmed to fit the Procrustean bed of a theory.

> The human understanding [he wrote], when it has once adopted an opinion (either as being the received opinion or as being

[1] *Novum Organum*, Aphorism xxiv, *Philosophical Works of Francis Bacon*, ed. J. M. Robertson, 1905, pp. 261-2.
[2] Ibid., Aphorism c, p. 289.

agreeable in itself) draws all things else to support and agree with it. And though there be a greater number and weight of instances to be found on the other side, yet these it either neglects and despises, or else by some distinction sets aside and rejects; in order that by this great and pernicious predetermination the authority of its former conclusions may remain inviolate. And therefore it was a good answer that was made by one who when they showed him hanging in a temple a picture of those who had paid their vows as having escaped shipwreck, and would have him say whether he did not now acknowledge the power of the gods, – 'Aye', asked he again, 'but where are they painted that were drowned after their vows?' And such is the way of all superstition, whether in astrology, dreams, omens, divine judgments or the like; wherein men, having a delight in such vanities, mark the events where they are fulfilled, but where they fail, though this happen much oftener, neglect and pass them by ... Besides, independently of that delight and vanity which I have described, it is the peculiar and perpetual error of human intellect to be more moved and excited by affirmatives than by negatives; whereas it ought properly to hold, itself indifferently disposed towards both alike. Indeed in the establishment of any true axiom, the negative instance is the more forcible of the two.[1]

That one who was not himself a practical scientist, or even a very coherent philosopher, should have grasped so firmly the basic principles of empirical science, and been able to state them in a way that impressed the imagination of the next two centuries, is surprising. In addition, not the least significant of Bacon's ideas was the plan, in his *New Atlantis* (1623), for a college of scientific investigators, whose researches were to be directed to changing man's material conditions. The connection between scientific progress and material improvement was a familiar thought to seventeenth-century scientists, and Bacon's views would have been less influential if they had not been put forward at a time when practical experimental science was itself developing rapidly under the pressure of utilitarian needs. The inadequacy of medieval science in respect of such arts as shipbuilding, military engineering, gunnery, aquatic works, navigation and the like, was becoming patent, and the

[1] *Novum Organum*, Aphorism xlvi, pp. 265–6.

problems involved in practical developments stimulated scientific inquiry and experiment.

The science in which the most marked empirical advances were made was perhaps that of anatomy. Here also, as in astronomy, the crucial steps were taken at the University of Padua, where anatomical studies had continued to follow the tradition of dissection handed down by Galen, until, in the sixteenth century, they moved beyond the teaching of the master. Vesalius, one of a notable group of anatomists, on the strength of his own observations challenged some of the long authoritative views of Galen. The same year, 1543, that saw the publication of the *De Revolutionibus Orbis* of Copernicus, also saw that of Vesalius' *De Humani Corporis Fabrica*.

There was doubtless more than one reason why Padua should have become such an important centre of the new scientific developments, but one at least may have been that it was under the anti-clerical rule of Venice. Its scientific illumination was not a mere flash in the pan. Nearly a century later, it was after working at Padua, in 1628, just when Galileo was publishing his *Dialogues*, that Harvey established the modern science of anatomy with his *De motu cordis*. Like Galileo, Harvey did not merely co-ordinate and reduce to a simple form a great mass of facts of observation and experiment, he also set anatomy firmly on a new scientific basis. He did for the human body what the new astronomy was doing for the heavenly bodies. He abandoned the attempt to provide an explanation in terms of 'vital spirits', and took the heart as simply 'a piece of machinery in which one wheel gives motion to another, yet all the wheels seem to move simultaneously'.[1] With Galileo and Harvey the scientific age had begun: the laws of mechanics held sway over macrocosm and microcosm alike, over the heavens and man.

Such advances as Napier's logarithms and Kepler's conic sections stimulated the mathematical approach to scientific problems in the seventeenth century. Indeed, mathematical theory was beginning to seem the key to the universe. But it was an abstract universe that it revealed. Mathematics, declared Descartes, he found it best to consider 'in the most general form possible, without referring them to any objects in particular.'[2] And Descartes, great as he was, himself exemplified the danger of wreck when the theoretical structure of

[1] Quoted in Butterfield, *Origins of Modern Science*, p. 50.
[2] Descartes, *Discourse on Method*, ii, p. 16. References to Descartes are to *A Discourse on Method, etc.* Everyman's Library, 1912.

mathematical thought was allowed to come adrift from its empirical moorings. His deductive reasoning from first principles, starting in particular from the Aristotelian view that there could be no such thing as 'empty' space, enabled him to construct, in his great theory of vortices, a magnificent mathematical structure, in which the only defect was the inadequacy of its empirical verification. The predominance, in Descartes' mind, of the a priori over the empirical was shown by his absence of concern at the fact that some of the observed movements of the planets did not correspond to his theoretical calculations, or at his inability to fit the comets – always a nuisance – into his vortices.

Meanwhile, William Gilbert's *De Magnete*, in 1600, had drawn attention to the phenomenon of magnetism. Both he and Kepler linked it with gravitation, and once again terrestrial and celestial mechanics seemed to be calling for a common explanation. But merely to mention all those who added, in greater or less degree, to the development of scientific thought in the seventeenth century would be to turn this slight sketch into a catalogue. The climax to the whole movement came when Sir Isaac Newton, after long meditation and verification of the ideas he had worked out in the mid-'sixties, at last, in 1687, published his famous *Principia*, the *Mathematical Principles of Natural Philosophy*. In Newton a mastery of experimental science, exhibited in his *Opticks*, was combined with insight into mathematical theory. An element of strangeness, illustrated by his obsession with the alchemists and his calculations of the chronology of world history, was not absent from his genius. This was perhaps what enabled him to base his mathematical structure on the theory of universal gravitation; for the idea that a force of attraction could be exercised across space, with no apparent material bodies intervening to bridge the gap, was almost a mystical hypothesis compared with the apparent common sense of Descartes' vortices. So it seemed to supporters of Cartesian mathematics, who fought a long rearguard action against the Newtonian system. Huygens and Leibniz, both eminent scientists, could not bring themselves to accept it. But an explanation which explained so much and left only some small and barely noticed empirical observations unaccounted for, was bound to win the struggle for scientific acceptance.

By the time of Newton scientific inquiry was a widespread and organized activity. The second half of the seventeenth century saw the foundation of the Royal Society in London and the Académie des Sciences in Paris. The scientific movement was now safely launched. My object has not been to give an account of it, but only to try to pick out the elements in it that seem more significant for the history of the European mind. From what has been said already it will be evident that its essential genius lay in the combination of conceptualization and experiment, or, in other words, of mathematical theory and empirical observation. If either of these elements had come to dominate the other the Newtonian synthesis could not have been achieved. The conviction that 'all which we clearly perceive is true',[1] and that mathematical patterns, regardless of empirical evidence, must embody the highest truths, since they are the clearest of all, had led Descartes to deduce too much from his first principles, to accept too many supposed facts without verification, and to neglect the observations or experiments necessary to provide other and relevant ones.

On the other hand observation, to be of value in the construction of a scientific pattern, had to be strictly selective, and in recognizing this Descartes was at one with such a scientist as Galileo. We can see in them both how the wide-ranging interest in fact, what might be called for our purpose the naturalism of the Renaissance world, had to be trimmed and narrowed before it could achieve results of value for science. For scientific analysis deals in mental constructions. The colours, scents and all the uncertain and changing appearances of the sensual world, had to be wiped out and forgotten before the austere vision of a Galileo could be seen by the mind's eye, with a sort of blinding clarity.

No sooner [he wrote] do I form a conception of a material or corporeal substance, than I feel the need of conceiving that it has boundaries and shape; that relative to others it is great or small; that it is in this or that place and in this or that time; that it is moving or still; that it touches or does not touch another body; that it is one, few or many; nor can I by any effort of imagination, dissociate it from these properties. On the other hand, I find no need to apprehend it as accompanied by such properties as to be white or red, bitter or sweet, sounding or silent, pleasant or evil smelling ... I hold that these tastes, odours, colours, etc., of the object in which they seem to reside, are

[1] Descartes, *Principles of Philosophy*, I, xxx, p. 177.

nothing more than pure names, and exist only in the sensitive being; so that if the latter were removed these qualities would themselves vanish.[1]

What remained was a universe that could be reduced to mathematical formulae. A teleological was replaced by a mechanistic science, which had both the certainty of a priori truth and the confirmation of empirical observation. It may be asked how this differed from the world of Aristotle or Ptolemy, whether it was not merely the creation of another rigid pattern, a new scientific dogmatism. If theory had dominated empirical observation, this would have been so, and Cartesianism did indeed solidify into an unyielding dogmatic faith. Modern science escaped this fate, and has never, up to the present, become stereotyped in a rigid pattern, because a principle of development was inherent, 'built in', to the new scientific thought. Its theoretical patterns, or 'laws', were a means of grasping and formalizing a great mass of empirical observations; but the very process which made their formulation possible ensured their progressive modification. With the rise of modern science the system of controlled experiment and observation became firmly established. The consequences of Newtonian science, when it passed into the minds of ordinary educated men, and of the new world-picture that it bequeathed to the following century, remain to be discussed; but enough has been said, I hope, to justify the view that the rise of modern science itself was a revolutionary change in outlook on the world. Before turning to its consequences, however, there were other great intellectual developments, proceeding contemporaneously, which have also to be taken into consideration.

---

[1] Quoted in *The Age of Reason*, ed. Stuart Hampshire, p. 33.

IV

Cartesianism

DESCARTES, though a major figure in the history of science, is hardly in the middle of the road of the scientific revolution, nor can he be regarded as one of its great seminal minds. He is more intimately associated with, and indeed was the initiating genius of another great intellectual revolution, in the realm of philosophy. As a young man he had – for reasons which will be mentioned later – abandoned literary and historical studies, but found himself 'especially delighted' with mathematics. He did not put into print all his scientific ideas, partly, it has been suggested, because of the condemnation of Galileo by the Holy Office; but his scientific studies in themselves are perhaps less significant than the motive which he gave for them. As soon as he had gained some knowledge of the principles of physics, he said, he realized that:

> I could not keep them concealed without sinning grievously against the law by which we are bound to promote, as far as in us lies, the general good of mankind. For by them I perceived it to be possible to arrive at knowledge highly useful in life; and in room of the speculative philosophy usually taught in the schools, to discover a practical, by means of which, knowing the force and action of fire, water, air, the stars, the heavens, and all the other bodies that surround us, as distinctly as we know the various crafts of our artisans, we might also apply them in the same way to all the uses to which they are adapted, and thus render ourselves the lords and possessors of nature.[1]

Without such a practical motive it may be suspected that empirical discovery might have played a smaller role in the scientific thought of the period. Descartes himself hardly put his own principles into practice in this respect, which is perhaps the reason why his essential contribution to the new intellectual world was made in the field of general ideas rather than in that of any particular science. But so much emphasis has been laid, correctly, on the strong a priori bent of his mind, that it is worth while pointing out that even the founder

[1] Descartes, *Discourse on Method*, vi, p. 49.

41

of Cartesianism was not uninfluenced by practical, utilitarian motives. As he wrote:

> It occurred to me that I should find much more truth in the reasonings of each individual with reference to the affairs in which he is personally interested, and the issue of which must presently punish him if he has judged amiss, than in those conducted by a man of letters in his study, regarding speculative matters that are of no practical moment, and followed by no consequences to himself.[1]

His 'earnest desire', he declared, was always 'to know how to distinguish the true from the false', and this in order that he 'might be able clearly to discriminate the right path in life, and proceed in it with confidence'.[2]

It was in this spirit, and as one who had mastered the new mathematical thought, that Descartes approached the problem of philosophy. Though attributing motives is dangerous, it may be suggested, reading between the lines of the *Discourse on Method*, that his essential aim in philosophy was to find a means of justifying the irresistible conviction which he felt, along with the other great scientists of his day, in the truth of mathematical knowledge. The natural bent of his mind away from empiricism, as well as reflection on dreams and illusions, prevented him from finding any sure foundation in the evidence of the senses. He shared the view, on which Galileo has already been cited, that the secondary qualities such as colour, sound, smell or taste, have no real existence; but he needed to demonstrate the objective reality of the primary quality of spatial extension, because if this were illusory the whole of mathematical thought became an illusion with it, and Descartes refused to believe that man could be a victim of illusions even in his most clear and unquestionable intellectual convictions. But mathematics could not itself provide any proof of its correspondence to objective reality. Only some power above both man and nature could do that, and this power must be God. The truth of mathematics was therefore dependent on the veracity and a fortiori on the existence of God. But this was not the end of the argument. It was significant of a new spirit that was rising that Descartes felt the need for a rational proof of God. He found this in the argument that the idea of a nature more perfect than his own, 'which even possessed within

[1] *Discourse on Method*, i, p. 9.   [2] Ibid.

itself all the perfections of which I could form any idea',[1] was a clear
and certain conception which could not be denied without self-
contradiction: 'I could not possibly be of such a nature as I am, and
yet have in my mind the idea of a God, if God did not in reality
exist.'[2] Consequently, the existence of God, he declares, is a truth
'at least as certain as I ever judged any truth of mathematics to be'.[3]
God and Pythagoras' theory stand or fall together.

But even God is not the ultimate, irrefutable reality in Cartesian
philosophy. Behind his 'infinite, independent, all-knowing, all-
powerful'[4] figure there is the lesser one of Descartes himself, for it
is in his mind that he knows the idea of God, as all other ideas; and
here, he believes, is something that requires no further proof. Even
the very act of doubting is an assertion of the existence of the doubt.
Assuming that thinking cannot exist without something that thinks,
the quality without the substance, Descartes is able to postulate the
ego – 'cogito ergo sum' – as a self-evident proposition, and one
which cannot be denied without self-contradiction. The innate ideas
of God and the self stand as the twin pillars of Cartesian philosophy.
Descartes has thus reversed the process of medieval scholastic
philosophy.[5] Starting from the certainty of the world, the schoolmen
inferred God. Descartes starts from his own ideas and proceeds, by
way of God, to deduce the existence of the world, at least as a mathematical construction; for his world, to return to the point from
which we started, is a world of spatial extension.

The philosophical merits or demerits of Cartesianism are not our
subject here, but it is necessary to attempt to indicate in conclusion
the major factors in the intellectual inheritance that Descartes bequeathed to his successors. Though it was not peculiar to him, of
course, that mechanical pattern of the universe, and the conception
of invariable laws of nature to which science owes so much, was
impressed firmly on the modern mind by his influence. It emerges
conspicuously in his anatomical observations. The human body,
he declares, should be considered

as a kind of machine, so made up and composed of bones,
nerves, muscles, veins, blood, and skin, that although there were
in it no mind, it would still exhibit the same motions which it

[1] Ibid., iv, p. 28.
[2] Descartes, *Meditations on the First Philosophy*, iii, p. 110.
[3] Ibid., v, p. 122.   [4] Ibid., iii, p. 104.
[5] S. V. Keeling, *Descartes*, 1934, p. 117.

at present manifests involuntarily, and therefore without the aid of the mind.[1]

This human machine is further evidence of the operation of a divine hand for it is 'incomparably better arranged' than any machine of human invention.[2] In this way Descartes laid the bases of the argument from design which was to be the corner-stone of deistic thought.

God is not only the guarantor of the reality of the world of extension, he is also the source of all truth, so long as we rightly employ the faculty of distinguishing truth from error that he has given us.[3] This is why Descartes could hold, as has been said above, that 'all which we clearly perceive is true'. Error arises when we attempt to assert something that we do not clearly perceive.[4] It is an act of will; and the possibility of error must be allowed because it is only on this condition that we can possess a free will.[5]

Thus far Descartes' thought is concerned exclusively with ideas, but he does not deny the existence of a material world, or that the ego as well as being a mind is also a body. The problem is to find some link between 'the mind and the body, or between a thinking and corporeal thing',[6] for the body belongs to that mechanical universe which is subject to unalterable law; the mind is free. They are substances of entirely different nature: the fundamental attribute of the mind is thought, of the body extension,[7] and the two are so different that how the one can be related to the other can hardly be conceived. Yet we know intuitively that there is a connection between them, says Descartes. Indeed he writes, in the *Discourse on Method*:

> The mind is so intimately dependent upon the condition and relation of the organs of the body, that if any means can ever be found to render men wiser and more ingenious than hitherto, I believe that it is in medicine they must be sought for.[8]

The relation of mind and body is yet another of the problems which Descartes bequeathed to posterity, for it cannot be pretended that his own solution, locating the gear-box, as one might say, of the human machine in the pineal gland, had much merit.

---

[1] *Meditations on the First Philosophy*, vi, p. 138.   [2] *Discourse on Method*, v, p . 44.
[3] Descartes, *Principles of Philosophy*, IV, xix, p. 228.
[4] Ibid., I, xxxiii-viii, pp. 178-9; *Meditations on the First Philosophy*, iv, p. 116.
[5] *Principles of Philosophy*, I, xxxix, p. 180.   [6] Ibid., I, viii, p. 167.
[7] Ibid., I, liii, p. 185.   [8] *Discourse on Method*, vi, p. 49.

Indeed whenever one approaches the realm of empirical fact the limitations of Descartes appear. His thought was naturally deductive. He had a noble faith in the supremacy of reason and believed that the maximum of deduction should be drawn from the minimum of premises. Only deductive reasoning was certain. This was why he early abandoned history: it was a work of the imagination. His own philosophical principles, he believed, were 'so clear and evident that the human mind, when it attentively considers them, cannot doubt of their truth.'[1] There is something a little reminiscent of dogma in this, and the hypotheses that his mathematical principles required – such as the famous vortices – were innocent of experimental verification. Reason had, for Descartes, a greater virtue than any empirical observation could possess: it was immutable, unquestionable and open to the understanding of all.

> I have observed [he wrote], on examining the natural constitutions of different minds, that there are hardly any so dull or slow of understanding as to be incapable of apprehending good opinions, or even of acquiring all the highest sciences, if they be but conducted along the right road. And this can also be proved by reason; for, as the principles are clear, and as nothing ought to be deduced from them, unless most manifest inferences, no one is so devoid of intelligence as to be unable to comprehend the conclusions that flow from them.[2]

Here was one of his most important contributions to the ideas of the future Enlightenment. It was also, Descartes said, the reason why he chose to write in French rather than in Latin, 'because I expect that those who make use of their unprejudiced natural reason will be better judges of my opinions than those who give heed to the writings of the ancients only'.[3]

He had appealed to the unprejudiced reason of men, but that reason was to carry them far beyond the principles which he had laid down. His religious arguments were to lead in a direction that would have alarmed him, for they were to open the door to deism and even atheism; his innate ideas were to prepare the way for, and to be rejected in favour of, the sensational psychology; the laws of mechanism that he had proclaimed were to extend their influence from matter to mind; experiment and observation were to dominate

---

[1] *Principles of Philosophy*, Preface, p. 148.
[2] Ibid., p. 155.   [3] *Discourse on Method*, vi, p. 61.

the natural sciences, and deduction to lose the primacy which he had attributed to it. But Cartesian rationalism had set its mark on the modern, and especially the French mind, and Descartes, if the Enlightenment was to repudiate many of his doctrines, remains one of its founding fathers.

V

Scepticism

MODERN science and Cartesian philosophy had, of course, to win their victory not only over intellectual opponents but also over those who would suppress them by force. On the whole there is more reason to be surprised at the slightness of the active persecution than at its existence. The work of Copernicus aroused a mild interest but no particular alarm in Rome. *De Revolutionibus* was dedicated to Pope Paul III. Luther's reference to its author as 'the fool who would overturn the whole science of astronomy' was perhaps typical of general scepticism; but on the whole, up to the latter years of the sixteenth century, the heliocentric theory received little attention.[1] Although the cause célèbre of the new science has been regarded as that of Giordarno Bruno, condemned and burnt at Rome in 1600, his prophetic speculations hardly come into the category of science, though he was condemned for teaching, among other heresies, the plurality of worlds. But the Counter-Reformation was now approaching its high-water mark and there was increased concern with the suppression of dangerous ideas. This was chiefly because orthodox religious thought was wedded to Aristotelianism and a bitter conflict between the old and the new scientific thought was developing.

By 1616 the dangers inherent in the Copernican theory were at last officially perceived and it was condemned by the Congregation. Galileo's *Dialogues*, as a frontal attack on Aristotelianism, incurred the consequential condemnation of the Church. Here may be one reason why scientific progress, which up to about the middle of the seventeenth century had been more marked in the Roman Catholic countries, now to some extent, though by no means exclusively, migrated to the Protestant nations. It was not until 1744 that Galileo's *Dialogues* could be printed with a papal licence at Padua, and then only on condition that the sentence on Galileo and his recantation were included in the volume. Only in 1757 did the Congregation of the Holy Office decide not to enforce any longer the decree condemning books which taught the movement of the world.[2] In spite of the

---

[1] Hall, *Scientific Revolution*, pp. 54-5.
[2] G. Maugain, *Étude sur l'évolution intellectuelle de l'Italie de 1657 à 1750 environ*, 1909, p. 82.

decree, as Galileo is alleged to have observed at the time, the world had been moving; and this was to open the stable door long after the horse had escaped. The Churches, in their struggle to maintain ecclesiastical authority over scientific truth, were fighting a losing battle. The intellectual assumptions of the ordinary educated man were increasingly falling under the influence of the new scientific outlook.

Descartes had provided new certainties in philosophy, Galileo, Newton and others in science. Old beliefs could not survive in the educated mind once the new world-picture had been presented to it by popularizers of the new science. One of the most influential of these was Fontenelle, who borrowed his facts and arguments from the austerer works of scientists and philosophers, gave them a witty dress, and presented them to the literary public in an easy and readable form. The frivolous tone of such works should not prevent us from detecting their serious motivation. "Tis the persecuting spirit', wrote Shaftesbury, 'has raised the bantering one.'[1] Fontenelle's *Histoire des Oracles*, in 1686, made mockery of what had formerly been a spiritual interpretation of natural phenomena, but which now seemed to be merely superstitious. Faced with an apparent exception to the mechanistic laws of nature, the new disposition was to assume that with further investigation a natural explanation would be found for it. The audience in the theatre, says Fontenelle, seeing Phoebus borne aloft in his chariot over the stage, may think that this is a miraculous suspension of the laws of nature. Those who are in the know, or in the stage pit, see the laborious apparatus of ropes and pulleys by which the miracle is being effected. Another embryo change in temper of mind is shown in the tendency to attribute supposed miraculous occurrences to conscious deceit. Fontenelle, thus, had no difficulty in disposing of oracles: they were a manifestation not of divine power but of priestly imposture.

In the second half of the seventeenth century grosser superstitions, such as the belief in witchcraft and sorcery, began to die out, even in the mind of the common man, at least in the towns. In the country older ways of thought survived to a later date, but even there pernicious and cruel superstitions were in due course to sink to the level of charming and poetical old customs. Perhaps the most notable of the attacks on superstition was the *Pensées diverses écrites à un docteur de Sorbonne à l'occasion de la Comète qui parut au mois de*

---

[1] Shaftesbury, *Characteristics*, 1711 (ed. of 1900), i, 50.

décembre 1680 by Pierre Bayle, but Bayle is a figure so important in our story that he will have to be treated separately.

Writers like Bayle and Fontenelle were, in one sense, carrying on the older sceptical tradition of the French libertines, but it had now acquired a more positive content under the influence of the new scientific ideas. Libertine thought had emerged rather from the geographical discoveries and the histories, which Descartes truly saw as the parents of uncertainty. The sixteenth and seventeenth centuries witnessed a great outpouring of accounts of voyages and missions to America, Asia, Egypt. Herodotus and Strabo added from the ancient world information which no longer seemed the mere product of uncontrolled fancy.[1] The diversity of human customs and ideas on religion, justice, property, social organization, morality, was thus revealed to the astonished and fascinated gaze of the European literati. Small wonder if some drew the conclusion that all was relative and norms of behaviour conspicuous by their absence, and some, like Montaigne with his *Que sais-je?*, took refuge in a generally amused wonder at the aberrations of the human race and a tolerant scepticism.

The religious version of the history of mankind, which had hitherto provided almost the only available record, was now challenged by the secular traditions of antiquity. Egypt, with its great monuments, and so far no readable accounts of barbarism or superstition to shock the student, provided an apparently preferable alternative to the sanguinary history of the Old Testament, or to Greece, identified with the shackles of classical authority, as the cradle of civilization. The Jesuit missions to China discovered a great civilization which had never known Christianity; and they reported a wonderful work of conversion, not unassisted by a generous adaptation of Roman Catholic practices to local conditions. This success was explained in 1697, by a Jesuit book, printed for the guidance of young missionaries to China, which exhibited the similarity of Confucianism and Christianity. Their affinities were more evident to the missionaries than they were to European theologians. In 1700 the dispute of the Chinese ceremonies broke out. The Jesuits were condemned by the Sorbonne for their tolerance of Chinese customs and for modifying Catholic rites to suit Chinese prejudice. Sceptics exploited the public controversy with glee. They solemnly agreed with Rome and the Sorbonne that the Chinese Confucianists were

Cf. A. Momigliano, 'The place of Herodotus in Historiography', *History*, xliii, 1-13.

not Christian; but despite or perhaps because of this they went on to find in them every other virtue. Free from superstition, elevating philosophy to the highest rank, cultivating art in tranquillity, the Chinese philosopher was to become an eighteenth-century stereotype.

The Huguenot jeweller, Chardin, wrote in 1686 an account of his travels in Persia, romantic land of learning and art – but more of the Persians later. Essays on the Arabs revealed that Mohammed was a philosopher. The less civilized nations were all the more virtuous. Simplicity, honesty, generosity, and natural morality seemed to be the general character of all the extra-European and non-Christian peoples. This belief persists in some quarters to the present day. The picture was not quite easy to reconcile with that of the strange, outlandish customs which at the same time made men wonder what was moral and what was not. However, the two pictures did not have to be presented at the same time, and on the whole the more pleasing representation of the noble savage won the day and became a stock model for the eighteenth century.

Imaginative writers took up the theme and used it for the purpose of social satire and criticism of their own society, sometimes, with Cyrano de Bergerac or Peter Wilkins or Swift, whose indictment of human nature, however, carries the story of Gulliver into a different class, sending their heroes to remote, legendary or planetary lands, where they could see the errors and crimes of their own society magnified and multiplied as in a set of distorting mirrors, or else discover a society which held up a clearer mirror to nature and reflected a purer image than their own corrupt civilization showed; sometimes bringing the child of a purer clime to Paris or London streets and reporting his naive misunderstandings and astonishment at the oddities and barbarities of the society that was revealed to him. Thus the alleged Turkish spy sent back his mocking accounts of the Paris of Louis XIV;[1] while, a generation later, the unspoiled Indian contrasted the simplicity and virtue of the Hurons with the corruption of European civilization.[2]

Among a host of examples the one which, because of its own merits as well as the subsequent work of its author, has kept its place in literature, is Montesquieu's *Lettres persanes*, appearing in 1721. Lively descriptions of the material charms of the denizens of a Persian harem, and their by no means spiritual consolations in the

[1] G. P. Marana, *L'espion du Grand Seigneur*, 1684.
[2] Delisle de la Drevetière, *Arlequin sauvage*, 1721.

absence of their lord and master, are alternated skilfully with astringent comments on the France of the opening decades of the eighteenth century. On Louis XIV the Persian of Montesquieu comments: 'The king of France governs with equal genius his family, his court and his state ... He has a minister of eighteen and a mistress of eighty.'[1] The Pope he sums up, of course knowing no better, as 'une vieille idole qu'on encense par habitude.'[2] Public Law is 'a science which teaches princes up to what point they can violate justice without injuring their own interests'.[3] The financier John Law is compared to the Persian astrologers and described as turning the State inside out as a tailor turns a coat.[4] A 'grand seigneur' is a man who sees the king, talks to the Ministers, and has ancestors, debts and pensions. Favour is the chief divinity of the French, and Ministers are its high priests.[5] All this and much more is in the true libertine tradition, though with perhaps a more conscious element of propaganda. Montesquieu is not merely mocking at everything, there is serious social criticism behind his wit; and one can detect the emergence of more constructive ideas; but these must be reserved for later treatment.

A significant development in the emancipation of thought, at the end of the seventeenth century, was what is known as the struggle of the Ancients and Moderns. This was primarily a literary episode, which only arose when the real issue was really already settled. It might be described as a revolt of the French seventeenth century, increasingly conscious of its own achievements, against the relics of the classical renaissance. Ancient science was being surpassed or discredited, French classical tragedy rivalled the Greeks on their own ground, philosophy was renovated. It seemed time to challenge the traditional superiority of classical letters. The dispute was exploited by Fontenelle in his *Digression sur les Anciens et les Modernes* of 1688. He shifted the emphasis and transformed the debate into an argument in favour of a new conception of the progress of society. Traditionally the life of a nation, or a civilization, had been compared to that of a man, vigorous in youth and early age, but declining and enfeebled in its later years. Against that view Fontenelle asserted the permanence of the forces of nature. The same conditions, he declared, will always produce the same results, hence reason and science will progress, if from no other cause, because of the simple accumulation

[1] *Lettres persanes*, xxxvii.   [2] Ibid., xxix.   [3] Ibid., xcv.
[4] Ibid., cxxxviii.   [5] Ibid., lxxxix.

of knowledge. Here we can see the negative, sceptical attitude of the libertines beginning to give way to a more positive faith in the future.

Increasing confidence in contemporary achievements added to the criticism of religious as well as of secular antiquity. The scepticism of the Renaissance had weakened or destroyed the faith of small literary coteries, but the real danger to the Churches came when the new scientific attitude began to spread to the general educated public. Science provided a new set of intellectual assumptions which changed the 'climate of opinion', even when they did not necessarily involve a direct attack on essential religious beliefs. Cartesianism was gradually reconciled with Catholic theology, and the quarrel of the Catholic Church with Galileo had arisen out of an historically comprehensible but otherwise somewhat unnecessary identification of Aristotelianism with Christianity. Scientific empiricism was certainly dangerous to religion, but the particular facts which presented the most immediate, though not the most basic threat, were not those of science but of history. The rise of historical criticism will have to be discussed later. For the moment it may perhaps be taken for granted and our attention directed to the results which followed when the methods which were derived from the study of secular history were turned to criticism of the Bible.

One very obvious problem appeared when the scholars of the Renaissance developed an interest in historical chronology. The new information obtained about ancient civilizations produced glaring anomalies. How were the thirty dynasties of Egyptian history to be fitted into the traditional chronology of the Old Testament from the creation of the world to the coming of Christ? The suggestion of one apologist, attempting to fit so much into four thousand years, that the dynasties overlapped or were perhaps even co-terminous, did not produce conviction. And then what of the alleged antiquity of Chinese civilization?

Textual criticism, both linguistic and historical, undermined belief in the historical accuracy of the Bible on a broader front. Two names that stand out in this field are those of the Dutch Jew, Spinoza, and the Catholic priest, Richard Simon. Spinoza, despite his early brilliance in rabbinical studies at Amsterdam, had to quit the Jewish synagogue in that city on account of his unorthodox views. There was hardly any thinker of the seventeenth century who drew a clearer or more devastating distinction between rational and theological thought. He wrote:

The sphere of reason is ... truth and wisdom; the sphere of theology is piety and obedience. The power of reason does not extend so far as to determine for us that men may be blessed through simple obedience, without understanding. Theology tells us nothing else, enjoins on us no command save obedience, and has neither the will nor the power to oppose reason: she defines the dogmas of faith ... only in so far as they may be necessary for obedience, and leaves reason to determine their precise truth: for reason is the light of the mind, and without her all things are dreams and phantoms.[1]

In this light Spinoza treats the Bible as though it were a secular text and open to the same critical treatment. He gives reasons for supposing that the Pentateuch could not all have been written by Moses, and challenges the authenticity of the other sacred books. Faced with the account of supernatural events, he is apt to suggest natural explanations: for example, an east wind may have brought the plague of locusts and a west wind have dissipated it. And if one accepts the evidence for miracles, what, he asks, of the equally well-authenticated miracles of the Greek gods?

Spinoza's criticism was influential, even though he himself might be discredited as an atheist. Richard Simon, on the other hand, was a Catholic priest, an Oratorian, a man with no sceptical or unorthodox intentions, simply bitten with the bug of textual scholarship and believing that it was not possible to read the Bible fruitfully unless one was 'in advance informed on the criticism of the text'.[2] He argued: 'It is impossible to understand perfectly the sacred books, unless one knows in advance the different states in which the texts of these books have appeared at different times and in different places.'[3] Orthodox thought was quite unprepared to face such a challenge. Like Spinoza, Richard Simon drew attention to the facts of internal evidence – alterations in style and language, the recording of events that occurred after the death of the supposed writer, repetition of descriptions of the same events in different terms – which threw doubt on the accepted attribution of the Pentateuch to the authorship of Moses. The Old Testament all through, he pointed out, offered many signs of alterations and transpositions, as well as

[1] Spinoza, *Chief Works*, trans. by R. H. M. Elwes, 1891, vol. i, *Tractatus Theologico-Politicus*, pp. 194-5.
[2] *Histoire critique du vieux testament*, 1678.
[3] Cf. P. Hazard, *La crise de la conscience européenne*, 1935, part ii, ch. 3, p. 190.

chronological difficulties. Furthermore, to understand the Bible properly, he held, some knowledge of the civilization of the ancient Hebrews was needed.

Simon did not deny the divine inspiration even of the alterations; he allowed that the tradition of the Church was necessary for the understanding of Scripture, and attacked the Socinians and Protestants. But despite such evidences of orthodoxy, his application of the methods of secular scholarship to the sacred books was more than the Church could stand. He was excluded from the Oratory, that least orthodox of religious orders, his work was placed on the Index and banned by the Royal Council, and copies of his books were seized by the police. Unfortunately Simon was one of those men who once they have seen what they believe to be true cannot give it up. Banned in France, he published a new version of his *Critical History* in Amsterdam, added to it a critical examination of the New Testament, and with a fanatical devotion went on accumulating and printing textual studies to his death.

Biblical criticism was by now well launched. Protestants were more influenced by it than Catholics, and sceptics seized on it gleefully as a new weapon. The Church of Rome itself was perturbed by the threat, which was so difficult to counter. More than forty refutations of Simon's *Critical History* were published.[1] The great Bossuet himself entered into the controversy. Indeed, the iniquities of Spinoza and Simon became almost an obsession with him. The Scriptures are not to be treated as a human text, he protested. But assertion was not enough. Unwillingly, he had to descend into the field chosen by his adversaries and argue about the scripture on their level. There *are* additions to the text of Moses, he was forced to admit, but they are only little ones. The smallest concession was dangerous.[2] The critical spirit was penetrating even into the very stronghold of orthodoxy. Beyond such minor concessions, of course, orthodox opinion could not accept the conclusions of biblical criticism, any more than it could accept the naturalistic interpretation of miraculous events. The result was to drive a wedge between the modern mind and the Churches, and — for those who accepted the new ideas — to identify religion with superstition.

---

[1] Hazard, pp. 201-2.   [2] Ibid., pp. 208-10.

VI

The Rise of Toleration

THE growing spirit of scepticism was strengthened by scientific opposition to the miraculous and by scholarly criticism of religious texts. There was a weakening of religious orthodoxy even inside the Churches. In the Protestant sects in particular, religious thought was becoming dangerously free. A name which for long covered with infamy those who rejected the dogmas of the Churches was provided by the Polish heretic, Socinius, who, at the end of the sixteenth century, condemned religious tradition and all the Churches. Only the Bible, interpreted by the individual conscience, he held, should be followed, and this taught simple, clear, universal truths. The ideas of Socinius found an echo in the independent sects of Puritan England.

In the Dutch republic the theologian Arminius abandoned the Calvinist doctrines of irresistible grace and predestination, while his follower, Grotius, the founder of international law, elevated secular Natural Law to a position apparently higher than, or at least independent of, the divine commands revealed by religious authority. Orthodox Calvinism was outraged by these teachings, and those who followed Arminius were condemned by the Dutch theologians at the Synod of Dort in 1618 and persecuted by the Calvinist pastors. The Arminians consequently looked for protection to the State, and so developed those views on the control of the Church by the secular power which are particularly associated with their name. From Holland their influence spread to England, where it proved a seed from which tolerant and latitudinarian attitudes were to grow.

In England the Cambridge Platonists – John Smith, Henry More, Ralph Cudworth – were also in revolt against the extremes of Calvinist dogma. They condemned the 'black doctrine' of predestination, were lukewarm on Original Sin and shaky on the Fall. Rationalism was now infiltrating into the very citadel of religion. For Cudworth and his friends reason was a divine enlightenment given to man: truth was to be discerned by the light of reason and confirmed in scripture – which was, from a strictly orthodox point of view, rather the wrong way round. The purpose of religion, they held, was to lead to good men and good lives. In a spirit not very different from that of Erasmus they called man away from 'dogmas and barren speculation', a dangerously mundane view for men of such sincere and even profound religious convictions.

On the other hand, although, to begin with, the Cambridge Platonists had not been immune from the influence of Descartes, their attitude to the world remained basically irreconcilable with his conception of a universe ruled by mechanical law, and of truth as concordance with the decrees of a deity whose arbitrary will constituted the essence of reason. On the God of Descartes, Cudworth wrote:

> This is that monstrous and prodigious idea or portraiture of God which Cartesius has drawn out of his metaphysics. That there is *nulla ratio veri aut boni* in nature antecedent to his will. So that according to him, God is both good and wise by will, and not by any nature; a being nothing but blind, indifferent and fortuitous will, omnipotent. And all divine perfections are swallowed up into will; that a triangle hath three angles equal to two right angles, that equals added to equals make equals, or that two and two are not four otherwise than according to his will, because they were made such by arbitrary decree of God Almighty.[1]

The materialism of Hobbes was the necessary corollary of the Cartesian attitude according to the Cambridge Platonists, and they condemned it in defence of their own view, which was still that of a world ruled by spiritual forces. But they were fighting a losing battle. The attraction of the new science was too great, and in a world dominated by immutable law, what was left of God's decree or man's free will? The animistic conception of the universe being eliminated, directly by the critique of the supernatural, and indirectly by the assertion of the laws of nature, what room remained for the operation of God's power? This was the problem which the new scientific conception of the universe presented to the seventeenth-century mind.

One answer, which satisfied for a time, was to see the discoveries of science as a revelation of the greatness of God. This implied the acceptance in advance of an optimistic, deistic view of the world.

[1] Ralph Cudworth, *A Treatise of Free Will*. Quoted by R. L. Colie, *Light and Enlightenment*, 1957, pp. 56-7.

It was successful so long as it was not realized that the rabbit which was being pulled out of the hat had previously been surreptitiously inserted into it. Spinoza had a contemptuous comment: 'In their endeavour to show that nature does nothing in vain, i.e. nothing which is useless to man, they only seem to have demonstrated that nature, the gods, and man are all mad together.'[1]

This was going too far. Apart from Spinoza, even the most advanced thinkers hardly ventured to challenge the demonstration of the wisdom of God in nature until well into the eighteenth century. In the meantime, Newtonian science and the world picture that went with it had changed the setting of religious thought. Where formerly had been seen the direct intervention of God, or of lesser spiritual powers, now only appeared the operation of superstitious beliefs. The particular dogmas of the separate Churches or sects began to seem irrelevant where they did not accord with the conditions of universal reason and the laws of nature. The result was to weaken the defences of orthodoxy all round and to prepare the ground for toleration.

Perhaps the decisive factor in crystallizing a new belief in toleration was an overwhelming demonstration of the nature and consequences of intolerance. The persecution of the French Huguenots by the Government of Louis XIV, reaching its climax with the Revocation of the Edict of Nantes in 1685, aroused the moral indignation of Protestant Europe, and even Catholics were not united in approving the actions of the French king. The Revocation was indeed something of an anachronism at the end of the seventeenth century. Huguenot refugees spread a hatred of religious persecution wherever they went; and by putting the ideas of toleration which had already developed in England and Holland into the universal language, French, they helped to give them wider circulation.

It must not be supposed that the Protestant Churches were necessarily more tolerant than the Catholic Church, or that toleration was in any sense an intended or direct consequence of the Reformation. Lutheranism had done much to increase the authority of the secular ruler in religious matters. Calvin established a theocracy in Geneva. The Huguenots, whose survival in seventeenth-century France clearly depended on the goodwill of the king, were for a time the strongest upholders of monarchical authority. As one pastor wrote: 'Our property, our bodies, our lives belong to the

[1] Quoted in Colie, p. 90.

king, and reserving only our consciences, which concern only God, everything remaining is entirely devoted to his service.'[1]

Even after the Revocation, the greatest of the refugee pastors, Pierre Jurieu, refused to extend to others the toleration which he claimed for the Huguenots. Their unchristian charity for heretics was one of the charges which he levied against the Arminians: 'That which causes us the greatest aversion for these Arminian churches is the criminal tolerance which they have for all sorts of errors, since they nourish in their bosoms Pelagians and Socinians'.[2] Such, he held, must be subject to the penal laws, 'not because of the plurality of opinions but because of the authority of the sovereign magistrate who is the master of the affairs of religion and especially because these laws are just and because they are true heretics'.[3] Conscience was not to be used as a justification for the denial of the fundamental truths of religion. Sects, like the Socinian, which repudiate these, or even those which introduce less fundamental false opinions but prepare the way for the diversity of religions, are not to be tolerated. Above the dictates of conscience, Jurieu proclaimed, are the laws of God.[4] 'It is faith which makes right reason, and not right reason faith.'[5]

For the classic statement of the principle of toleration which emerged out of the seventeenth-century debate, we have to turn to a thinker whose ideas were derived not from orthodox Calvinism but from the English Independents and Dutch Arminians. This was John Locke, whose Letter concerning Toleration, published in Latin in 1689, was rapidly translated into Dutch, French and English. Since Locke sums up in a concise form the conclusions of what we may call the 'enlightened' thought of the seventeenth century on toleration, and since he exercised so great an influence on the succeeding century, a brief summary of his main arguments seems justifiable here.

It is significant that Locke's opening appeal should be to the spirit of humanity, which suggests not only that it was the first consideration in his own mind, but also that he believed that it would come first with his readers:

That any man [he writes] should think fit to cause another man – whose salvation he heartily desires – to expire in torments,

[1] Quoted in G. H. Dodge, The Political Theory of the Huguenots of the Dispersion, 1947, p. 6. Cf. ibid., pp. 6, 10, 18.
[2] Jurieu, Traité de la puissance de l'église, 1677, p. 215. Dodge, p. 168, n. 10.
[3] Dodge, p. 115.   [4] Ibid., pp. 200-1, 204.
[5] Jurieu, Défense de la doctrine universelle de l'Eglise, p. 11. Dodge, p. 226.

and that even in an unconverted state, would I confess, seem very strange to me, and, I think, to any other also. But nobody, surely, will ever believe that such a carriage can proceed from charity, love or good-will.[1]

His positive arguments begin with the assertion that religion is a matter of the conscience, which cannot be forced:

I may grow rich by an art that I take not delight in, I may be cured of some disease by remedies that I have not faith in; but I cannot be saved by a religion that I distrust, and by a worship that I abhor.[2]

For this reason articles of faith are not to be imposed by law.[3] A church is 'a free and voluntary society';[4] the civil magistrate can only deal in matters affected by outward force, he has no authority over souls:[5]

For the political society is instituted for no other end, but only to secure every man's possession of the things of this life. The care of each man's soul, and of the things of heaven, which neither does belong to commonwealth nor can be subjected to it, is left entirely to every man's self.[6]

To allow a man's religion to be dictated by the ruler would be to make his salvation dependent upon the chance of his birth in one country or another.[7]

Toleration, of course, does not mean that everything is to be permitted:

If some congregations should have a mind to sacrifice infants, or (as the primitive Christians were falsely accused) lustfully pollute themselves in promiscuous uncleanness, or practice any other such heinous enormities, is the magistrate obliged to tolerate them, because they are committed in a religious assembly? I answer, No. These things are not lawful in the ordinary course of life, nor in any private house; and therefore neither are they so in the worship of God, or in any religious meeting.[8]

[1] Locke, *A Letter concerning Toleration*, in *The Second Treatise of Civil Government, etc.*, ed. J. W. Gough, 1946, p. 125.
[2] Ibid., p. 141. Cf. pp. 125, 127.   [3] Ibid., p. 150.   [4] Ibid., p. 129.
[5] Ibid., p. 127.   [6] Ibid., p. 153.   [7] Ibid., p. 128.   [8] Ibid., p. 145.

He adds, however, that the magistrate ought to be 'very careful' not to use his authority to oppress any religion on the pretext of public good.[1] Again, a Church ought not to be tolerated if it acknowledges the authority of a foreign ruler.[2] Locke gives as his example of this the Mohammedans, who acknowledge the authority of 'the Mufti of Constantinople'; but it is clear that he is really thinking of Catholicism and its allegiance to Rome. He also excludes from toleration atheists, because they cannot be bound by any oaths or promises and indeed have no religion to be tolerated.[3] It is worth noting that these exceptions are based upon supposed facts, and stand or fall with the correctness of these. He makes no other qualifications.

> If solemn assemblies, observations of festivals, public worship be permitted to any one sort of professors, all these things ought to be permitted to the Presbyterians, Independents, Anabaptists, Arminians, Quakers, and others, with the same liberty. Nay, if we may openly speak the truth, and as becomes one man to another, neither Pagan nor Mahometan, nor Jew, ought to be excluded from the civil rights or the commonwealth because of his religion.[4]

To the undogmatic mind these arguments may seem strong, to the Calvinist Jurieu they spelt only religious indifference.[5] Certainly they are difficult to reconcile with any belief in the overriding importance of religious dogma.

The new attitude to religion which was developing, when it stopped short, as it generally did, of absolute scepticism, was to find a name for itself in the term deism. Foreshadowed in such writers as Bodin and Montaigne, deism was denounced by Bossuet as a 'disguised atheism'. Its growth in England was shown by the publication, in 1677, of Bishop Stillingfleet's *Letter to a deist*, the first definite attack on English deism.

The meeting-place of many currents of thought, deism, like the principle of toleration, received its most moderate and comprehensive exposition and defence from Locke, in his *Reasonableness of Christianity*. While scepticism, science and even the spirit of tolerance, had undermined the faith of advanced thinkers in the dogmas of religion, for the most part they did not yet venture to

---

[1] Locke, *A letter concerning Toleration*, p. 146.   [2] Ibid., p. 155.
[3] Ibid., p. 156.
[4] Ibid., p. 160.
[5] Dodge, *Political Theory of Huguenots*, p. 220.

challenge the idea of deity. For Locke the existence of God was
evident as it was for Newton and on much the same grounds.

This most beautiful system of the sun, planets, and comets, could
only proceed from the counsel and dominion of an intelligent
and powerful Being ... He endures forever, and is everywhere
present; and by existing always and everywhere, he constitutes
duration and space.[1]

It was more a poetical than a mathematical conception, and
Addison turned the argument for deity into often quoted verse:

> The Spacious Firmament on high,
> With all the blue Etherial Sky,
> And spangled Heav'ns, a Shining Frame,
> Their great Original proclaim.

It did not matter if the picture of the heavens was a little old-
fashioned –

> What though, in solemn Silence, all
> Move round the dark terrestrial Ball.

(Copernicus and Galileo would not have been quite happy about
this, but a poet should not be expected to be quite up to date in his
science.)

> What tho' no real Voice nor Sound
> Amid their radiant Orbs be found?

(At least the harmony of the spheres had ceased.)

> In Reason's Ear they all rejoice,
> And utter forth a glorious Voice,
> For ever singing, as they shine,
> 'The Hand that made us is Divine'.

This is the famous watchmaker argument, and it is to be noted that
a significant change has intervened since the time of Descartes. He
had deduced the truth of nature from the existence of God: Locke
and his followers deduce the existence of God from nature. There
was one difficulty, however, to which Locke draws attention:

Though the works of nature, in every part of them, sufficiently
evidence a Deity; yet the world made so little use of their reason,

[1] Hall, *Scientific Revolution*, p. 271.

that they saw him not, where, even by the impressions of himself, he was easy to be found ... Reason, speaking ever so clearly
to the wise and virtuous, had never authority enough to prevail
on the multitude.[1]

Natural religion was nowhere adequately 'taken care of' by natural
reason, nor for that matter was natural morality. 'It is no diminishing
to revelation', Locke writes, 'that reason gives its suffrage too to the
truths revelation has discovered.'[2]

> The greatest part of mankind want leisure or capacity for
> demonstration ... And you may as soon hope to have all the
> day-labourers and tradesmen, the spinsters and dairy-maids,
> perfect mathematicians, as to have them perfect in ethics this
> way.[3]

What is needed, therefore, is 'a religion suited to vulgar capacities'.
'If the poor had the Gospel preached to them, it was, without doubt,
such a Gospel as the poor could understand; plain and intelligible.'[4]
It follows that theological controversy is only a source of confusion
and conflict about the fundamentals of religion:

> All the effect of it will be just the same it has been these
> thousand years and upwards; schisms, separations, contentions,
> animosities, quarrels, blood and butchery ... There is nothing
> more ridiculous, than for any man, or company of men, to
> assume the title of orthodoxy to their own set of opinions, as if
> infallibility were annexed to their systems, and those were to be
> the standing measure of truth to all the world ... The considera-
> tion of human frailty ought to check this vanity.[5]

He has been charged, he says, with having spoken against all systems.
'And always shall', Locke replies, 'so far as they are set up by
particular men, or parties, as the just measure of every man's faith.'[6]

The orthodox were profoundly suspicious, not without justification, of such views, and John Toland's *Christianity Not Mysterious*,
which appeared in 1696, the year after Locke's book, seemed to
them an exposure of the real implications of Lockian thought.
Toland assembles all the stock anti-religious arguments of the
Renaissance libertines, and it might seem that there is nothing new

---

[1] Locke, *The Reasonableness of Christianity* in *Works*, 1823, vii, 135.
[2] Ibid., p. 145.   [3] Ibid., p. 146.   [4] Ibid., pp. 157, 8.
[5] *A Second Vindication of the Reasonableness of Christianity,* in *Works*, vii, 358, 376.
[6] Ibid., p. 387.

in him. But because he was an Irish Catholic, educated, he says, in superstition and idolatry, we meet in Toland an aspect of the attack on religion which hardly appears elsewhere in English thought. This is a virulent hatred of the Church and its priests, in fact anticlericalism, which is a phenomenon peculiar to Catholic countries. For Toland all religion is priestcraft, and all the clergy conscious rogues. Locke, on the other hand, had plenty of religious and even clerical friends and never spoke ill of them.

Deism was met half-way by the latitudinarian movement in the Church of England and by the increasing laxity of the old dissenting sects. But, lacking the stimulus of persecution and without any inherent religious fervour, it could be no more than a half-way house to complete religious scepticism, though comparatively few in England were bold enough to pass on to that destination. Among those who did was Anthony Collins, who continued the use of historical criticism.[1] Since it was an age of empirical thought, all controversialists had to appeal either to science or to history; and since science was apparently committed to a formal deistic pattern, religious apologists and sceptics tended to fall back on historical arguments, all the more because Bossuet had apparently made the truth of Catholicism dependent on the evidence of history. Anthony Collins seriously discusses the proofs of Christianity as established by the prophecies of the Old Testament, arguing 'that if those Proofs are invalid, then is Christianity false'.[2] Of course, he shows that the proofs are indeed inadequate, and that the irreligious conclusion is unavoidable, but it was the orthodox themselves who had made the truth of Christianity apparently depend on the historical accuracy of the Old Testament.

The New Testament was exposed to criticism chiefly on the ground of the miraculous occurrences it reported, which were difficult to reconcile with the scientific conception of the universe. As the influence of science spread, so the miraculous was gradually eliminated from everyday life, at least in Protestant countries, and confined to the past. Consequently the argument over miracles also became an historical one. Thomas Woolston, in his *Six Discourses on the miracles of our Saviour* (1727–30), argued that they were merely allegorical. Other writers drew attention to the existence of equally

---

[1] Cf. *A Discourse of Free Thinking*, 1713; *A Discourse of the Grounds and Reasons of the Christian Religion*, 1724.

[2] *A Discourse of the Grounds and Reasons of the Christian Religion*, p 31.

strong evidence for pagan miracles. Conyers Middleton's *Letter from Rome* (1729) extended the field of controversy by showing the similarity between Catholic observance and the pagan superstitions of Greece and Rome.

The last word was said by Hume in his *Essay on Miracles*. He, also, adopted an historical point of view: the argument in favour of miracles, he said, must depend on the testimony for them. He drew attention to the occurrence of pagan miracles, apparently equally well authenticated historically. He asked sarcastically why miracles were of such common occurrence in primitive societies, whereas in more civilized ones they tended to disappear? The argument which was decisive to Hume, however, was a logical one. The uniformity of nature, he said, is the sole ground of the reliability of our reasoning. To argue for a breach of this uniformity is therefore a self-destructive argument. Moreover, there must be uniform experience against any miracle, otherwise it is not one. Such uniform experience can only be overthrown by superior evidence for the miracle; which it is patently impossible to have; besides, no historical evidence can ever pass from probability to certainty. Add to this the belief that Christianity cannot be accepted by any reasonable person without accepting at least one miracle as a fact, and the conclusion is obvious.

In England, opinion on the whole stopped before it reached the point of complete scepticism in religious matters; the controversy died down for lack of fuel, and ultimately, with the rise of a different approach to the problems of religion, the conditions of the argument were fundamentally altered. In France there developed an anti-Church militant, perhaps because it still had a Church militant and an actively persecuting one to fight against. It is no accident that the campaign in France against religion, and more particularly against the Catholic Church, was led by an exiled Huguenot.

Pierre Bayle,[1] born in 1747, the son of a Protestant pastor, must have had religious questionings from an early age, since for a period of eighteen months he became a Catholic convert and studied at a Jesuit college, one of the first of many sceptics to be produced by the great schools of the Society of Jesus. This experience, though it may have further undermined Bayle's Calvinism, did not convince him of the truth of Catholicism; but it did mean that when he left

---

[1] On Bayle, I have found particularly useful Jean Delvolvé, *Religion, Critique et Philosophie Positive chez Pierre Bayle*, 1906; and *Selections from Bayle's Dictionary*, edited by E. A. Beller and M. du P. Lee, 1952.

the Jesuits, as a relapsed heretic he had to fly the country. He went to teach, first at Sedan, and when the college there was closed by the pressure of Louis XIV, to Rotterdam, where he held a chair until the great Huguenot pundit, Jurieu, secured his dismissal because of his unorthodox opinions. 'God deliver us from the Protestant inquisition,' wrote Bayle then, 'it will be so dreadful in five or six years that one will long for the Roman as after a blessing.'[1] In his famous Dictionary he denounced the French refugee ministers:

> As soon as they are come into another Country, they have pronounced their Anathema against Those, who condemn the use of Penal Laws, in order to suppress Errors. This should serve for an Example of the Instability of human Things; and may furnish matter for much moral Reflexion.[2]

The first of Bayle's important writings – his *Pensées diverses sur la comète* (1682) – was stimulated by the outbreak of superstition that accompanied the appearance of a comet in 1680. At the same time he was directing his critical powers to the history of the Religious Wars in France, comparing the differing accounts of Catholics and Protestants.[3] In 1684 he founded his *Nouvelles de la République des lettres*, the first of many such literary and scientific periodical reviews, in which new contributions to letters and the sciences were summarized and discussed, and the views of the editor directly or indirectly propagated. Bayle was, with Fontenelle, who was made of lighter metal, among the first of the great propagandists of the Enlightenment. His sceptical mind exercised a powerful influence over the following generation, above all through his monstrous and unclassifiable *Dictionnaire historique et critique* (1697), a vast reservoir of corrosive erudition.

A few examples of Bayle's criticism must suffice. Thus, his historical criticism, applied to the Bible, produces the comment:

> If such a Narrative as this should be found in Thucydides, or in Livy, all the Critics would unanimously conclude, that the Transcribers had transposed the Pages, forgot something in one Place, repeated something in another, or inserted some preposterous Additions in the Author's Work.[4]

The clergy suffer at Bayle's hands by a technique that was to become

[1] Dodge, *Political Theory of Huguenots*, pp. 209-10.
[2] Art. 'Augustin', Beller and Lee, pp. 64-5.
[3] *Critique générale de l'histoire du Calvinisme*, 1682.
[4] Art. 'David', Beller and Lee, p. 99.

familiar. He is speaking of the Japanese Bonzes, who, he says, profess celibacy. There follows a reference to a footnote, if notes that often occupy the greater part of the page can be so called:

> But they do not always observe it very exactly. They abstain from flesh and fish, shave their beards and hair, and conceal their debaucheries under the appearance of an austere life ... They who would draw a parallel between the east and the west ... could not chuse but say inwardly to themselves 'thus it is with us'.[1]

Without equal literary genius, it is in all other respects the pen of Voltaire; and like Voltaire, Bayle is more inspired by a hatred of cruelty than by a love of truth. His article on David concludes sardonically:

> It is generally believed, that his Adultery with Bathsheba, the murder of Uriah, and the Numbering of the People, are the only faults he can be charged with. But it is a great Mistake. There are many other things in his life that deserve Censure. It would be doing an Injury to the Eternal Laws, and consequently to the True Religion, to give libertines occasion to object, that when a Man has been once inspired by God, we look upon his conduct as the Rule of Manners; so that we should not dare to condemn the Actions of People, though most opposite to the notions of Equity, when such an one has done them. There is no Medium in this Case; either these Actions are not Good, or Actions like them are not evil.[2]

A new element can be detected in this last extract. Bayle is condemning the Bible not only as irrational but also as immoral. Conscience for him is the judge of morality, and it is a higher judge than revealed religion or the Churches, for it is the expression of that 'natural idea of equity which ... illumines every man coming into the world'.[3] He anticipates the sceptics of the eighteenth century in being essentially a moralist. No metaphysician, he is concerned with practical questions. To theories he opposes facts, for example the fact that a pagan is as capable of being virtuous as a Christian. He attacks the Churches because they are based on false history and irrational superstition; but this criticism provides the weapon rather

---

[1] Art. 'Japan', Beller and Lee, p. 143.   [2] Art. 'David', ibid., p. 107.
[3] Quoted in J. Delvolvé, *Religion, Critique et Philosophie Positive chez Pierre Bayle*, 1906, p. 101.

than the motive. Basically, Bayle hates the Churches because they are cruel and persecuting, destroy what he believes to be the natural equity in man, and violate his conscience. The ultimate lesson of his scepticism is therefore toleration, and a toleration even broader than Locke had thought to be possible.

VII

Locke's Theory of Knowledge

THE years from 1680 to 1715 have been identified by Hazard with 'the crisis of the European conscience'. This was the generation during which the new scientific, philosophical and religious ideas of the seventeenth century began, very slowly and in limited circles, to be popularized, and to move from the sphere of intellectual speculation to that of practice. It was also the period in which a marked shift can be detected from a primary concern with the discovery of a priori truth, which can be called rationalism, to an empirical attitude. The progress of scepticism contributed to this change. The Cartesian certainty, amounting in its long-range influence to something rather like intellectual arrogance, in which the methodological doubt of Descartes eventuated, was replaced by an awareness of the limitations of the human mind. The philosopher in whom this transformation appeared most plainly was John Locke, and seldom has a great revolution in matters of the mind been presided over by a man of such intellectual modesty. Whereas most philosophers, of even minor distinction, are conspicuous by their awareness of their powers and of the questions they can answer, Locke's genius lay in his consciousness of the many questions he could *not* answer. Every young philosopher can, and usually does, make rings round Locke, which must be very flattering for them, seeing that he was for so long the dominant figure in European thought.

Locke's *Essay concerning Human Understanding* of 1690 is primarily epistemological. It is an inquiry into 'the original, certainty and extent of human knowledge'. The first step, Locke said, must be:

> to take a survey of our own understanding, examine our own powers, and see to what things they were adapted. Till that was done, I suspected we began at the wrong end, and in vain sought for satisfaction in a quiet and sure possession of truths that most concerned us, whilst we let loose our thoughts into the vast ocean of being; as if all that boundless extent were the natural and unbounded possession of our understandings, wherein there

was nothing exempt from its decisions, or that escaped its comprehension.[1]

This is not an abnegation of the understanding: our minds, Locke says, are broad enough for our use, why should we quarrel that their powers are not unlimited?[2] 'Our faculties being suited not to the full extent of being, nor to a perfect, clear, comprehensive knowledge of things, free from all doubt and scruple, but to the preservation of us, in whom they are, and accommodated to the use of life.'[3]

It is evident that with Locke scepticism has penetrated into philosophical thought and Cartesianism is being challenged in its basic principles. The object is no longer to achieve certainty, nor is Locke concerned with the problem of existence. He will not set sail on the 'vast ocean of being'. His investigation is psychological, not metaphysical; and even in this respect his concern is not with the mind that thinks but with the 'phantasm, notions, species, or whatever it is, which the mind can be employed about in thinking'.[4] He calls the subject of thought ideas, and he assumes that all mental processes are conscious, for, as he puts it, to suppose the soul to think and the man not to perceive it would be 'to make two persons in one man'[5] – a possibility which it was reserved for a later age to envisage.

Locke's ideas are like empirical facts, they are events. Put together they make up our stream of consciousness. How do they arise, or whence do they come? Before he answers these questions, Locke proceeds to demolish the view that among these ideas are some that are innate – 'characters, as it were, stamped upon the mind of man, which the soul receives in its very first being; and brings into the world with it'.[6] His refutation takes the form of the assertions, first that general consent to an idea does not prove that it is innate, and secondly that there are no ideas 'to which all mankind give an universal assent', for at least children and idiots must be excepted.[7] Innate ideas could at best be only an assumption and one that is unnecessary; for, he says, 'men, barely by the use of their natural faculties, may attain to all the knowledge they have, without the help of any innate impressions'.[8] Copying, perhaps consciously, the attitude of mind of the scientists, he refuses to introduce into his explanation of the operation of the mind an hypothetical factor

[1] *An Essay concerning Human Understanding,* book I, ch. 1, §7.
[2] Ibid, I, i, 5.   [3] Ibid., IV, xi, 8.   [4] Ibid., I, i, 8.   [5] Ibid., II, i, 19.
[6] Ibid., I, ii, 1.   [7] Ibid., I, ii, 3-5.   [8] Ibid., I, ii, 1.

which merely complicates the issue and for which he can see no
empirical evidence, when a simpler explanation is available to him.

For such a determined onslaught on innate ideas, however, we need
to find a motive, as well as an intellectual justification, especially
since, in Locke's argument, the latter is not without its weaknesses.
The most obvious influence is, as has just been suggested, the
empiricism of natural science. Even deeper, we may suspect, lies
the desire to eliminate what Locke calls 'innate practical principles' —
ideas of morality or religion which, so long as they have to be
accepted as a basic element in human nature, are not subject to
question. Such practical ideas, Locke points out, vary from country
to country. After a rather Voltairian enumeration of peculiar
customs, he concludes:

> Where, then, are those innate principles of justice, piety,
> gratitude, equity, chastity? ... He that will carefully peruse the
> history of mankind, and look abroad into the several tribes of
> men, and with indifference survey their actions, will be able to
> satisfy himself, that there is scarce that principle of morality to
> be named, or rule of virtue to be thought on ... which is not,
> somewhere or other, slighted and condemned by the general
> fashion of whole societies of men governed by practical opinions
> and rules of living, quite opposite to others.[1]

Ideas of God are subject to similar variation.[2] If all these different
conceptions are somehow to be identified with innate ideas there
can be no scope for a scientific treatment of the human mind, and
the principle of the uniformity of nature would have, so far as man
is concerned, to be repudiated. There may be a less drastic explanation. Indicating, near the beginning of his inquiry, what was to
emerge as one of its most important practical conclusions, Locke
speculates that upbringing and education in a different society and
country is perhaps all the difference there is between an Englishman
and a Hottentot.[3]

That there is a practical motivation behind Locke's argument may
be the more easily suspected, because later in his book he comes
dangerously close to the position of Descartes. This is when he speaks
of intuitive and demonstrative knowledge: we have an intuitive
knowledge of our own existence, and a demonstrative knowledge

---

[1] *An Essay concerning Human Understanding*, I, iii, 9, 10.
[2] Ibid., I, iv, 14.   [3] Ibid., I, iv, 12.

of the existence of God.[1] He has little to say of the former, save to wonder how the self can be an idea and thus be a subject of its own knowledge. As for God, Locke adopts the cosmological argument for an intelligent first cause. He is really more concerned, however, with a third kind of knowledge, which he calls sensitive. His problem, assuming that no ideas are innate, is whence they come, and he answers:

> Let us then suppose the mind to be, as we say, white paper, void of all characters, without any ideas; how comes it to be furnished? Whence comes it by that vast store which the busy and boundless fancy of man has painted on it, with an almost endless variety? Whence has it all the materials of reason and knowledge? To this I answer in one word, from experience; in that all our knowledge is founded; and from that it ultimately derives itself. Our observation employed either about external sensible objects, or about the internal operations of our minds, perceived and reflected on by ourselves, is that which supplies our understandings with all the materials of thinking. These two are the fountains of knowledge, from whence all the ideas we have, or can naturally have, do spring.[2]

In other words, Locke puts forward the sensational theory of knowledge. In spite of metaphors comparing the mind to a white paper or a *tabula rasa*, however, he does not think of it as purely passive. The senses provide the simple ideas, but the mind can go beyond these:

> When the understanding is once stored with these simple ideas, it has the power to repeat, compare, and unite them, even to an almost infinite variety, and so can make at pleasure new complex ideas. But it is not in the power of the most exalted wit, or enlarged understanding, by any quickness or variety of thought, to invent or frame one new simple idea in the mind.[3]

The working out of this theory involves Locke in considerable philosophical difficulties, especially when he has to account for general ideas, which he does by the assumption of a process of abstraction from simple ideas. Even simple ideas, he holds, however, do not reveal the true essence of substances, because the mind can

---

[1] Ibid., IV, iii, 21; IV, ix, 2.
[2] Ibid., II, i, 2.   [3] Ibid., II, ii, 2.

have no other object but its own ideas, which, if they are a result of real things, are not the things themselves.[1] These must remain unknowable.

Locke stands at the opposite extreme from Descartes. He is sceptical of the capacity of the human mind for reaching absolute truth in any form. He warns us: 'Most of the propositions we think, reason, discourse, nay, act upon, are such as we cannot have unundoubted knowledge of their truth.'[2] They fall into the 'twilight of probability'. Even this is not the end of his doubts. What do we know of the mind itself, or its relation to the body? Perhaps, he speculates, we shall never know whether a purely material body can think.[3] Even the most obvious general statements about the world fall short of certainty:

> We cannot, with certainty, affirm, that all men sleep by intervals; that no man can be nourished by wood or stones; that all men will be poisoned by hemlock; ... We must in these, and the like, appeal to trial in particular subjects, which can reach but a little way. We must content ourselves with probability in the rest.[4]

If Locke could go as far as this the ground was already well prepared for the destructive analysis of Hume.

Descartes was a greater philosopher than Locke, but Locke had laid the mine under Cartesianism which later philosophers were to explode. So far as ordinary enlightened opinion went, Locke's own writings served to destroy the validity of Descartes' arguments. Inadequate in his analysis of human psychology, halting and confused in his logic, Locke yet dominated the thought of the succeeding generation, and was the inspiration of a whole century. One cannot but wonder if he was quite as stupid as is sometimes said. It may, of course, be argued that his influence is attributable not so much to the theoretical merits of his discussion as to the practical consequences that could be drawn from it. The age of theory and rationalism was coming to an end, and an age that was concerned above all with practice was taking its place; though eighteenth-century empiricism should not be interpreted merely as a 'reaction' against the rationalism of the seventeenth century nor Locke as merely a precursor; he was the eighteenth-century Enlightenment in full force.

[1] *An Essay concerning Human Understanding*, III, vi, 6; IV, i, 1.
[2] Ibid., IV, xv, 2.   [3] Ibid., IV, iii, 6.   [4] Ibid., IV, vi, 15.

Never, perhaps, was there a philosopher who answered more completely to the needs of his day. Locke provided just the theoretical pattern which seemed to be called for by the practical interests and aims of his contemporaries. By extending scientific analysis to the mind, he asserted that man is a part of nature and subject to the same empirical investigation. By concentrating his attention on problems of epistemology, he let metaphysics go the way of religious dogma. By insisting that all we can really know is what is of use to us, he justified the growing utilitarian spirit and its concern with practical consequences. By rejecting innate ideas he cleared the ground at one blow of the inheritance of the past, and with the sensational psychology opened the gate to a different future. Immediately, and even in the long run, the greatest significance of Locke's theory of knowledge lay in its practical corollaries. Innate ideas being ruled out, the contents of the individual mind, it followed, were determined by the environmental influences to which it was subjected, or, using the term in its broadest sense, by its education. Appropriately, Locke's practical conclusions are indeed to be found most explicitly in his writings on education. 'Of all the men we meet with', he writes, 'nine parts of ten are what they are, good or evil, useful or not, by their education.'[1] And the power of education, if it could be used, could also be abused:

> There is, I know, a great fault among all sorts of people, of principling their children and scholars; which at last, when looked into, amounts to no more but making them imbibe their teacher's notions and tenets, by an implicit faith ... What colours may be given to this, or of what use it may be when practised upon the vulgar, destined to labour, and given up to the service of their bellies, I will not here inquire.[2]

'I imagine the minds of children', says Locke, 'as easily turned, this or that way, as water itself.'[3] This is not to be interpreted as a denial of individual freedom of choice, or responsibility. It must be read in conjunction with the insistence that every man has the touchstone of his natural reason with which to try all things.[4] But it does mean that there is a basic equality among men. Apparent differences in intelligence arise mainly from differences in powers of attention

[1] Some Thoughts concerning Education, 1693, §1.
[2] Of the Conduct of the Understanding, 1706, §41.
[3] Some Thoughts concerning Education, §2.
[4] Of the Conduct of the Understanding, §3.

and concentration,[1] which, Locke believed, were to some extent susceptible of training. It follows that by education man can become, within reasonable limits, the master of his destiny in this world. 'Men's happiness or misery is most part of their own making.'[2] This was truly a revolutionary conclusion.

[1] *On the Conduct of the Understanding*, §30.
[2] *Some Thoughts concerning Education*, §1.

VIII

The Problem of Good and Evil

IT would not be entirely fanciful to describe the seventeenth and eighteenth centuries as a second age of the sophists. At the time their intellectual achievements must have seemed similarly destructive to those who clung to any of the various orthodoxies. Religious faith was the principal victim of the new ideas, and the undermining of religion had far-reaching results, for the whole existing pattern of political and moral behaviour seemed to be based on religion, and to survive only by virtue of the religious sanction. Morality was equated with the commands of God. What was good in politics and morals was so because such was the teaching of religious authority. With the loss of this, an alternative source had to be found. This is why, as in the ancient world, the decline of religious faith was accompanied by the rise of moral philosophy, and of course in other periods the inverse process can be seen. Never perhaps has there been any century so intensely concerned with the problem of social morality as the sceptical and infidel eighteenth century.

The trend had set in strongly even earlier. In the sixteenth century humanist writers had brought Epicurean ideas back into currency, and these were to form one important strand in the growth of a new pattern of moral speculation. By the first half of the seventeenth century there was a fairly pronounced current of hedonistic thought. Pierre Gassendi (1542–1655), a French cleric, theologian, philosopher and mathematician, might be mentioned in many different connections, and particularly as a critic of Aristotle and advocate of experiment. He opposed the views of Descartes, and anticipated Locke in proclaiming 'Nihil in intellectu quod non prius fuerit in sensu'. Like many others his scientific thinking was strongly influenced by Lucretius, whose *De Natura Rerum* went through some thirty editions between the *editio princeps* of 1473 and 1600.[1] Gassendi did not make any important contributions to science, but he is significant as the author of a life of Epicurus, in which he

[1] Hall, *Scientific Revolution*, p. 206, n.1.

75

defended Epicurean doctrines, proclaimed that virtue and pleasure
are not opposites, and declared that the end of life is happiness.

A more systematic hedonistic morality appeared in the *Leviathan*,
where Hobbes stated unequivocally:

> Whatsoever is the object of any man's appetite or desire, that is
> it which he for his part calleth *good*; and the object of his hate
> and aversion, *evil* ... there being nothing simply and absolutely
> so; nor any common rule of good and evil, to be taken from the
> nature of the objects themselves.[1]

Locke put equally plainly the principle that the terms good and evil
are to be used only with reference to pleasure and pain. For him,
happiness, pleasure and good were equated.[2] He held also that moral
truths possess the same certainty as mathematical and are similarly
capable of demonstration, though he did not demonstrate any.[3]

The search for moral principles independent of religion was now
well started, but there was one preliminary question to be answered
– it had been implicitly posed by the extremer libertines – whether
and why there was such a thing as morality at all. If there were good
and evil in the world, and the good was preferable to the evil, why
was this so? God could not be left out of this argument: it was still
felt by all except a very few advanced thinkers that he was necessary
as a basis for morality. The problem therefore was that of justifying
belief in the existence of a deity in the absence of religious faith. As
has been suggested above, science, which had largely caused the
difficulty, seemed to offer the solution.

The wonders of nature were called in as evidence of the existence
of God. A host of books elaborated on this theme. Their titles tell
us really all we need to know about them – Burnet's *Sacred Theory
of the Earth*, Clarke's *Demonstration of the Being and Attributes of God*,
John Ray's *Wisdom of God in the Creation*, *La vérité de la religion
chrétienne démonstrée par l'ordre géométrique*, *The Christian Philosopher:
a Collection of the best discoveries in Nature, with religious improvements*,
L'existence de Dieu démonstrée par les merveilles de la Nature, *Théologie
des insectes*, and so on. *Le spectacle de la nature* (1732–50) by the abbé
Pluche, which passed through many editions, was the most successful
of all the zoological theologies. Pluche wrote: 'The Prospect of
Nature then is a kind of vulgar Theology ... The whole world is

---

[1] *Leviathan*, Part I, ch. vi.
[2] *Essay concerning the Human Understanding*, II, xx, 2.   [3] Ibid., IV, iii, 18, 20; iv, 7.

one great Picture, in which are displayed the Perfections of God.'[1] Or again: 'Providence has formed some Animals to live with Man, and be serviceable to him; and has created others to people Woods and Deserts, animate every Part of Nature, and chastise Mortals when they grow impious and abandoned.'[2]

The intellectual level of Pluche, it will be seen, was not a high one. The mathematician Maupertuis satirized the argument from design by reference to those who found God in the folds of the skin of a rhinoceros, because the animal's hide being so hard it would not be able to move without these folds. Conyers Middleton was more savage:

> As to the other part of the Cavil, that *God does nothing in vain*; you answer; that the *Foreskin was not made in vain*; that in *ordinary cases it was better to have it on, than off; but for extraordinary,* it was wisely contrived, that there might be *something to spare, something to cut off as occasion should require*: A most *admirable Solution*; which amounts just to this; that had not *God wisely provided it*, he could never have order'd it to be *cut off*.[3]

A frontal attack on the whole argument from design was made by the French writer Formey in his *Examen de la preuve qu'on tire des fins de la nature pour établir l'existence de Dieu*. And in such an iconoclast as the abbé Meslier it is inverted and the defects of the human organism used to prove either the wickedness or the non-existence of God.

From the religious point of view the argument from design was a dangerous way of demonstrating the existence and the goodness of God, and thus providing a moral foundation for the universe. Glorifying God in nature was only a step from glorifying nature. This step was taken by Locke's pupil, one of the most influential, if not profoundest, moralists of the eighteenth century, the third Earl of Shaftesbury. 'O glorious nature!' he exclaims, 'Supremely fair and sovereignly good! all-loving and all-lovely, all divine! ... O mighty Nature! wise substitute of Providence', etc., etc.[4] This comes a little unexpectedly from the author of *A letter concerning Enthusiasm*, but the merits or demerits of enthusiasm depended on what one was enthusiastic about. Religious enthusiasm, Shaftesbury thought, could

---

[1] N. A. Pluche, *Spectacle de la Nature*, trans. Humphreys, 1757, iii, 303-4.
[2] Ibid., i, 204.   [3] *A Letter to Dr Waterland*, 1731, pp. 35-6.
[4] *Characteristics*, ii, 98.

have undesirable consequences – there was some historical justification for this view. On the other hand nature was a harmless object
of adoration. Nature, Shaftesbury held, is good. Evils only appear
as such because we cannot see the whole. It follows that man as part
of nature is also good. Supernatural influences are hence not needed
to make him moral, and in fact the belief in them is destructive of
real virtue. True religion is based on nature, virtue consists in following nature, and beauty and goodness are ultimately the same.
Whereas morals had been for Locke demonstrative, comparable to
a geometrical theorem, for Shaftesbury they are 'as natural to us as
natural affection itself'; because there is a 'natural moral sense'.[1]
The importance of the step that Shaftesbury took should not be
underestimated. 'Delight in beholding torments, and in viewing
distress, calamity, blood, massacre and destruction,' he wrote, 'can
now be condemned as unnatural.'[2] Nature can thus take the place
of God as the basis of morality. Moreover, by means of the moral
sense the chief difficulty in hedonistic morals is solved, for it identifies
self-love and social good: 'Thus the wisdom of what rules, and is
first and Chief in Nature, has made it to be according to the private
interest and good of everyone, to work towards the general good.'[3]

The optimistic[4] view of the world and man represented by
Shaftesbury's moral theory was put into elegant verse by Pope in
his *Essay on Man* (1732–4), which rejected, denied, and ruled out as
irrelevant or misunderstood, all considerations that might seem to
contradict the optimistic faith:

> All Nature is but Art, unknown to thee;
> All Chance, Direction, which thou canst not see;
> All Discord, Harmony not understood;
> All partial Evil, universal Good;
> And, spite of Pride, in erring Reason's spite,
> One truth is clear, *Whatever is, is right.*

This was good orthodox theology for the time. Pope might have
found it in Archbishop King's *De Origine mali*, printed in Latin in
1702 and translated into English in 1731, just before the publication
of his *Essay*.

The older idea of the Chain of Being, which joined all existences

---

[1] *Characteristics*, i, 260, 262.   [2] Ibid., i, 331.   [3] Ibid., i, 338.
[4] A word which is said to have been first used in 1737. Hazard, *La Pensée européenne au XVIIIe siècle*, 1946, ii, 59.

in a divinely planned hierarchy, and in which the lower subserved
the ends of the higher, contributed to the same stream of thought.
The true philosopher is one who is —

> Slave to no sect, who takes no private road,
> But looks thro' Nature up to Nature's God,
> Pursues that chain which links th'immense design,
> Joins Heav'n, and earth, and mortal, and divine.

Universal harmony also solves the problem of the conflict of
individual interest and social morality:

> Thus God and Nature link'd the gen'ral frame,
> And bade Self-love and Social be the same.

But it would be unfair to Pope to represent him with these quotations alone. The laureate of optimism was too good a poet not to be
capable of better poetry and more pessimistic sentiments, though
they are less relevant to our theme. In the same poem, but in a
different mood he sees man —

> Plac'd on this isthmus of a middle state,
> A being darkly wise and rudely great:
>
> . . . . .
>
> Sole judge of Truth, in endless Error hurl'd;
> The glory, jest, and riddle of the world!

As the shadows darken, Pope finds it difficult to keep his courage up
the whole time. Philosophers could do that better than poets, but
even they only so long as they continued their whistling in the dark.
A poet could not but touch reality:

> Behold the child, by Nature's kindly law,
> Pleas'd with a rattle, tickled with a straw:
> Some livelier plaything gives his youth delight,
> A little louder, but as empty quite:
> Scarfs, garters, gold, amuse his riper stage,
> And beads and pray'r-books are the toys of age:
> Pleas'd with this bauble still, as that before;
> Till tir'd he sleeps, and life's poor play is o'er.

Pope's optimism declines into a quiet melancholy. Other eighteenth-century moralists faced the problem of suffering and evil
more seriously. It weighed heavily on the minds of men like Swift
and Voltaire and Dr Johnson. The problem of evil was not a new

one: it had been coped with, after a fashion, by the religious thought of the past, with the aid of the Devil, Original Sin and a future state of rewards and punishments. Unfortunately in enlightened thought these were all discredited. Wesley's vigorous faith in the Devil and all his works came to the rescue of the common man, but the Devil's future career was destined to be on a rather lower level of society than he was accustomed to. For enlightened men, the Devil and Original Sin disappeared into the limbo of unbelief along with the serpent and the apple, Adam and Eve, and the rest of the fascinating Jewish-Christian mythology. They left a void: somebody had to be responsible for all the evil in the world; and if the Devil became a myth, and man was naturally good, who remained but God? This was a terrifying thought. If God were the author of evil, how could he function as the sanction for morality? And how could a perfect being be responsible for evil? Or if he were not responsible for it, what had happened to his omnipotence? These questions were easier to pose than to answer.

One way of dealing, after a fashion, with the dilemma appeared in 1705, in a little anonymous verse pamphlet of twenty-six pages and costing sixpence. It was called *The Grumbling Hive: or Knaves Turned Honest*. Enlarged and republished in 1714 as Mandeville's *Fable of the Bees*, with the sub-title 'Private Vices – Public Benefits', it had many subsequent enlargements and additions until it had swollen to the size of two volumes. Mandeville's theme is well known. He draws a picture of a prosperous and happy but far from moral hive, in which all the little bees, each pursuing his (or her) own selfish and amoral interest, gather honey while they may and so contribute to the general weal. However, a few ruthless moralists are not content with this condition and fill the air with their complaints about the prevailing vice. Jove, tired of their importunities, at last 'rid the bawling hive of fraud'. What happens? Industry weakens, trade decays, all the professions fall out of employment, population declines, foreign enemies and rivals triumph, and finally a pathetic remnant of the once great and flourishing community takes refuge in a hollow tree. The moral is drawn in Mandeville's own words:

> Then leave complaints: Fools only strive
> To make a great an honest hive.
> T'enjoy the World's Conveniences,
> Be fam'd in War, yet live in Ease,

Without great Vices, is a vain
Eutopia seated in the Brain!

. . . . .

Bare Vertue can't make Nations live
In Splendour; they, that would revive
A Golden Age, must be as free
For Acorns, as for Honesty.

Mandeville, writes Leslie Stephen, 'puts in its most offensive form the dogma that what we call virtue is but selfishness masquerading'.[1] But his views should not be written off merely as witticisms. Montesquieu wrote 'I would willingly enter into the ideas of the author of the *Fable of the Bees*'.[2]

The same strain appears in the *Beggar's Opera* (1728) of John Gay, whose rogues and whores play out, on a sordid stage and in tattered finery, the tragi-comedy that their betters enact in Court and Parliament. In France, *Gil Blas* (1715) teaches the same lesson. It must not be supposed that the cynical phase in literature necessarily reflected any general deterioration in conduct. It was rather a reflection of the growth of scepticism about traditional moral principles; but a more philosophical treatment of the problem of evil was also needed.

Among those who attempted this was Soame Jenyns, in *A Free Enquiry into the Nature and Origin of Evil* (1757). He began with what was by now the general assumption, of which he provides one of the most striking statements in eighteenth-century literature, that good is the same as happiness, and evil as unhappiness:

> To say truth, Happiness is the only thing of real value in existence; neither riches, nor power, nor wisdom, nor learning, nor strength, nor beauty, nor virtue, nor religion, nor even life itself, being of any importance but as they contribute to its production. All these are in themselves neither Good nor Evil; Happiness alone is their great end, and they desirable only as they tend to promote it.[3]

Morality he defines, logically, as the pursuit of happiness, though he adds to it, as a kind of bonus, the virtue acquired by obeying the decrees of religion. Jenyns, however, does not put us off with the

---

[1] Leslie Stephen, *English Thought in the Eighteenth Century*, 2nd ed. 1881, i, 38.
[2] Montesquieu, *Pensées*, in *Œuvres complètes*, ed. A. Masson, 1950, ii, 449.
[3] Soame Jenyns, *A Free Enquiry into the Nature and Origin of Evil*, 1757, p. 46.

superficial optimism of a Shaftesbury or Pope. He recognizes as a fact the existence of evil on an extensive scale. He has been blamed for this instead of being praised for his intellectual honesty; but this is because, as well as accepting it, he tries to fit it into the eighteenth-century pattern of a rational world, presided over by a benevolent deity. His explanation is that even God cannot create good without evil.[1] For Jenyns, necessary evil takes the place of Original Sin; and with the aid of the old 'Chain of Being idea he revives, in an extreme form, the view that partial evils contribute to greater good. But because Jenyns did not pretend that the evils were other than they were, the result seemed to some of his contemporaries peculiarly shocking. He writes, in the strain of Mandeville: 'Luxury maintains its thousands, and Vanity its ten thousands ... and thus private vices become publick benefits by the force only of accidental circumstances.'[2] This seems comparatively harmless, but he also says:

> Poverty ... is what all could not possibly have been exempted from ... ; for had all been rich, none could have submitted to the commands of another, or the necessary drudgeries of life; thence all governments must have been dissolved, arts neglected, and lands uncultivated, and so an universal penury have over-whelmed all, instead of now and then pinching a few.[3]

This was the kind of explanation that stood in the way of any attempt at amelioration of human conditions. There is no reason to believe that Soame Jenyns was other than an humane man, but he has to argue that ignorance being the opiate of the poor, they should not be deprived of it by 'an ill-judged and improper education'.[4] Or even that 'There is something in the abstract nature of pain conducive to pleasure; [so] that the sufferings of individuals are absolutely necessary to universal happiness.'[5] The goodness of nature begins to be almost as mysterious as the way in which God moves to per-form his wonders. Ruthlessly optimistic to the last, Soame Jenyns speculates that the sufferings of the lower forms of creation may subserve, and therefore be justified by, the happiness of the higher. Perhaps even the evils with which the face of man is disfigured, he suggests, may contribute to the pleasure of higher beings.

This aroused the indignation of Dr Johnson, who knew from

---

[1] Soame Jenyns, pp. 17, 67.
[2] Ibid., p. 87.   [3] Ibid., p. 50.   [4] Ibid., p. 34.   [5] Ibid., p. 60.

personal experience, better than Jenyns, what these sufferings were. In a review he let fly with Johnsonian wrath:

> Many a merry bout have these frolic beings at the vicissitudes of an ague, and good sport it is to see a man tumble with an epilepsy, and revive and tumble again, and all this he knows not why. As they are wiser and more powerful than we, they have more exquisite diversions, for we have no way of procuring any sport so brisk and so lasting, as the paroxysms of the gout and stone, which undoubtedly must make high mirth, especially if the play be a little diversified with the blunders and puzzles of the blind and deaf.[1]

The difference between Soame Jenyns and Dr Johnson does not lie in the inhumanity of the one and the humanity of the other, but in the fact that the former was still trying to maintain the optimistic world-view of Pope's *Essay on Man*, and to integrate the facts of evil that he recognized into the picture; while the latter had abandoned the attempt to build a theoretical system that would justify the nature of things. Dr Johnson fell back, in *Rasselas*, on a stoical acceptance of the misfortunes of life. What else can be said of a tale that begins:

> Ye who listen with credulity to the whispers of fancy, and pursue with eagerness the phantoms of hope; who expect that age will perform the promises of youth, and that the deficiencies of the present day will be supplied by the morrow; attend to the history of Rasselas, prince of Abyssinia.

And ends: 'Of these wishes that they had formed they well knew that none could be obtained.'

The pessimism of Dr Johnson does not belong to the story of the Enlightenment; but equally its moral theory does not end with the blind optimism of Shaftesbury or the optimism *malgré tout* of Jenyns. This kind of optimism was only a phase, mainly confined to England, and not a lasting one even there. Dr Johnson himself noticed the parallel between his own story *Rasselas* and Voltaire's *Candide*, which was published almost at the same time. There is no reason to believe that Dr Johnson, poverty-stricken, ugly and ailing, had ever shared the world-view of the *Essay on Man*; but Voltaire, as a young writer enjoying premature and astonishing success, with the world at his

[1] Quoted in Basil Willey, *The Eighteenth-century Background*, 1940, p. 53.

feet, had admired the honeyed verse of Pope and condemned the tragic vision of Pascal. In the *Lettres philosophiques* he wrote: 'I dare to take the side of humanity against this sublime misanthrope; I dare to assert that we are neither as wicked nor as unhappy as he says.[1]

The young Voltaire hymned the praise of luxury and proclaimed 'le paradis terrestre est où je suis',[2] or, as an earlier version put it, 'le paradis terrestre est à Paris'. Age and experience brought a remarkable change. The Lisbon earthquake of 1755 finally forced the problem of evil on his notice, and like Dr Johnson he found he could not pretend that evil was really good, even indirectly or in disguise. In the preface to the poem evoked by this disaster, he still praised Pope, whom, he said, he continued to admire and love; but the belief that 'tout est bien' had since Pope been so perverted that it had become 'an insult to the sufferings of our life'. Bayle was the better guide, because he had taught men to doubt. In a spirit of Johnsonian stoicism Voltaire concludes:

> Dans une épaisse nuit cherchant à m'éclairer
> Je ne sais que souffrir, et non pas murmurer.[3]

Even the *Poème sur la loi naturelle*, which accompanied the poem on the Lisbon earthquake and was intended to rescue the deistic ideas of natural religion and universal morality, is something closer now to Pascal than to Pope:

> Dans nos jours passagers de peines, de misères,
> Enfants du même Dieu, vivons au moins en frères,
> Aidons-nous l'un et l'autre à porter nos fardeaux:
> Nous marchons tous courbés sous le poids de nos maux;
>
> .   .   .   .   .
>
> Ah n'empoisonnons pas la douceur qui nous reste.
> Je crois voir des forçats dans un cachot funeste,
> Se pouvant secourir, l'un sur l'autre acharnés,
> Combattre avec les fers dont ils sont enchaînés.

The last lines bring to mind the second great shock that completed the undermining of Voltaire's optimism – the Seven Years War. The subsequent appearance of *Candide* is not a chronological accident, for by now he had come to detest the optimistic world-view

---

[1] *Lettres philosophiques*, 1734, XXV.   [2] *Le Mondain*, 1736.
[3] *Poème sur le désastre de Lisbonne.*

with its implied justification of so much suffering. His long pre-occupation – one might almost call it an obsession – with Leibnizian optimism comes to a head in the bitter satire he directs against Dr Pangloss, though rather than Leibniz Pangloss may have represented his egregious popularizer Christian Wolff, whose ideas Voltaire would have known well enough through Mme du Châtelet.[1] Voltaire's own view is summed up when Cacambo asks, 'What is optimism?' 'Alas,' said Candide, 'it is the mania for pretending that all is well when all is ill.'

He returns to the subject in the article 'Tout est bien' in the *Dictionnaire philosophique*, which sums up Leibniz as teaching that this is the best of possible worlds, and one ingredient in it is necessary evil. Mock-seriously, Voltaire presents various explanations of the existence of evil: – the theory he attributes to Lactantius, that evil is necessary, because without it God could not have given us good; the view of Bolingbroke, Pope and Shaftesbury that all is well, which means that all is governed by immutable laws, and particular evils add up to general good; the Manichaeist dualism, with good and evil as the two equal powers that rule the world; the box that Pandora opened; or, finally, the suggestion that perhaps the world was made by inferior angels and so is a sub-standard article. He ends with the conclusion that the 'all is well' theory cannot but represent God as an all powerful and evil-doing ruler. The existence of evil remains inexplicable: it is something we do not understand, but 'Il faut cultiver notre jardin'.

The stoical resignation of a Dr Johnson or the resigned pessimism of a Voltaire were not for the ordinary man, who was less acutely aware of the deeper issues. A subsidiary but more practical problem, that of reconciling self-interest with the utility of the public, pressed more consciously on the minds of those who continued to pursue the moral debate. One of the most influential attempts at a solution is that proffered by David Hartley in his *Observations on Man* (1749). Hartley takes his start from some suggestions that Locke had thrown out. He picks up the passing suggestion of Locke that possibly a material being can think and proceeds to interpret the operations of the mind in terms of material vibrations. With this beginning it is not difficult for him to look for some force which will play the part in mental activity of gravity in Newtonian physics. In place

[1] For a thorough discussion of Voltaire's reaction to Leibnizian optimism see W. H. Barber, *Leibniz in France from Arnauld to Voltaire*, 1955.

of the active function of reflection, which Locke allows to play on the simple ideas acquired by the senses, Hartley hypothesizes an entirely automatic process of association:

> Any Sensations A, B, C, etc. by being associated with one another a sufficient Number of Times, get such a Power over the corresponding Ideas a, b, c, etc. that any one of the Sensations A, when impressed alone, shall be able to excite in the Mind b, c, etc. the Ideas of the rest.[1]

Now God, who is 'the Cause of all Things', has so arranged that the desire of happiness is the necessary result of the universal principle of association in the human mind; and it follows from this that the tendency of Benevolence is 'to augment itself without limits' and of Malevolence to destroy itself ultimately. This, says Hartley, 'appears to be a very strong Argument for the infinite Benevolence of God'.[2] From which, he concludes: 'It is probable from Reason, that all Mankind will be made happy ultimately.'[3]

Religion found another solution to the dilemma in terms of utilitarianism, by bringing in the pains and pleasures of a future life to redress the balance of the present one. This 'other-worldly' morality was perhaps not a new element in religious thought except in the terms in which it was stated, which were sufficiently plain. Archdeacon Paley's *Moral and Political Philosophy* (1785) was its classic statement, which Leslie Stephen has summarized rather cruelly:

> Christ came to tell us that we should go to hell if our actions did not tend to promote the greatest happiness of the greatest number; and the Almighty has contrived a means for giving him satisfactory credentials. The man at whose order the clock strikes thirteen must be in the secret of the artificer, and we may trust his account of a hidden part of the machinery.[4]

Another line of approach to the problem, which took the form of a combination of Shaftesbury's moral sense and Locke's moral new-tonism, is to be found in the theory of Francis Hutcheson.[5] God, he held, has implanted in the individual a moral sense by which he is

---

[1] David Hartley, *Observations on Man, his Frame, his Duty, and his Expectations*, 1749, i, 65.
[2] Ibid., ii, 21, 31.   [3] Ibid., ii, 419.   [4] Stephen, *English Thought*, p. 416.
[5] *System of Moral Philosophy*, 1747.

able to see, and when he sees to desire, that which is for the common good, which Hutcheson defined, in a phrase which was to become famous when a greater thinker used it, as 'the greatest happiness of the greatest number'. Adam Smith's *Theory of Moral Sentiments* (1759) adopts a similar line of argument, except that without denying the moral sense, he takes ethical behaviour as the product of all the other sentiments, moderated by the operation of social sympathies. Its result is that happiness of mankind which 'seems to have been the original purpose intended by the author of nature'.[1] The superficial optimism which, in Soame Jenyns, aroused the wrath of Dr Johnson, is echoed by Adam Smith. Despite the appearances of disorder in this world, 'yet even here every virtue naturally meets with its proper reward'.[2] It is true that wealth is unequally distributed, but as a result of the expenditure of the rich:

> They are led by an invisible hand to make nearly the same distribution of the necessaries of life which would have been made had the earth been divided into equal portions among all its inhabitants.[3]

By now, however, the eighteenth century had doubtless had enough of this kind of thing. It was becoming clear that the debate in England was petering out, and it might be thought that all that could be said on these lines had already been said, almost ad nauseam; but in fact a major contribution to ethical thought has still to be mentioned. The work of most lasting value in the field of moral philosophy published in the eighteenth century was that of Richard Price in his *Review of the Principal Questions and Difficulties in Morals*.[4] Price set the whole discussion of the moral sense on a sounder basis by refusing to go behind the fact of the moral judgment. We know, he declared in effect, that we do make moral judgments continually. 'To *behold* virtue', he declares, 'is to *admire* her ... to *perceive vice* is the very same as to *blame*.'[5] This is to say that morality is intuitive: it is derived from an inner sense. At the same time, he does not yield up moral behaviour to the uncontrolled sway of some hypothesized and vague moral emotion. The application of these intuitive judgments, the assessment of their relevance when, as is often the case, more than one comes into play or their transference into action is not clear, calls for the employment of, and indeed control by, reason.[6]

---

[1] *Theory of Moral Sentiments*, Part III, ch. v.   [2] Ibid.   [3] Ibid., Part iv, ch. i.
[4] *Review of the Principal Questions and Difficulties in Morals*, 17,8.
[5] Ibid., p. 95.   [6] Ibid., pp. 129-30.

Price's theory of intuitive ethics is the most logical statement of one trend in eighteenth-century ethical thought. The stricter utilitarian view, on the other side, was to culminate in Bentham. Neither remained quite independent of, or uninfluenced by, the other; and the combination of the two was perhaps more fruitful than either would have been by itself.

In France the debate had followed rather different lines, as may be seen by a glance at the treatment of the question of morality in the *Encyclopédie*.[1] The basic moral problem which appears in its pages is whether there is a natural morality, preceding society and the institution of laws, or whether all ideas of morality are the product of society. Excluding a religious basis for morality or any innate moral ideas, and seeing man as a part of nature, Diderot and his collaborators gave an affirmative answer to the first question. It followed that it should be possible to discover the nature of the necessary moral rules from a study of the facts. Natural morality should be scientific, positive and sociological. In practice the Encyclopaedists' line of inquiry was nothing of the sort. They made no serious attempt at an empirical inquiry. The mass of information that existed on the social customs of the various peoples of the world they largely ignored. Anything that they could not understand was dismissed as a product of human folly or roguery, probably of priestcraft. The Cartesian faith in first principles, and their own preconceived notions, were too strong for them. Their belief in a natural morality was a belief in a theoretical pattern, of universal validity, which merely needed to be discovered to be applied. Diderot himself saw better than many modern thinkers the difficulty of the attempt to derive a moral theory from the fantastic varieties of human behaviour, which seemed to lead to the conclusion that there was scarcely any supposed vice that was not a virtue somewhere.

The *philosophes* are not necessarily to be criticized for their failure to build up a scheme of morality on the shifting and contradictory bases of the facts of differing societies. If they looked to the physical and psychological needs of man to provide a system of morals, the result was hardly more encouraging; societies were so rarely natural, and universal, unchanging human nature could seldom be detected in actual customs. Thus they fell back on speculation. Their discussion of the origin of moral sentiments was hypothetical rather than historical or practical. Some sought to discover by psychological

[1] Cf. R. Hubert, *Les Sciences sociales dans l'Encyclopédie*, 1923, Part II, ch. v.

analysis how morality *must have* originated. Others, like de Jaucourt, clung to the traditional moral ideas of the Natural Law school of thought. Under the influence of Cartesianism they all tended to believe that what was clear, simple and universal was true, in morals as in mathematics. They were, indeed, trying to achieve the deductive system of morals that Locke had proclaimed, and were no more successful than he was in giving it a positive content.

Utilitarians, like Helvétius and d'Holbach, and intuitionists like Rousseau, were to carry on the debate, within the limits of their systems, more profitably. Diderot, combining both tendencies, and adding a special insight of his own, summed up the contributions and contradictions of a century in his writings. These later developments remain to be discussed, but already it will be evident that eighteenth-century thinkers gave no final answer to the problem of morality, any more than they had to the problem of evil. They are not to be criticized too severely for this failure. It can hardly be claimed that their successors have answered the questions that the eighteenth century had at least the credit of raising, or that later generations deserve higher praise for abandoning a debate of which the greatest merit lay simply in the fact that it was carried on with such sincerity and intensity. If a serious debate over moral problems, as distinguished from an unquestioning acceptance of views established by tradition or authority, is any test of morality, then the age of the Enlightenment was the most moral of all ages.

IX

The Rise of Political Liberalism

THE discussion of the problem of morality has led us far into the eighteenth-century Enlightenment. But before we can leave the seventeenth century there remains for investigation another major field in which it sowed the seeds from which later ideas were to grow. The decline of orthodox religious thought, as well as provoking speculation on the nature and sanction of morals, necessitated a rethinking of the bases of government. Ethics and political thought, merely subordinate branches of theology since the decay of classical civilization, were reborn in the fifteenth and sixteenth centuries, but they only became really independent of theological thought in the seventeenth. The Churches themselves, after the Reformation, played a large part in the revival of political thought, by way of the reaction against the bitter civil strife which had been waged in their name. As in other respects, however, we must be careful not to antedate the development of political thinking.

The test of the emancipation of politics is perhaps to be found in the development of the idea of the secular State, which means in one form or another the idea of sovereignty. Medieval political theory, Gierke holds, never reached 'the legal concept of the personality of the State as a unitary whole'. For this reason, he argues, it did not achieve the idea of the sovereign State.[1] In the sixteenth, and to some extent even in the seventeenth century, according to him, it was still held 'that what makes a statute a law lies in the formal determination of the sovereign that its content accords with the idea of justice', not in the will of the sovereign that such and such should be law.[2]

Admittedly, the sixteenth century had seen a great increase both in the fact and in the theoretical justification of monarchical authority, in the course of which the idea of sovereignty, which had reappeared in the controversies over imperial and papal claims in the later Middle Ages, developed farther. Both Lutheranism and Catholicism, looking to secular rulers for protection and support,

---

[1] O. Gierke, *The Development of Political Theory*, trans. B. Freyd, 1939, p. 150.
[2] Ibid., p. 308.

promoted the growth of sovereignty, in theory and practice. There were, of course, contrary currents. The French Religious Wars, the massacre of St Bartholomew, and the alliance with the Huguenot nobles, produced ideas of justifiable resistance among the French Calvinists, such as were expressed in the *Vindiciae contra tyrannos*. The people as a corporate body, it was held, acting under its natural leaders, had a right of resistance in certain cases. But when Henry IV became the heir to the throne, Huguenot thought reverted to strict monarchical principles. The Jesuit writer, Suarez, now claimed in his turn that sovereignty was derived from the community, which therefore had the right of resisting tyrants;[1] while another Catholic writer, Mariana, even justified tyrannicide.[2] The whole process was summed up by Figgis in the phrase: 'Political liberty is the residuary legatee of ecclesiastical animosities.'[3]

While such views were finding expression in theory, however, practical developments were moving in the opposite direction, with the rise of more powerful rulers. On the continent of Europe only in the Dutch Republic did the idea of the absolute sovereignty of the ruler fail to obtain general recognition. In England, despite the survival of Parliament, the Tudors put forward higher claims to sovereignty, and asserted them more effectively in practice, than any previous English dynasty. Only the accession of the Stuarts, and their failure to crush the Parliamentary opposition that had already been appearing under Elizabeth I, prevented the triumph of the idea of monarchical authority in England as in Europe. And when Parliament, having won the Civil War, tried to establish its own sovereignty in place of that of the king, the Independents turned against the Parliamentarians the arguments that the latter had employed against the king.

In the course of the English Civil War the individualist element in Calvinist thought was extended from the religious to the political field. Revolutionary conditions make for a rapid, even feverish, development in political ideas. Sovereignty was now claimed for the people as 'under God the original of all power'. The extremist group of the Levellers, as well as demanding sovereignty for the people, called for it to be put into practice by biennial parliaments with redistribution of seats and equality before the law. Antinomian and millenarian ideas carried the agitation into extremes which

---

[1] *De Legibus*, 1619.   [2] *De Rege*, 1599.
[3] J. N. Figgis, *From Gerson to Grotius*, 2nd ed. 1931, p. 118.

provoked a reaction and contributed to the restoration of Charles II; but the effects of the Civil War and Commonwealth could not be undone. When the country was faced with the succession of the Catholic James, Duke of York, a dissenting and anti-monarchical agitation broke out again in the Exclusion Bill controversy. It has recently been shown that John Locke then wrote his famous treatises on government, though they were only published in 1690. The date of writing is not without significance, for it shows that they were originally composed not simply to justify an accomplished revolution, but to support a projected one. In this light Locke's proclamation of a doctrine of resistance is even more striking. And once again we have to turn to him for a summing-up of the intellectual achievements of the seventeenth century in yet another field.

Locke's *First Treatise of Civil Government* is an attack on Filmer's *Patriarcha*, which had just been published in 1680, long after its date of composition. The strength of the divine right theory of monarchical authority is suggested by the fact that Locke should have troubled to devote a whole book to its refutation. But though Filmer is less contemptible than has been suggested, in criticizing him Locke was looking to the past. The *Second Treatise* lays down the principles of the politics of the future.

Locke's problem, given the decline of the religious sanction of government and the abandonment of ideas of divine right, was to find 'another rise of government' which would provide an alternative to treating it as the simple product of force.[1] He begins by giving his definition of political power:

> Political power, then, I take to be a right of making laws with penalties of death, and consequently all less penalties, for the regulating and preserving of property, and of employing the force of the community in the execution of such laws, and in the defence of the commonwealth from foreign injury, and all this only for the public good.[2]

This definition is the clue to the whole argument. It embodies Locke's basic assumptions about government, and by rigorously limiting the ends of political power determines in advance the line his thought shall take. In his initial assumptions are encapsulated his final conclusions, in which Locke is perhaps not very different from other political theorists.

---

[1] *Second Treatise on Civil Government*, ed. J. W. Gough, 1946, §1.   [2] Ibid., §3.

A summary of so well known a work as Locke's *Second Treatise* is unnecessary, but the influence it exercised over the political thought of the Enlightenment was so great that an attempt must be made to indicate some of the more significant features in the argument. In the first place, Locke's State of Nature, unlike that of Hobbes, is one of freedom, equality and obligation to mutual love; it is not a state of licence and it is ruled by a Law of Nature, which is reason.[1] Whether the State of Nature is, or is not, conceived by Locke as an historical state is a comparatively minor question; the seventeenth century was not particularly conscious of this issue. The State of Nature is, however, certainly a way of defining his basic assumptions about *human nature*. And just as Hobbes's human nature is so anti-social that it is only by adducing the previously unrevealed factor of reason that the possibility of social life can be envisaged, so Locke's State of Nature is so idyllic that it comes very unexpectedly when he puts forward the need 'that all men may be restrained from invading others' rights, and from doing hurt to one another.'[2] One had hardly anticipated any such dangers from his previous description. Whatever the justification, he argues that there is a need to prevent disorder by the creation of an authority with power to judge between men.[3] This can only be set up by means of a compact, which itself must be limited by the same conditions as, in Locke's initial definition, limit all political power:

> The only way by which anyone divests himself of his natural liberty and puts on the bonds of civil society is by agreeing with other men to join and unite into a community for their comfortable, safe, and peaceable living one amongst another in the secure enjoyment of their properties, and a greater security against any that are not of it.[4]

As a preliminary to the contract, it follows, Locke has to justify property, which he does by the labour theory of value. Starting from the assumption that the earth was given to mankind in common, he proceeds to argue that, 'As much as anyone can make use of to any advantage of life before it spoils, so much he may by his labour fix a property in.'[5] The limit of property is set by 'the extent of men's labour and the convenience of life'.[6] He proceeds from this to justify great inequalities of property and elsewhere even excuses slavery

---

[1] Ibid., §§4, 5, 6.   [2] Ibid., §7.
[3] Ibid., §13.   [4] Ibid., §95.   [5] Ibid., §31.   [6] Ibid., §36.

by patently fallacious arguments, but these weaknesses in his argument were only to be taken up seriously in the nineteenth century.

Politically, it must be emphasized, Locke's is a revolutionary theory. His contract is not intended primarily to stabilize a new regime but to overthrow an old one. Nor does he simply justify a 'once for all' revolution. The right of resistance is a permanent right, the duty of obedience is what is temporary and provisional:

> Nor is it now any more hindrance to the freedom of mankind that they are born under constituted and ancient polities that have established laws and set forms of government, than if they were born in the woods amongst the unconfined inhabitants that run loose in them.[1]

No contract can bind posterity,[2] nor does it abrogate the rights of nature, embodied in the Law of Nature.[3]

The greatest safeguard of these rights, in Locke's theory, is the fact that after the establishment, by contract, of the political society, the setting up of the legislature is equated to the constitution of a trust. Thus, though he treats the legislature as the supreme power, it is only within strictly defined limits: 'All power given with trust for attaining an end, being limited by that end, whenever that end is manifestly neglected or opposed, the trust must necessarily be forfeited.'[4]

Political authority is also limited by its division between three different powers — legislative, executive and federative in Locke's definition.[5] Moreover, the distinction between the contract of society and the trust of government enables Locke to distinguish between changing a political regime and the dissolution of society.[6] It follows that the right of revolution may be upheld without the fear that every time the people assert it they incur the penalty of a relapse into anarchy. In any case, the fear of revolution, Locke argues, is an exaggerated fear: 'People are not so easily got out of their old forms as some are apt to suggest.'[7] As for the charge that his theory will provoke frequent rebellions, he answers:

> No more than any other hypothesis. For when the people are made miserable, and find themselves exposed to the ill-usage of arbitrary power, cry up their governors as much as you will for

---

[1] *Second Treatise on Civil Government*, §116.   [2] Ibid.
[3] Ibid., §135.   [4] Ibid., §149.   [5] Ibid., §§143–8.
[6] Ibid., §211.   [7] Ibid., §223.

sons of Jupiter, let them be sacred and divine, descended, or authorized from heaven, give them out for whom or what you please, the same will happen. The people generally ill-treated, and contrary to right, will be ready upon any occasion to ease themselves of a burden that sits heavy upon them. They will wish and seek for the opportunity, which in the change, weakness, and accidents of human affairs seldom delays long to offer itself.[1]

The ultimate question is 'Who shall be judge whether the prince or legislative act contrary to their trust?' Locke's answer is: 'The people shall be judge.'[2] Beyond this, 'God in heaven is Judge ... but every man is judge for himself.'[3] This is not so very different from Cromwell's 'my calling is from God and the people'. Locke's theory summed up what moderate men could accept of the ideas of the Commonwealth, and looked forward, over the constitutional monarchy of the eighteenth century, to the parliamentary democracy of the nineteenth. Its outstanding features are the absence of any idea of absolute sovereignty, the insistence on division of authority, and the limitation of government to strictly utilitarian ends.

That Locke should have laid down liberal principles of government when he did was particularly important, for political thinking and positive institutions in Europe were developing in quite the opposite direction. In France the tradition of Natural Law was checked by the influence, especially after the Renaissance, of Roman Law, whereas in England it had been aided by the survival of the Common Law; the Catholic Church was hostile to the application of the ideas of Natural Law to politics, because of a suspected connection with Protestantism; and, in the seventeenth century the French royal lawyers, under the Cardinals, systematized the theory of absolute sovereignty.[4] Even the Huguenots, seeing, as has been said above,[5] their only hope in the protection of the Crown, proclaimed the absolute authority of the king in the most exaggerated terms.[6] The exception to this statement is, of course, Bayle, who, as well as putting forward dangerously unrestricted ideas of toleration, argued that subjects and sovereigns were in a contractual relationship with one another, and hence if the ruler broke his side of the

[1] Ibid., §224.   [2] Ibid., §240.
[3] Ibid.; §241.
[4] Le Bret, *Traité de la souveraineté du roi*, 1632. Cf. W. F. Church, *Constitutional Thought in Sixteenth Century France*, 1941.
[5] Cf. p. 57.   [6] Dodge, *Political Theory of Huguenots*, pp. 6, 7, 10, 18.

contract, his subjects were released from the duty of obedience.[1] For Bayle, also, in the last resort, private individuals have a right of resistance.[2] Even the representative of orthodox Huguenot thought, Jurieu, admitted that human nature has inherent rights.[3] The Huguenots of the dispersion, as has been said, 'have an important place in this gradual transmission of ideas of liberty from the religious plane to the temporal'.[4] But the ultimate tendency of Jurieu's thought is hardly in the same direction as that of Locke or Bayle. He reverts to the earlier Calvinist idea that resistance is allowable in defence not of the rights of individuals but only of those of the community, which he identifies with a representative assembly.[5] His objective is not political liberty, but the triumph of the true religion.[6] He allows that the people can surrender all their rights to a sovereign, with the exclusion only of the ultimate right of preservation of the community and of religion.[7] For him the power of the people, and consequently by deputation of the ruler, can legitimately be absolute, though in the respects just mentioned not unlimited.[8] It seems fair to conclude that 'Jurieu was prepared to endow the monarchy with a far more absolute character than his contemporary Locke, since it must be powerful enough to establish the true faith in both France and England'.[9]

However, the political ideas of Calvinism do not come to the end of their development with Jurieu and the more orthodox Huguenots. The Dutch Arminians were less authoritarian in their views. The greatest of their political writers, Grotius, in *De jure bello ac pacis* (1625) employed the ideas of Natural Law in the interest of the protection of the individual in international conflicts. He also contributed greatly to the secularization of the idea of Natural Law. He allowed a right of resistance against any ruler who alienated the State or made himself into a total enemy of society. All communities, he held, have a natural right to their own preservation. If, by the established constitution, the right of sovereignty is shared, each party can protect its own share. It has been said that Grotius does not arrive at a clear conception of State personality.[10] On the other hand he allows that the rights of the people can be alienated to the sovereign. Sovereignty is assimilated by Grotius to a property right, and though the alienation may be based on a contract he does not,

[1] Dodge, p. 95.   [2] Ibid., p. 99.
[3] Ibid., p. 230.   [4] Ibid.   [5] Ibid., pp. 64, 69-70.   [6] Cf. Ibid., p. 93.
[7] Ibid., p. 111.   [8] Ibid., p. 52.   [9] Ibid., p. 233.
[10] O. Gierke, *Natural Law and the Theory of Society*, trans. E. Barker, 1934, p. 55.

except in the cases mentioned above, allow of any right of resistance. All this is doubtless not unconnected with the fact that Grotius was an Arminian who had fled from Calvinist intolerance in the Dutch Republic to France and who dedicated his classic work to Louis XIII.

It remains to mention the most influential of all seventeenth-century political theorists on the continent, Pufendorf, whose *De jure naturae et gentium* appeared in 1672. Pufendorf starts with a contractual basis for government. The contract gives the subject rights and the sovereign obligations, he agrees; but as his thought develops it is seen that these amount to little in practice. For Pufendorf sovereignty, like the soul, is indivisible – the separation of powers is a monstrosity. Law is command. Sovereignty is absolute:

> The Sovereign is not obliged to render account of his conduct to any person here below ...
>
> Sovereign Powers are above all human behaviour and civil law, considered as such; and in consequence these sorts of laws do not put the Sovereign under any direct obligation. Indeed, they depend on the will of the Sovereign both for their origin and duration ... Finally, the Sovereign Power is sacred and inviolable, so that not only is it evil to resist or disobey it, when it only commands what is legitimate, but also subjects must patiently endure the caprices and cruelties of their Sovereign, as a well-bred child suffers the bad temper of his father or mother. If an individual is even threatened by his Prince with the most atrocious and humiliating treatment, he must try to seek safety in flight, or resolve himself to accept all kinds of ills, rather than draw the sword against his Sovereign.[1]

Thus even if the contractual rights of the subject are infringed, he has, according to Pufendorf, no right of resistance; and the rights of the individual are a good deal less secure when he is allowed no right of defending them.

In Pufendorf and his followers the contractual and Natural Law theories begin to turn into mere formulae. If they were to retain any effective value it was essential for the dualism between ruler and subject to be maintained. The individual could only have rights so long as he continued to be conceived as a distinct moral entity, separate from the State; but monarchical theories of sovereignty

[1] Pufendorf, *Les Devoirs de l'homme et du citoyen*, trans. by Jean Barbeyrac, 5th ed. 1735, II, ix, 2-4.

were beginning to disintegrate this kind of individualism. Bodin, in the sixteenth century, had taken a long step towards the idea of a ruler who embodies in himself the whole personality of the State. In the theory of Pufendorf the conception of a unitary State personality is dominant: sovereignty, at first asserted in defence of the independent territorial government against external challenge, becomes an attribute of the governing authority against all internal rivals.

French and German thought was now committed to absolute sovereignty. There were some exceptions. Leibniz criticized the view of Pufendorf that compulsion is essential to the nature of law, and argued for the priority of 'Recht' to 'Gesetz'. Even of divine law, he said, it is not law because God has willed it, but because God is just.[1] On the whole, however, liberal ideas of government were disappearing in seventeenth-century Europe. The Enlightenment of the eighteenth century had to look for the inspiration of its political thinking across the Channel to Locke, whose ideas were rapidly becoming known in Western Europe -- as early as 1691 a detailed analysis of the *Treatises on Civil Government* appeared in Le Clerc's *Bibliothèque Universelle* – but the influence of Lockian political ideas belongs to the history of the eighteenth century.

[1] Gierke, *Development of Political Theory*, pp. 89-90, n. 44.

X

Montesquieu and the Rule of Law

AFTER Locke, the second great seminal mind of eighteenth-century political thought is Montesquieu. A Gascon noble of the robe, born in 1689, educated at a school of the Oratory, for a short while *président à mortier* in the Bordeaux parlement, Montesquieu resigned while still a young man to devote himself to a literary career. His *Lettres persanes* (1721) gave him early fame and he joined the circle of unorthodox thinkers that centred on the Club de l'Entresol. There he entered into close relations with Bolingbroke, whose influence on him is at present difficult to estimate, but may have been great.[1]

Montesquieu was hailed as a wit in youth and a sage in later life. In each capacity he wrote a book marred by gross faults, and had each book hailed as a masterpiece by his contemporaries and the verdict endorsed by posterity. In a lesser work, the *Considérations sur les causes de la grandeur et de la décadence des Romains* (1734), the theme that was to dominate his speculation clearly emerged: 'It is not Fortune that governs the world: that is proved in the history of the Romans.' Behind all particular events, it was his profound conviction, we must seek for general causes. Montesquieu's view of the world is founded on a Cartesian rationalism so deeply embedded as to be below the level of conscious questioning. His greatest work, *De l'esprit des Lois* (1748), begins: 'Those who have said that *a blind fatality has produced all the effects that we see in the world* have uttered a great absurdity: for what greater absurdity is there than a blind fatality which has produced intelligent beings?'[2]

Yet he believed himself to be, and to some extent truly was, an empiricist. What he set out to create was a sociology of law, based on the facts. The combination of rationalism and empiricism which runs right through the Enlightenment is nowhere more striking than in Montesquieu's analysis of the nature of law:

> Law, in general, is the human reason, in so far as it governs all the peoples of the earth; and the political and civil laws of

[1] Cf. J. Dedieu, *Montesquieu et la tradition politique anglaise en France*, 1909, ch. ix.
[2] *Esprit des Lois*, I, i.

each nation ought to be only particular cases of the application of this human reason ... They have to be relative to the physical conditions of the country, to the climate, icy, burning or temperate; to the quality of the land, to its situation, to its size, to the manner of life of the people, agricultural, hunting or pastoral; they must be related to the degree of liberty that the constitution can allow, to the religion of the inhabitants, to their inclinations, their wealth, their number, their commerce, their social customs and manners.[1]

Behind the laws, thus, there is the whole framework of society, which is shaped by them and in its turn shapes them. Montesquieu does not attempt to isolate the political structure artificially from other aspects of social life and organization. Since what he is trying to achieve is a science of society, it follows that for him *mœurs* are more important than positive laws. As he had said in the *Lettres persanes*: 'les mœurs font toujours de meilleurs citoyens que les lois'.[2]

This attempt to combine rationalism with empiricism was bound to lead to some confusion between what is and what ought to be. Nature, and the laws of nature, are for Montesquieu sometimes the one and sometimes the other, as is very apparent when he is dealing with such an institution as slavery. It is against nature, he writes, but also that in some countries there is a natural reason for it.[3] Again, after having observed that in a country in which there were many more women than men, polygamy would be less unnatural than elsewhere, he adds: 'In all this I do not justify customs. I give the reasons for them.'[4] The basic dilemma of sociology has in fact already appeared in Montesquieu. The natural scientist can observe and classify phenomena, abstract common features, group them under general scientific hypotheses, without materially affecting the behaviour of the subjects of his study. Nor indeed does he want to change their natural behaviour. On the other hand the social scientist introduces a new factor into the situation that he is studying, which will inevitably influence future reactions, just as a theory of past revolutions can alter future ones. The knowledge that his studies will do this cannot but affect his work. As a scientist he is not concerned to pass moral judgments, but moral disinterestedness is impossible for anyone whose actions will affect other men. The moral responsibility of the social scientist is therefore inevitably

---

[1] *Esprit des Lois*, I, iii.   [2] Letter lxxix.
[3] *Esprit de Lois*, XV, vii; cf. VI, xvii.   [4] Ibid., XVI, iv.

engaged in his work: he is part scientist and part moralist. This appears very clearly in the way in which Montesquieu uses some of his basic terms. Nature is for him 'la nature des choses', the way things work, but it is also the way in which they *ought* to work. Right – 'droit' – is based on eternal law, but it is related to the conditions of each society. 'Devoir' is what ought to be, and also what *must* be.

Montesquieu does not attempt to evade this issue; he is a social scientist with a sense of moral responsibility, a cynic who believes in humanity. Men are rogues in little things, but in big things, he says, they are 'de très honnêtes gens'. This fundamental faith in human nature is what makes a secular theory of politics possible; whereas Calvinism and Catholicism had both relied on Original Sin as the ultimate explanation of the need for government, from which it followed that since rulers also were men and tainted by the same innate defects, anything better could only be expected from them by virtue of a special endowment of divine grace or right.

The theory of divine right of kings may be said to have reached its apogee in France under Louis XIV, and it is significant that whereas earlier writers had attacked divine right, Montesquieu merely ignores it. Already, in the later years of Louis XIV, there were signs that scepticism was dropping its corrosive acid, in a few secret cenacles, even on the ideology of the roi soleil, though the only serious, if undergound, opposition that existed in France was the little aristocratic group known, because it looked for reform to the heir to the throne, as the Duke of Burgundy's faction. The aim of its members was the restoration of the aristocratic constitution which France was supposed to have enjoyed before the bureaucratic tyranny of the Cardinals destroyed free, by which they meant aristocratic, institutions. The parlements also, though their power had been reduced to a nullity under Louis XIV, not long before in the Fronde had openly challenged royal authority. Montesquieu was subject to such influences as these, and above all to the sense of relief and outburst of criticism that the death of the old king brought with it. We might almost say that the shadow of Louis XIV dominates his thought on politics. Like all important works of political theory, De l'esprit des lois does not consist of mere academic musings; it is an attempt to change the conditions and ends of political action. It is inspired by a burning hatred of the system of Louis XIV, and by extension of all arbitrary government.

This prime motive accounts for the special nature of Montesquieu's analysis of forms of government. There are three kinds, he argues – republican, that in which the people as a whole or any part of it has sovereign power; monarchical, in which one man rules, but by fixed and established laws; and despotic, also the rule of one man, but without any law and with all government reduced to simple will or caprice.[1] Travel literature and histories, reporting the nature of Eastern or ancient despotisms, undoubtedly influenced Montesquieu, but as the *Lettres persanes* show, the real target of his criticism was the monarchy of Louis XIV. The same theme appears, in a more moderate form, in the *Esprit des lois*. For example:

> The enemies of a great prince, who ruled for such a long time, have a thousand times accused him, rather, I think, as a result of their fear than their reason, of having formed and put into operation the project of universal monarchy. If he had succeeded nothing would have been more fatal to Europe, to his own subjects, to himself, and to his family. Heaven, which knows what is truly to men's advantage, served him better by his defeats than it could have done by victories.[2]

In more general terms, Montesquieu transfixes despotism with the deadly shafts of his epigrams:

> The principle of despotic government unceasingly corrupts itself, because it is corrupted by its nature.[3]

> When the savages of Louisiana wish for fruit, they cut down the tree and pick the fruit. There you have despotic government.[4]

> No one is a tyrant without being at the same time a slave.[5]

And, in language which anticipates that of Burke and Acton:

> It is an eternal experience that every man possessing power is tempted to abuse it.[6]

It is evident that Montesquieu is more concerned to denounce despotism for its practical consequences than to provide a theoretical condemnation of it in principle. Similarly, for a better form of government he did not draw on theory, though he was not uninfluenced by Locke, but looked to a practical example, which he

[1] *Esprit des Lois*, II, i.   [2] Ibid., IX, vii.
[3] Ibid., VIII, x.   [4] Ibid., V, xiii.   [5] Ibid., IV, iii.   [6] Ibid., XI, iv.

found in England. Chief among the agents who conveyed a favourable picture of the English political system to France must be reckoned the Huguenot exiles, such as, for example, Rapin-Thoyras, whose *Dissertation sur les Whigs et Tories* (1717), and *Histoire de l'Angleterre* (1723–5) were widely read and influential. Montesquieu was familiar with these, but he also knew the English political scene at first hand; and his notebooks show that he was not unaware of its less creditable features. In the *Esprit des lois* he paints a somewhat idealized picture of the British constitution and its effects.[1] The English, he says, is the one nation in the world which has political liberty as the direct object of its constitution.[2] From the English example he derives his basic theory of the division of powers – legislative, executive and judicial.[3] The legislative power must be in the hands of the people, or, if the State is too large for this, of their representatives; it embodies what Montesquieu calls the 'volonté générale', the General Will of the State; the executive, in the hands of a monarch, carries out this General Will; and the judiciary, which must be independent of the other two powers, enforces the laws.

It may be noted that Montesquieu does not propound a theory of the separation of powers. He writes: 'In order that power shall not be abused, it is necessary that, by the arrangement of things, power shall check power.'[4] They overlap and limit one another. The system he is describing is one of checks and balances, not of rigid separation.

Political liberty is not only a matter of the relation of constituted authorities to one another, it also depends on their relation to the individual citizen. In this aspect liberty is equated with the security of the individual from the actions of arbitrary power. This security, says Montesquieu, is never more imperilled than in public or private criminal charges. He concludes: 'It is then on the goodness of the criminal laws that the liberty of the citizen principally depends.'[5] In the course of the nineteenth century this came to be so much taken for granted that it was almost forgotten. A generation ago it was a platitude. Now that the results of the abandonment of the judicial

---

[1] Ibid., XI, vi; XIX, xxvii.   [2] Ibid., XI, v.

[3] Montesquieu begins by calling them the legislative power, the executive power over those affairs which deal with the law of nations, i.e. foreign affairs, and the executive power over those which deal with the civil law, i.e. internal affairs. This is a close restatement of Locke's division into legislative, federative (i.e. foreign relations and war) and executive (i.e. judicial and police powers); but he soon modifies this into the now classsic division of legislative, executive, and judicial.

[4] Ibid., XI, iv.   [5] Ibid., XII, ii.

safeguards of the individual against police tyranny or ideological inquisition have become apparent again, it has regained its relevance.

As a sociologist, what Montesquieu was attempting was far beyond the possibilities of his time – or possibly of later times. It was his strength that – as was practically inevitable in the eighteenth century – in trying to be a social scientist he did not cease to be a moralist. He never lost sight of the ethical nature and ends of society. This moral preoccupation qualifies all that he says of liberty. He writes:

> Political liberty does not consist in doing whatever one wills. In a state, that is to say in a society in which there are laws, liberty only consists in being able to do what one ought to, and in not being forced to do what one ought not to.[1]

Political morality is above all needed in a republic, that is to say, in a·State in which political power is divided between various bodies, especially if it is a popular State, where political virtue, 'l'amour de la patrie, c'est-à-dire l'amour de l'égalité', is the essential condition of survival.[2]

But this is not his last word. Dare I say it, he comments, even virtue needs to be taken in moderation.[3] Unlike most political writers of the eighteenth century, Montesquieu does not exaggerate the powers of government. 'Customs', he wrote in the *Lettres persanes*, 'always make better citizens than laws',[4] and in the *Esprit des lois*, in words that explain the affinity that Burke felt for him, he declares that to recall men to ancient maxims is ordinarily to bring them back to virtue.[5] Again in Burkian language he declares that political liberty is to be found only in moderate governments[6] and that the excess even of reason is not always desirable.[7]

Montesquieu sums up, at a critical stage in the development of European thought, the tradition of liberty and law, of power balancing power, and of the limitation of all rightful authority. The roots of this tradition were buried deep in the past, but it needed restatement in the eighteenth century, when claims to a more absolute sovereignty than had been known since the ancient world were finding the possibility of realization in the new bureaucratic and military apparatus of the absolute monarchies. His influence, along with that of Locke, ensured that the political thinking of the Enlightenment should not turn into an apologia for absolutism.

---

[1] *Esprit des Lois*, XI, iii.   [2] *Avertissement*; IV, v.
[3] XI, vi.   [4] Cf. note 2, p. 100.   [5] *Esprit des Lois*, v.7.
[6] Ibid., XI, iv.   [7] Ibid., XI, vi.

XI

The Historiography of the Enlightenment

ONE more strain in the inheritance of the eighteenth-century Enlightenment remains to be discussed. It was in the nature of things that the development of an empirical interest in the facts of the natural world should be accompanied by a similar interest in the facts of history. This historical interest has its bearing on the sociological investigation of morals and politics such as Montesquieu attempted, and indeed on the general political and social thinking of the period; for to dismiss the thought of the Enlightenment as fundamentally unhistorical, as has sometimes been done, is a superficial error.

History, as distinct from chronicle, revived at the time of the Renaissance, when the historical writings of the humanists followed the lines laid down by the classical historians. This meant that their history was not aimed at the discovery of new information about the past, but rather at the retelling of an accepted story. What we should regard as its strictly historical content did not really count. The aims of humanist history were, first, the production of a work of literary value, and secondly, the provision of examples by means of which to inculcate moral and political lessons. This can be shown both by actual histories, and by the positive declaration of historians. Thus Bodin put forward as the 'most important fruit of history' that by it 'some can be incited to virtue and others turned away from vice'.[1]

The rationalism of the seventeenth century, however, provided an unsuitable climate for the growth of history. The view of Descartes has already been referred to. It was that:

Even the most faithful histories, if they do not wholly misrepresent matters, or exaggerate their importance to render the account of them more worthy of perusal, omit, at least, almost always the meanest and least striking of the attendant circum-

[1] Bodin, *La Méthode de l'histoire*, avant-propos. *Œuvres Philosophiques*, ed. P. Mesnard, 1951, p. 278.

stances; hence it happens that the remainder does not represent the truth.[1]

The libertines found ample scope for their scepticism in the discrediting of all history as mere imagining. La Mothe de Vayer wrote, in 1668, *Du peu de certitude qu'il y a dans l'histoire*. Bayle himself belongs, to some extent, with the sceptics. History lies before him, says Cassirer, like an enormous heap of ruins, and he finds nowhere evidence of rational purpose.[2] But Bayle is also one of the founders of historical criticism. Although he recognized the impossibility of certainty in history, he none the less concluded that truth is 'the soul of history'. His explanation of the nature of critical history is well worth repeating even today.

> History, generally speaking [he wrote], is the most difficult type of writing that an author can undertake, or one of the most difficult. It requires a great judgment, a noble, clear and considered style, a good conscience, a perfect probity, many excellent materials, and the art of placing them in good order, and above all things the power of resisting the instinct of a religious zeal which prompts one to cry down what he thinks to be false, and to adorn and embellish what he thinks to be true … An Historian can never stand too much upon his guard; and it is almost impossible for him to be altogether free from prejudices … I conclude, that none can be well qualified to write a good History, unless he be such an enemy to lying, that his conscience does not permit him to tell lies even to the advantage of his religion, and dearest friends, nor to the disadvantage of an impious sect, and of his most implacable persecutors.[3]

Bayle was more than a sceptic, he was also an *érudit*. Historical erudition has a continuous tradition from the fifteenth century, when the humanists began to apply their critical spirit to the legends of the Church. In sixteenth-century France philology became a methodological and historical science. In France, Italy, England, Germany, a vast historical documentation was collected and edited. By the time of Bayle, at the end of the seventeenth century, the principles of critical history were well established. Locke, writing to his Dutch friend, Philip van Limborch, to praise him for his

[1] *Discourse on Method*, pp. 6-7.
[2] E. Cassirer, *The Philosophy of the Enlightenment*, trans. 1951, pp. 203-4.
[3] *Dictionnaire*, art. 'Remond', Beller and Lee, pp. 230-1, 233, 235.

Historia Inquisitionis, declared that it was 'written just as history should be ... Everything is established and supported by authorities and documents.[1] Rather later Lenglet du Fresnoy declared:

He who speaks of History speaks of a faithful narration, an exact and sincere account of happenings, supported by the witness of our own eyes, or certain and indubitable documents, or the report of persons worthy of credence.[2]

With a strong interest in historical facts, and especially the problem of origins, and a sophisticated conception of the nature of historical criticism, it might have been expected that the eighteenth century would become a great age in historiography. If it did not, we must look not to some hypothetical anti-historical spirit but to positive and stronger factors which prohibited a concentration of attention on historical scholarship. The fact is that the men of the Enlightenment, while not indifferent to history, thought that there were better things.

Moreover it was difficult for history in the eighteenth century to become a merely academic discipline, for the more interest was aroused in historical problems, and the greater the tendency to look to historical origins, the more difficult it became to treat it in terms other than those of contemporary controversy. In a sense, the Enlightenment was not too little but too much conscious of history. Given its even more pronounced bent towards practical reform, the temptation to use history primarily for purposes of propaganda became almost irresistible.

Even the great Bossuet had found himself forced to the defence of Catholicism in terms of universal history.

This church [he wrote], always attacked and never conquered, is a perpetual miracle, and a striking testimony to the immutability of the counsels of God. In the midst of the agitation of human affairs it sustains itself always by an invisible force, so that in an uninterrupted sequence of nearly seventeen hundred years we see it go back to Jesus Christ, through whom it succeeds to the inheritance of the ancient people, and is united with the prophets and patriarchs.[3]

What authority, Bossuet asks, can be greater than that of the

[1] Quoted in M. Cranston, *John Locke*, 1957, p. 383.
[2] *L'histoire justifiée contre les romans par M. l'abbé Lenglet du Fresnoy*, 1735, p. 24.
[3] *Discours sur l'histoire universelle*, ed. of 1855, p. 300.

Catholic Church, uniting in itself the authority of all centuries past, and the ancient traditions of the human race. No religion which cannot show credentials going back to the creation of the world, he declared, can be from God.[1] 'No one can change the centuries past or give himself predecessors ... The Catholic Church alone fills all previous centuries with a succession which cannot be challenged.'[2] There is an element of circularity in Bossuet's argument. He bases the truth of history on the traditions of the Church, and then justifies the Church in the light of its history. Moreover, the appeal to history was more dangerous than he realized. He was closer to being a predecessor of Montesquieu than he could have believed, when he wrote: 'Except for certain extraordinary actions in which God wanted his hand alone to appear, no great change has happened which has not had its causes in the previous centuries.'[3]

In the eighteenth century history began to be used in France, as during the seventeenth century it had been in England, also for the purpose of political controversy. Boulainviller's *Histoire de l'ancien gouvernement de la France* (1727) revived sixteenth-century discussions of the origins of the French monarchy. The original rulers of France, Boulainviller claimed, were a conquering Frankish aristocracy, equal among themselves but subjecting the Gallo-Roman population to serfdom, from which he drew the conclusion that the rightful government was an aristocratic one, in the hands of the descendants of the Frankish nobles. This thesis was challenged by Dubos in his *Histoire critique de l'établissement de la monarchie française dans les Gaules* (1734). The Frankish settlement, Dubos claimed, was on the contrary the result of negotiations and treaties. It was not a conquest and did not change the existing system of government in Gaul. The Frankish kings were the legitimate heirs of the Roman Empire. Feudal society only developed several centuries later. Hence the true government of France was monarchical.

Montesquieu tended to agree, on historical grounds, with the facts of Dubos, but his aristocratic leanings led him to favour the conclusions drawn by Boulainviller. The Encyclopaedists, on the contrary, accepted Boulainviller's history, but rejected his aristocratic conclusions.[4] Influenced by Tacitus, they saw the early Germanic societies as communities of free men, ruled by laws to which they had consented. We need not pursue the argument further, for it

---

[1] *Discours sur l'histoire universelle*, pp. 330-1.   [2] Ibid., p. 332.
[3] Ibid., p. 342.   [4] R. Hubert, *Les Sciences sociales dans l'Encyclopédie*, 1923, I, ch. vi.

already illustrates clearly the tendency of such discussions to move out of the sphere of history and into that of politics.

In the historical writing of the Enlightenment, on the whole the humanist tradition prevailed over that of the *érudits*. The emphasis was on the utility and the literary merits of history. In Bolingbroke's well-known definition, history is 'philosophy teaching by examples'. If it does not serve some useful end, why study it at all, he argued. 'An application to any study, that tends neither directly nor indirectly to make us better men and better citizens, is at best but a specious and ingenious sort of idleness.'[1] Correspondingly the cult of erudition was declining. Voltaire advises the historian: 'If you have nothing to tell us other than that one Barbarian succeeded another Barbarian on the banks of the Oxus or Iaxartes, of what use are you to the public?'[2] Or, more succinctly, he exclaims: 'Woe to details. They are a vermin that destroys great works.'[3]

The historical writing of the Enlightenment also suffered from the inadequacy of eighteenth-century psychological theories. J. B. Black writes of Hume:

In virtue of his theory of uniformity he takes his stand on the existence of a normal historical man, as arbitrary and fanciful as the so-called economic man of the old political economy. And the error vitiates his conception of the past as it vitiated Voltaire's ... Every character he meets in history must be reduced to type.[4]

The merits and defects of the historiography of the Enlightenment are all exemplified in the greatest, save one, of all its historians, Voltaire. In his first historical work, *Charles XII*, he is writing humanist history, but he soon progresses beyond this. From Fontenelle he learnt that it was important to verify facts before arguing about them: 'Assurons-nous bien du fait avant de nous inquiéter de la cause.'[5] Although with reference rather to the accounts of supposed marvels than to the methods of secular history, Bayle taught Voltaire the critical use of sources. In the catalogue of writers appended to the *Siècle de Louis XIV*, Voltaire commends one author for citing his authorities: 'an absolutely essential precaution when one is not

---

[1] Bolingbroke, *Letters on the Study and Use of History*, 1735, Letter II.
[2] *Dictionnaire philosophique*, art. 'Histoire'.
[3] Lettre à J. B. Dubos, 3 Octobre 1738, *Œuvres*, 1877–85, xxxv, 30.
[4] J. B. Black, *The Art of History*, 1926, pp. 98–9.
[5] J. H. Brumfitt, *Voltaire Historian*, 1958, p. 141.

writing the history of one's own times, unless one is only repeating well-known facts'.[1] It is a precaution he rarely takes himself. Still, he has the utmost contempt for the kind of romanticized history that is so prevalent in our own day. He quotes the author of one such work:

> Mademoiselle de la Vallière, in a flimsy déshabille, flung herself down in an arm-chair; there she meditated undisturbed on her lover; often the day came to find her still sitting in the chair, her elbow on the table, her eyes fixed in an ecstasy of love.

Upon which Voltaire cries out: 'Hè mon ami, l'as-tu vue dans ce déshabille léger? l'as-tu vue accoudée sur cette table? est-il permis d'écrire ainsi l'histoire?'[2] Like Bayle he holds that historical truths are only probabilities.[3] We must set against all this the frequency with which Voltaire used history merely as propaganda. It will doubtless not necessarily be considered a defect that he had no philosophy of history. What he wrote under the title 'Philosophie de l'histoire', and added as an introduction to the Essai sur les mœurs in 1769, is mere deistic propaganda.[4] Moreover, although the Essai sur les mœurs exhibits a limited conception of the progress of mankind, he has no real sense of development in history or of the necessity to take into account changing standards and ideas.

As he became more pessimistic with age, so Voltaire became increasingly obsessed with the role of chance in history and the dominance of petty causes, what has been called the Cleopatra's nose theory of history. Thus, a dish of mushrooms eaten by Charles VI in 1740 changed the face of Europe. Or again: 'Some pairs of gloves of an unusual style which she [the Duchess of Marlborough] refused the Queen, a drop of water which she spilt in her presence, by a pretended mistake, on the dress of Mme Masham, changed the face of Europe.'[5] We may remember his tale of the Brahmin who, leaving his house one day, stepped out with his right foot instead of his left, and thus started the chain of events that led to the assassination of Henry IV.[6] What clue have we to guide us through this maze? As Voltaire puts it, in another analogy: '[Fortune] makes us play her terrible game like blind men: we never see the face of the cards.'[7]

---

[1] Brumfitt, *Voltaire Historian*, p. 129.   [2] Ibid., p. 163.
[3] *Dictionnaire philosophique*, art. 'Vérité', Œuvres, xx, 360.   [4] Brumfitt, p. 85.
[5] *Siècle de Louis XV*, Œuvres, xiv, 402; Brumfitt, p. 107.
[6] *Dialogue entre un Brahmane et un Jésuite, sur la nécessité et l'enchaînement des choses*, 1756.
[7] *Dictionnaire philosophique*, art. 'Théodose', Œuvres, xx, 513.

Increasing pessimism leads him to find something worse than merely the rule of chance in human history. In the end man's life becomes for him, as it was for Bayle, a record of crime and folly.

Voltaire's achievement as an historian should not be underestimated. But in sum the verdict on the historiography of the Enlightenment could not be a high one were it not for a single name. We should look for the historiography of the Enlightenment rather to England, where the Cartesian tradition was negligible, than to France where it still exercised a strong anti-historical influence. Historians such as Robertson and Hume are not to be forgotten, but the name that outshines all others is of course that of Gibbon, who, combining the intellectual attack of the *philosophes* with the erudition of the scholars, proved that the Enlightenment, when it wished, could also write great history.

PART THREE

THE ENLIGHTENMENT OF THE
EIGHTEENTH CENTURY

XII

Materialism

THE eighteenth century was not as great an age of original
thinkers as the seventeenth century had been, but this does not
mean that it merely repeated, in slightly different language,
the ideas of the previous age. The historic significance of the Enlightenment can only be understood when the basic creative ideas of
the seventeenth century, and their elaboration and modification in
the following period, are taken together. The order in which it will
be most helpful to study this second phase is not necessarily that
which chronology has dictated for the former. I have already broken
across what is largely an imaginary boundary with chapters following up the development of moral philosophy and history in the
eighteenth century, for in these fields the story is too continuous to
allow of a break; but there are some important differences in the
intellectual climate of the two centuries. Whereas the new ideas of
the seventeenth century began with science and philosophy, the key
to the understanding of the second phase of the Enlightenment is to
be found in the psychological theories of the eighteenth century.

Locke had laid down the ground plan of much eighteenth-century
thought, nowhere more clearly than in the dominant sensational
psychology. The ablest exponent of Lockian psychological theories
in mid-eighteenth century was Condillac, best remembered for his
famous statue analogy. He imagines a statue, organized within like
a man, but sealed in by a covering of marble. As this unromantic
Galatea is gradually given senses, so with each one the development
of its mind is traced. In turn Condillac's statue acquires the capacity
for attention, pleasure and pain, memory, awareness of succession,
comparison, judgment, wonder, desire, imagination, will, personality. Finally:

Our statue being capable of memory, there is not one odour which will not recall to it another. Here is its personality: for if it can say *I*, it will say it in all the instants of its existence, and each time its *I* will embrace all the moments of which it preserves the memory.[1]

Condillac illustrates admirably, also, the practical conclusion which the eighteenth century drew from Lockian psychology. This was the rejection of all metaphysical systems in favour of empiricism. In a chapter on 'the uselessness of abstract systems' he writes:

What could be more ridiculous than that men, coming out of a profound sleep, and finding themselves in the midst of a labyrinth, should lay down general principles for finding the way out? Yet that is the conduct of philosophers.[2]

In psychological theory, the one point on which the successors of Locke advanced beyond him was in a tendency to ignore the positive role he had attributed to reflection in the formation of ideas. The English moralist Hartley, who has been mentioned earlier,[3] completed the elimination of the creative element from the operations of the mind by his theory of an automatic association of ideas. The most influential development of Locke's psychology in the eighteenth century, however, arose out of his suggestion that possibly a material being could think. A strain of materialism had run through the libertine thought of the sixteenth century, stimulated in part by the influence of Lucretius. Similar possibilities were implicit in Cartesian thought, as the Cambridge Platonists had realized,[4] though Descartes himself evaded this consequence by his assertion of the dualism of mind and matter in man, along with the belief that animals were simple automata. The distinction between man and animal was essential if Cartesianism were to be compatible with religious reaching. It was challenged by Gassendi in the seventeenth century, and in the eighteenth the dilemma was posed plainly in the controversy over 'l'âme des bêtes'.[5] Either animals were mere machines, and if so why – apart from religious revelation which taught otherwise – was not man the same? Or if a man had a soul, why should not an animal?

Cartesian dualism did not prove a permanently satisfactory

---

[1] *Traité des sensations*, 1754, ch. vi, §1. [2] *Traité des systèmes*, 1749, ch. ii.
[3] See above, pp. 85-6. [4] Cf. Colie, *Light and Enlightenment*, ch. iv.
[5] Cf. R. R. Palmer, *Catholics and Unbelievers in Eighteenth Century France*, 1939, pp. 149-53.

solution of the problem of mind and matter. In England, David Hartley abandoned it, but on the basis of a kind of materialism reached a deistic conception of the world. In France, materialism was pushed to more ruthless conclusions in the extraordinary writings of the country curé Meslier, composed probably about 1722-3 and circulated surreptitiously in manuscript copies, of which Voltaire declared he had seen over a hundred long before they were printed. When they were in part published, much later in the century, by Voltaire, he even then felt it necessary to suppress their bitter social criticism.[1] With Meslier we return to the problem of evil. He declares that theology makes of its God 'a monster of unreason, injustice, malice and atrocity'.[2] He entitles one chapter, 'The World is not governed by an intelligent being'.[3] As for the argument from design:

> Has not this human machine, which is exhibited to us as a masterpiece of the workmanship of the creator, a thousand ways of going wrong? Are we to marvel at the skill of a mechanician who shows us a complicated machine which is liable to stop at any instant, and which after a short period will end by breaking down of itself?[4]

Materialism could hardly do other than undermine the deistic optimism with which the eighteenth century had opened. Its most notorious expression was in the short but incisive *L'Homme machine* (1747) of La Mettrie, appropriately an anatomist and doctor, who was brought to Potsdam by Frederick II and made a member of the Berlin Academy of Sciences. La Mettrie is not at bottom particularly original, but only more outspoken than his contemporaries. He begins by insisting on an empirical method: 'Let us then follow the direction of experience, and not trouble our heads with the history of the opinions of philosophers.'[5] The human machine, he holds, cannot be understood a priori, but only a posteriori, 'by disentangling the soul from the organs of the body'.[6] Form and motion being the essence of matter, God is not needed to bestow motion on inert matter, as Descartes had supposed. Matter has in itself the capacity for motion and sensation, and thus for thought. In a Lucretian

---

[1] There are many and varying editions of the writings of Meslier. See A. R. Morehouse, *Voltaire and John Meslier*, 1936.
[2] *Le Bon Sens du curé J. Meslier*, 1802, ch. lxii, p. 82.
[3] Ibid., ch. liv, p. 72.   [4] Ibid., ch. li, p. 68.
[5] La Mettrie, *L'Homme Machine*, trans. as *Man a Machine*, 1750, p. 6.   [6] Ibid.

manner La Mettrie conceives of the divine order of phenomena as due to the greater or less complex organization of matter. Just as Leibniz spiritualized matter so, it has been said, did La Mettrie materialize the psyche. It naturally follows that the only difference between man and animal is in complexity of organization, like that between, say, an astronomical clock and an ordinary one. The soul is an empty term. 'Man is but an animal, made up of a number of springs, which are all put in motion by each other.'[1] Thought is a property of organized matter, like extension. Innate ideas are an illusion: 'In vain would the *Cartesians* come here to attack me with their *innate ideas*; I certainly should not give myself a fourth part of the trouble, that Mr *Locke* has taken to explode such chimaeras.'[2] As for the kind of problems that religion is concerned with, how it all started is a question not worth worrying our heads about: perhaps man is a simple product of chance:

> Let us conclude boldly then, that man is a machine; and that there is only one substance, differently modified, in the whole universe ... This is my system, or rather, this is the truth, if I am not much mistaken. It is short and plain: let who will dispute it.[3]

The principles of morality that follow from La Mettrie's materialism are laid down in equally stark sentences. Virtue is defined as self-love; natural morality is based on self-interest. Crime brings with it its own penalty, for the criminal loses the pleasures of virtue; he is not to be punished but cured: 'It is much to be wished that we had none for judges, but the most skilful physicians.'[4] Though La Mettrie has abandoned deism, he does not abandon the optimism that went with it. The end of life is happiness: 'Nature has created us all to be happy; all I say from the worm that creeps, to the eagle that soars aloft in the clouds.'[5] And since sensation is the essential quality of living beings, the sensual pleasures are the basis of happiness.[6] Measured on this scale, La Mettrie has to admit, culture and learning may be only a waste of time, though reason, he allows, can be of use in dissipating prejudices and so helping us to achieve happiness. Tradition, of course, insisted that he put into practice what he preached and an appropriate death was invented for him as a consequence of eating a huge pheasant pie at one sitting.

Voltaire feared the influence of such frank materialism and

[1] La Mettrie, *L'Homme Machine*, p. 66.   [2] Ibid., p. 32.
[3] Ibid., pp. 85, 87.   [4] Ibid., pp. 43-4.   [5] Ibid., p. 46.
[6] La Mettrie, *Discours sur le bonheur*, in *Œuvres Philosophiques*, 1796, pp. 156-7.

atheism, either because of the damage La Mettrie's open avowals might do to the cause of the *philosophes*, or because of a genuine hostility to his ideas. What we might call official *philosophe* opinion, as represented in the *Encyclopédie*, was much more moderate, or less frank. Its contributors accepted Lockian psychology, as expounded by Condillac, without question, but left their readers to draw the more dangerous conclusions for themselves if they wished to. However, ten years after *L'Homme machine*, in 1758, appeared Helvétius' *De l'esprit*, which is in effect La Mettrie's short pamphlet blown out to the size of three volumes and written in pompous turgidities, instead of the pithy epigrams of La Mettrie.

Helvétius begins his book, typically, with the sentence: 'Up to the present the mind has been studied only under some of its aspects. Great writers have only cast a rapid *coup d'œil* over this subject.'[1] Like La Mettrie, he materializes Cartesianism, equating 'apercevoir' with 'sentir'. Sensibility is the general property of nature, the only difference between man and animals is in complexity of organization, and all pleasure is primarily physical pleasure.

The limitations of Helvétius' conception of human nature were indicated with some truth, however inappropriately and priggishly, on the occasion of his death, by the unpleasant baron Grimm who wrote of him in terms of cold moral condemnation:

> As he passed his life with women of gallantry, and sometimes with women without principles and without morals, he thought all women to be the same, and believed that the end of all their actions was sensual pleasure. A chaste woman was in his eyes a monster which had no real existence; in this respect his ideas were so restricted that he could not feel ... that there might exist, or ought to exist, an infinite variety in the moral character, as in the physical organism.[2]

In a posthumous work, *De l'homme*, which does little more than elaborate and draw further conclusions from the same principles, Helvétius declares:

> Physical sensibility is the unique cause of our actions, our thoughts, our passions, our sociability ... It is to clothe himself, to deck out his mistress or his wife, to procure them their amusements, to feed himself and his family, and finally to enjoy the

[1] Helvétius, *De l'esprit*, *Œuvres complètes*, 1795, i, 115.
[2] Grimm, *Correspondance littéraire*, 1812, ii, 141.

pleasure attached to the satisfaction of physical needs, that the artisan and the peasant think, exercise their imaginations, and labour ... Pleasure and pain are, and will always be, the only principle of the actions of men.[1]

Self-love, he says, following La Rochefoucauld, is a sentiment graven on us by nature; it is the source of both vice and virtue.[2] However, this does not lead to a purely individualistic hedonism. Like Mandeville, Helvétius makes egoism the basis of social solidarity. All laws must be related 'to a simple principle, such as that of the utility of the public, that is to say, of the greatest number subject to one and the same government'.[3]

His lack of subtlety and capacity for reiteration made Helvétius a successful propagandist for some of the simpler ideas derivable from the system of Locke. From Locke's picture of the mind at birth as a *tabula rasa* came the view that education and environment make all the difference between men: discoveries in the arts and sciences, concludes Helvétius, are the result of chance.[4] It is solely through good laws that virtuous men can be formed.[5] The last word is with the educator: 'goodness and humanity are not the work of nature, but only of education'.[6]

But who is to be the effective agent of this transformation? Because in the introduction to *De l'homme*, Helvétius praised Catherine II and Frederick II for their somewhat debatable services to humanity, he has been written down as an advocate of benevolent despotism. But what is arbitrary power, Helvétius asks? He replies that it is a germ of calamities which, deposited in the bosom of the State, only grows there into the fruit of misery and devastation. 'The most dangerous enemy of the public welfare is not troubles or sedition, but despotism.'[7] On the other hand, where powers are divided in the State, a free people, whose strength is drawn from its very constitution, can achieve great things.[8] We can hardly follow Bentham in describing Helvétius as the Bacon of the moral world, but we can see in him more clearly than we might in a more sophisticated thinker the practical implications of the materialist psychology and its links with utilitarianism, which will need fuller treatment in a subsequent chapter.

[1] Helvétius, *De l'homme*, iii, 139, 163. [2] *De l'esprit*, i, 163. [3] Ibid., i, 323.
[4] *De l'homme*, iii, 283, 285. [5] *De l'esprit*, i, 394-5.
[6] *De l'homme*, iii, 439. Cf. *De l'esprit*, ii, 257-9.
[7] *De l'homme*, iii, 304, 305. [8] *De l'esprit*, ii, 183.

XIII

Voltaire and the War on Religion

I F the sensational psychology constituted the basic theoretical element in the eighteenth-century Enlightenment, its most immediately obvious practical object was the attack on religion. To reduce the whole movement to this would be a gross over-simplification, but it is justifiable to see this as its keynote. And in the anti-religious campaign the leading figure is undoubtedly Voltaire. He is also the person who most clearly links the Enlightenment of the eighteenth century with its seventeenth-century origins.

Voltaire was closer to the seventeenth century than we are apt to think. He was twenty-one when Louis XIV died and to that extent belonged to the age of the great king whose reign he was to record. He passed his early twenties in the atmosphere of Regency libertinage and scepticism, which he carried with him to his death in 1778. His origins were bourgeois, his father a lawyer and his mother descended from very minor provincial nobility, but at the Jesuit College of Louis-le-Grand he made friends with the sons of the Court nobility. While still in his teens he was known as a wit and writer of society verse. His tragic drama, *Oedipe*, in 1718, at once put him in the fore-front of French dramatists. Satirical verse epigrams and witticisms about nobles got him beaten by lackeys and put into the Bastille, after which, partly for safety, he resorted to England. Already Voltaire had come to share the unorthodox religious ideas of the time. He expressed his deistic views in 'Le Pour et le Contre', a poem composed in 1722 which he only admitted to his acknowledged works fifty years later.

The sojourn in England introduced Voltaire to a new society and a world of new ideas, which he was to be one of the chief agents in transmitting to France. In 1734, soon after his return, appeared the *Lettres anglaises* or *Lettres philosophiques*, which proved that Voltaire was a whole-hearted convert to Lockian psychology, Baconian empiricism and Newtonian mathematics and physics. The boldness of his breach with prevailing ideas in France should not be under-estimated. Unorthodox religious views were already fashionable, but the rejection of the whole Cartesian system was a revolutionary step. Voltaire was perhaps the only great French thinker in the eighteenth century to emancipate himself completely from Cartesian ways of thought.

As much as by ideas, Voltaire was impressed in England by facts. He saw a country in which different religious sects lived peacefully together in the same State. 'Every man', he writes, 'can here serve God in his own way.'[1] Adopting thus early the dialogue form which he was to exploit so successfully later, he reports a long discussion with a Quaker, in which Voltaire puts forward all the orthodox objections and the Quaker gets the better of all the arguments. He admits that in England to hold many posts one must be a member of the Church of England; it follows, he adds, that nineteen-twentieths of the population is Anglican. But its clergy is serious and only attains high positions with age; one does not hear of boys becoming bishops as soon as they leave college, as in France. That indefinable being, neither religious nor secular, called the abbé, does not exist in England. When the English hear about our debauched young priests, he says, they thank God that they are Protestants; but, he concludes ironically, they are all wretched heretics and of course ought to be burned at the stake.[2]

Turning to another field, Voltaire observes that the rich are not exempted from paying taxes in England. Younger sons of the nobility go into the City and engage in commerce. Trade is free and flourishing. The farming population is prosperous.

> The peasant does not have his feet crippled by sabots; he eats white bread; he is well dressed; he is not afraid to increase the size of his flocks and herds nor to tile his roof lest his taxes be increased the following year. There are many peasants here who have property worth some 200,000 francs and who do not disdain to continue to cultivate the land which has enriched them and on which they live in freedom.[3]

The application of all this to French conditions is barely concealed: and the influence of a successful example adds enormously to the power of an idea.

Three of the letters are devoted to an exposition of the Newtonian system, which Voltaire did much to introduce to France. In 1734, also, began the fifteen years of intimate collaboration with Mme du Châtelet, primarily, though not exclusively, in science and

[1] Voltaire, *Lettres philosophiques*, V.   [2] Ibid., v.   [3] Ibid., ix.

philosophy, which ended only with her tragic death. There followed the short period with Frederick II; but at bottom Frederick was mainly interested in having one of Europe's leading men of letters at his Court, while Voltaire was unable to control his gifts for sarcasm and for making money by dubious means — among his many other activities he was accumulating a large fortune — so that their association was not an entire success and they parted with mutual expressions of disesteem. Voltaire settled for the rest of his life with his niece and mistress, Mme Denis, at Ferney, there, like Luther at Wittenberg, or Calvin at Geneva, to be the patriarch not of a new religion but of the French Enlightenment, his greatest contributions to which were still to come.

In 1756, at the age of sixty-two, he produced the *Essai sur les Mœurs*, long in preparation, and the poems on the Lisbon earthquake and on Natural Law; in 1759 *Candide*; and in 1764 the first version of the *Dictionnaire philosophique*. In the midst of dealing with a constant flow of visitors and with a European-wide correspondence, he poured out an unending stream of writings, mostly hidden under rather thin disguises of anonymity, attributed to dead authors, or purporting to be translations. In 1778 he was given a triumphal welcome in Paris as the grand old man of letters, and shortly after, at the age of eighty-four, he died.

Increasingly, and in his latter years almost exclusively, Voltaire had devoted himself to his campaign against the Catholic Church. This was, naturally, destructive rather than constructive. He had no system himself and hated systems, as befitted the heir of the libertines and Bayle. Some influence may also be attributed to Bolingbroke, who joined all those who were guilty of a priori, metaphysical or religious thought — Plato and Descartes, Leibniz and the theologians — in a common condemnation.[1] Voltaire was a sceptic and empiricist who did not believe it was possible to know the nature of things. Let us conclude, he writes, that we should employ our mind, the nature of which is unknown to us, 'to perfect the sciences which are the object of the *Encyclopédie*, as watch-makers use springs in their watches, without knowing what makes a spring work'.[2] When he met with a philosopher like Berkeley, he dismissed him, in Johnsonian fashion, with 'le paradoxe de Berkeley ne vaut pas la peine d'être réfuté'.[3]

[1] Cf. Leslie Stephen, *English Thought*, i, 179.
[2] *Dictionnaire philosophique*, art. 'Âme', *Œuvres*, xvii, 141.
[3] Ibid., art. 'Corps', *Œuvres*, xviii, 274.

Voltaire's own religion was a vague and unsystematic deism – a natural religion engraved on men's hearts by that God whom all nations, he alleges, originally recognized, who rewarded virtue and punished crime, and whom they worshipped in a simple cult.[1] The theoretical justification of his deism is rather thin. An ontological proof would be inconsistent with his general standpoint, and he mocks at the absurdities into which the argument from design led such theological scientists as the abbé Pluche; but he himself falls back on the Newtonian conception of the universe to justify his belief in the existence of an intelligence behind it. His deistic views had been formed in the intellectual climate of the opening years of the eighteenth century, and he clung to them obstinately for the rest of his life. It might be argued, though not with certainty, that deism was upheld by Voltaire chiefly as a basis for social morality. 'No society can exist without justice', he writes. Let us therefore proclaim a just God. If the law of the state punishes detected crimes, let us proclaim a God who punishes undetected ones. A philosopher may be a Spinozist (i.e. atheist) if he will; the statesman must be a theist.[2] We do not know what God is, or how he operates, says Voltaire, but we know that he must be the sovereign reason and justice: it is enough. Proclaim this, he advises: 'no man has the right to oppose you, since you say a thing which is probable, and necessary to the human race'.[3] He even goes so far as to argue that deists are not disrespectful of Christ: they revere in him a Jewish theist: but of course he instituted nothing that has the slightest relation with so-called Christian dogma. 'What is the least bad of all religions? That which has the least dogma and the most virtue.'[4]

How far is all this sincere, and how far is it a camouflage for Voltaire's anti-religious propaganda? With him it is always difficult to tell. He certainly feared open atheism as likely to bring discredit on the *philosophes;* possibly also he saw in it a threat to social stability. Yet he could also say that a bad conception of God is worse than none at all: though both are bad, fanaticism is more dangerous than atheism, which even in its error retains an element of reason to 'trim its claws'.[5] His particular detestation was reserved for the Old Testament. He sardonically observes: 'It must be admitted that if the Holy Ghost wrote this history, it did not choose a very edifying

[1] *Dictionnaire philosophique*, art. 'Dieu, Dieux', *Œuvres*, xviii, 359 ff.
[2] *Dieu et les hommes*, ch. xliv: Axiomes, *Œuvres*, vii, 243.   [3] Ibid.   [4] Ibid., p. 244.
[5] *Dictionnaire philosophique*, art. 'Athée', *Œuvres*, xvii, 457; art. 'Dieu', ibid., xviii, 380.

subject.'[1] There has been some discussion whether Voltaire's anti-religious campaign, carried on under the banner of 'Ecrasez l'infâme', was directed against all Churches, or only against the Church of Rome. The latter, undoubtedly, was his main target, because he associated it with the acts of persecution which aroused his bitterest hatred.

Voltaire's unremitting attack, and the corrosive effect of his satire, have led to the identification of the anti-religious campaign with his name; but it was an essential element in the Enlightenment as a whole. Nor was it confined to the more extreme *philosophes*. As moderate a man as Montesquieu held fundamentally the same ideas, though he expressed them with greater caution. Montesquieu, indeed, for this reason, illustrates more clearly just what the basic ideas were. Unlike Bayle, and probably Voltaire, he does not believe that it is better to have no religion at all than a bad one:[2] even a false religion is some guarantee of probity.[3] The truth or falsity of a religion, he says, is less what makes it useful or pernicious than the use or abuse to which it is put.[4] Thus, instead of justifying morality by religion, he justifies religion by morality; its chief function is to make men better citizens.[5]

Montesquieu also – and here he differs from Voltaire – attempts to provide a sociological explanation of religious differences, even suggesting that climate has fixed the limits of Christianity and Mohammedanism.[6] Because religion is justified only by its social utility, it follows that 'anti-social' religious usages are to be condemned, for example the excessive number of fêtes, which harm productive industry and agriculture and lead to debauchery.[7] Excessive encouragement of the contemplative life could also have a deleterious effect on the material standards of a society.[8] Again, a great accumulation of property in the hands of the Church was harmful to production.[9] Religion should not, said Montesquieu, on the pretext of gifts, exact from the people the necessities of life.[10] Cautiously declaring that he did not attack the principle of celibacy in itself, he warned against carrying it to excess.[11] The *philosophes* were less cautious; for them chastity, or celibacy on religious principles, was an assault on nature and shocked their sense of morality.

Finally, there was the issue, which the seventeenth century,

[1] Ibid., art. 'Histoire', Œuvres, xix, 368.
[2] De l'esprit des Lois, XXIV, ii.   [3] Ibid., viii.   [4] Ibid., xix.   [5] Ibid., xiv.
[6] Ibid., xxvi.   [7] Ibid., xxiii.   [8] Ibid., xi.   [9] Ibid., XXV, v.
[10] Ibid., vii.   [11] Ibid., iv.

culminating in Locke, had made the central one, of toleration. Some placid general observations on the subject lead up to what is, for Montesquieu, a uniquely passionate chapter. He begins:

> A Jewess, eighteen years old, burnt at the last *auto-da-fé* in Lisbon, gave rise to this little piece of writing: and I believe that it is the most useless that has ever been composed. When one is concerned to prove things which are so obvious, one is sure never to convince.

There follows a powerful plea for tolerance, put in the mouth of a Jew and addressed to the Inquisitors. It ends:

> You must be warned of one thing; this is that, if anyone in the future ever ventures to say that in the century in which we live the people of Europe were civilized, you will be cited to prove that they were barbarians; and the idea that will be held of you will be such that it will disgrace your century and bring down hatred on your contemporaries.[1]

Voltaire's treatment of religion also centres, and even more persistently, on the point of intolerance. It should be remembered that ceremonial burnings of heretics were still common in the Iberian peninsula, that Protestant ministers were still being hanged in France, that sacrilege was still occasionally punished with death, that men could be sent to the hulks and women to prison for many years or life for attending Huguenot assemblies. The cases of Calas, Sirven and La Barre, which were seized on by Voltaire partly for propaganda purposes, did not stand alone.

The fact that Calas and many others were tortured to death should not be unduly emphasized. It was normal legal procedure. The novelty lay in the views of Voltaire and the other *philosophes*, and, even more than in their objection to religious persecution as such, in the fact that, under the influence of their hedonistic psychology, they had altogether ceased to believe that torture was a good thing. This was a new moral judgment, which, in the course of the century, spread far beyond the bounds of the philosophic sect. Educated men, throughout Western Europe, were losing their faith in cruelty, even for religious ends. Voltaire claimed, in the preface to his play *Alzire*, that in nearly all his writings would be found that spirit of humanity 'which ought to be the prime character of a thinking

---

[1] *Esprit des Lois*, XXV, xiii.

being'.[1] It was no ignoble or unjustified boast; and it was unfortunate that the Catholic Church, like the law, clung to older ethical ideas and cruel practices which, in the degree to which they were stripped of their moral justification began to appear, to use an only slightly anachronistic term, as mere sadism. Indeed, it was not an accident that the idea of sadism, cruelty for its own sake, or for the sake of the sexual or other pleasure it could confer, appeared at the end of the century, just when it had lost most of its moral and religious justification.

A hatred of the institutionalized cruelties with which religion was associated, and which it defended, and what can only be described as a consciousness of ethical superiority to those who perpetrated such cruelties, gave Voltaire and the *philosophes* the moral fervour to carry on their crusade. If he had ever been conscious of the need of defending himself for his war on the Churches, Voltaire would have said that it was hardly his fault that they were identified with cruelties and superstitions which, if they were explicable on historical grounds — though of course he would not have understood that — could not but revolt the conscience of an age of Enlightenment.

[1] *Œuvres*, ii, 379.

XIV

The French Utilitarians

PROGRESS is a question-begging term, but it is reasonable to describe the eighteenth century as an age of progress in humanitarian ideals. The Enlightenment is sometimes associated with the idea of progress in a more far-reaching sense, as a result of identifying it exclusively with the ideas of Condorcet and a few other minor eighteenth-century writers. That the pessimism of Rousseau or the very qualified optimism of Voltaire cannot be reconciled with this interpretation hardly needs to be stressed. Yet a widely accepted historical view is seldom without some justification, and the Enlightenment may at least be said to have prepared the ground for the idea of progress. We have seen how Fontenelle established the possibility of scientific progress. The historical scepticism of Bayle, the Lockian rejection of innate ideas, the belief that man is moulded by education and environment and by changing these can in effect change himself – such ideas freed the human race from automatic bondage to the past, and broke the chains of tradition. Education and legislation were now the keys to the reform of society. As early as 1751, long before Condorcet, in an *Essai sur la perfection* Formey saw man as led by nature and the law written in his heart to a harmonious life. In 1772 the chevalier de Chastellux's *De la félicité publique* linked progress with intellectual enlightenment. There was a general belief that the nature of man was good. Moralists who condemned man as a victim of his passions were mistaken. 'I do not fear to advance', wrote Toussaint, taking a long step beyond the rationalism of the seventeenth century, 'that on the contrary it is our passions which are innocent, and our reason which is guilty.'[1] Social evils, it followed, were not the penalty of Original Sin but were due to ignorance and prejudice, and there was a reasonable expectation of reducing or even eliminating them. Even religious influences temporarily operated in the same direction. Jansenism, it it true, upheld older ideas of man's corruption, but Molinism, influential through the Society of Jesus, deprecated Original Sin and emphasized God's grace to man. Missionaries

[1] Toussaint, *Les Mœurs*, 1748 (new ed. of 1760), pp. 65-6.

126

provided material for a favourable view of human nature in narratives which helped to build up the legend of the noble savage. The contribution of deism and the argument from design to an optimistic world-view has already been mentioned. All that was necessary for happiness, or so it seemed to more superficial thinkers, was to discover the laws laid down by a benevolent deity, according to which man and society should be ruled, and obey them. The positive facts of a limited but noticeable material advance in the countries of Western Europe encouraged hope of further improvement. It was an age of invention, social as well as mechanical. Change and reform were in the air, even though established institutions and vested interests stood in their way.

The aim which the Enlightenment had set before itself was to promote happiness, and in the pleasure-pain motivation it believed there was a built-in pilot in human nature to steer it in the right direction, so long as it was allowed to operate freely. In this, as in most other respects, the seventeenth century had anticipated the eighteenth. Bacon and Descartes had justified scientific inquiry partly by its usefulness. Hobbes and Locke both propounded psychological theories of pleasure and pain; though Hobbes's very peculiar hedonism took the negative form of avoidance of evil, or rather of one particular evil – violent death at the hands of other men; while in Locke's theory the ideas of natural law and natural rights took precedence over the strictly utilitarian conception of happiness. Already in the last years of the seventeenth century, however, we meet the abbé de Saint-Pierre (1658–1743), deist and Cartesian, an associate of Fontenelle and later a member of the free-thinking Club de l'Entresol, who was the very model of philanthropic utilitarianism. To Saint-Pierre is attributed the introduction into general use of the word 'bienfaisance'.[1] He devoted his life to the invention of schemes for improving the lot of mankind. Among his *projets* were those for perpetual peace, for a graduated land tax, for diminishing the number of lawsuits, for improving schools, for reforming spelling, for extirpating the Barbary corsairs, for rendering dukes and peers serviceable, for making honorific titles more useful to the State, for a system of annuities, for making the writing of bad books – romances, catechisms, sermons and the like – more honourable for their authors and more useful to posterity, for improving the system of government, for making roads passable

[1] P. Hazard, *La Pensée européenne au XVIIIe siècle*, 1946, i, 232-3.

in winter, for dealing with beggars, and many others, down to a project for a patent portable armchair. It is easy to make fun of Saint-Pierre, and would be still more so if he had been less benevolently disinterested, or if so many of his projects had not in the end turned out to be quite practicable. D'Alembert, in his Eulogy, wrote of him:

> Utility was indeed the sole aim of his labours. Never was any author, even among those who profess themselves most indifferent to fame, less occupied wih his own glory, or less susceptible to the most secret illusions of self-love.'[1]

Saint-Pierre – anticipating Bentham – devoted himself systematically to a way of thought in which the whole Enlightenment was to become engaged. It was the expression of a general, diffused utilitarianism, under the influence of which a host of reforms were elaborated. This was what the Enlightenment meant by progress. Its expectation of the realization of its hopes was perhaps naive. The opposition of those whose attachment to the existing ways of doing things, and even more to the advantages which, however much against the general interests of society, they brought to individuals or groups, kept many – though not all – of the projected reforms mere paper schemes; but they were not to remain inoperative permanently. The nineteenth century inherited and began to put into practice the legacy of this great wave of reforming idealism, the influence of which is yet far from exhausted.

For a systematic exposition of the utilitarian approach to social problems England had to wait for Jeremy Bentham. In France, the completest and most sophisticated expression of utilitarianism is to be found in the writings of the baron d'Holbach, though compared with the enormous influence exercised by Bentham, the practical effect of d'Holbach's writings was negligible. D'Holbach (1723–89) was a Palatinate baron settled in Paris. The happy and benevolent ménage of the d'Holbachs became a centre for the more advanced *philosophes* in the latter part of the eighteenth century. The abbé Galiani called him the maître d'hôtel of philosophy. His first book, *Christianisme dévoilé* (1767) was a frank exposition of atheism, which aroused Voltaire's indignation but contains nothing particularly new or interesting. Religion being brushed on one side, d'Holbach turned to the problems of secular morals and utilitarian

---

[1] *Eloges de d'Alembert*, 1779, p. 101.

politics in his *Système de la Nature* (1770) and *Système social* (1773). D'Holbach is of course a materialist, though in a note he admits that 'the most extravagant of systems -- that of Berkeley' is also the most difficult to refute.[1] The soul, he says, is merely the body envisaged in respect of some of its more obscure functions: it should be studied anatomically.[2] Morals, therefore, can be reduced to scientific laws in the same way as physics,[3] and by doing so we can bring man back to nature. Man is made, as La Mettrie and all the materialists believed, to be happy, and is only unhappy because he has abandoned nature, by which they meant his own nature. It is a vulgar error to suppose that for the Enlightenment 'follow nature' meant 'return to the life of the primitive savage'; on the contrary, nature was identified with reason, and reason with the principle of utility. The important result was the exclusion of a priori truth from the field of morals, or so at least it was thought. This does not mean that there is no criterion of good and bad. D'Holbach makes this clear. Virtue, he says, is the fulfilment of the end of society, which is utility, that is the happiness of its members.[4] It rests 'on the eternal and invariable relations which subsist between beings of the human species living in society, and which will subsist as long as men and society do'.[5] His is, in fact, a sociological morality, which looks back to Montesquieu and forward to Bentham.

The utilitarianism of d'Holbach, besides being essentially social, is based on a recognition of human differences, both physical and moral. Because of these, men need one another's co-operation in society. The imaginary state of nature, in which they lived in isolation from one another, if it ever existed, says d'Holbach, would have been a state of 'misery, imbecility and unreason'. 'Man is, naturally, the being most useful to man.'[6] Useful, of course, is equated with the production of happiness, but d'Holbach has a broader definition of this than Helvétius. It is not transient pleasure: the greatest happiness is the most lasting.[7] Happiness, he sums up, is 'la coordination de l'homme avec les causes qui agissent sur lui'[8] – which might be interpreted as harmony between man and his environment. Where d'Holbach is open to criticism is in his unduly limited conception of both man and the influences operating on him; but with a kinship with the basic ideas of La Mettrie and Helvétius,

---

[1] *Système de la nature*, 1770, i, 158, n.46. [2] Ibid., i, 186.
[3] *Système social*, 1774, i, 1-2. [4] Ibid., i, 134. [5] Ibid. [6] Ibid., i, 190, 192.
[7] *Système de la nature*, i, 135. [8] Ibid., i, 136.

the social philosophy of d'Holbach is much less crude and more susceptible of development.

He is also much more aware of the difficulties in the way of the practical application of utilitarian ideas, and is led into a much more serious discussion of social and political questions. For d'Holbach, as for the whole Enlightenment, politics is the practical application of morals, and they cannot be separated without danger.[1] Nature does not make men either good or bad; parents, teachers, education as a whole does that.[2] The art of politics is that of regulating the passions of mankind and directing them to the good of society,[3] which is the general interest, interpreted, of course, in strictly individualistic terms; it means ensuring the advantages of society for the greatest number, and these advantages are liberty, property and security[4] – so close are we still to Locke. The political ideas of d'Holbach will have to be discussed later. His view of existing governments is a gloomy one, but it does not lead to pessimism. Everywhere, he believes, can be detected signs of the progress of lumières.

D'Holbach represents the highest point of the utilitarian spirit in the French Enlightenment. Moderate as his views may seem to us, he had gone too far for many of the philosophes. What most of all aroused alarm was the social consequences that could be drawn from utilitarian premises; for the utilitarian idea could not be confined within the limits that had seemed proper when Voltaire was a young man, nor could it be kept strictly to the fields of government and law. There was a latent egalitarianism in it which could not be ignored permanently. To describe the attitude of the Enlightenment to the unenlightened masses as, in the words of Anatole France, 'cette charité froide qui on nomme altruisme' is comprehensible but hardly just. The narrow social sympathies of a rigid individualism were based on the optimistic assumptions of the natural identification of interests, according to which, if each individual pursued his own interest, the greatest happiness of all individuals would be achieved. But this principle was itself to be tested by its results. Utilitarianism was bound to the principle that the end of society is the happiness of individuals, but not to any particularly individualist method of reaching this end. Moreover, the prevailing humanitarian sentiment which, as was demonstrated by Saint-Pierre and Bentham, went hand in hand with the utilitarianism of the Enlightenment, was not

---

[1] Système social, i, 7-8.   [2] Système de la nature, i, 149.
[3] Ibid., i, 140.   [4] Ibid., i, 142.

permanently to be confined within the bounds of self-interest, and in the course of the two centuries we can watch a steady broadening of sympathies. Thus the institution of slavery had been excused, however awkwardly and inconsistently, by Locke; but Montesquieu, although a citizen of the great slaving port of Bordeaux, wasted no words to qualify his condemnation. Later in the century, Raynal's *Histoire des deux Indes* (1772) was an armoury of arguments against slavery, which before the French Revolution had been totally discredited, intellectually and morally, in the enlightened mind. While, admittedly, few if any of the French or English writers of the Enlightenment were slave-traders or owners, at least we can say that in this respect they were not the 'hirelings of their bourgeois masters'.

The egalitarian implications of the Enlightenment were not confined to what might be regarded as a remote problem. The *philosophes* shared, in varying degrees, a rather vague, but undeniable, admiration for the republican ideal, derived largely from reminiscences of the classics, with which was associated the idea of economic equality. The connection can clearly be seen in such writers as Montesquieu, Rousseau and Mably. A utopian literature, portraying the ideal egalitarian republic, is represented in Fénelon's *Télémaque* (1699), Montesquieu's Troglodytes in his *Lettres persanes* (1721), Morelly's *Code de la Nature* (1755), and various other works.

Similarly, the criticism of 'luxe' was common enough to evoke the well-known defence of it in Voltaire's *Mondain*. It derived, as did most social Utopianism, largely from classical sources, and was to some extent a mere literary fashion. But it would be a mistake to dismiss the whole tendency in this way. The right of property was, of course, taken for granted: it was to be embodied in the French Declaration of Rights as 'sacred and inviolable'; but it was generally recognized that the laws of property were civil and not natural laws, the result of convention, and therefore liable to be changed if the interests of society so required. As conservative a thinker as Montesquieu approved of sumptuary legislation[1] and of taxation in proportion to capacity to pay;[2] he held that the State had responsibilities to care for the aged, invalids and orphans[3], and argued that the laws of inheritance could be altered.[4] Indeed there are few of the practical economic reforms of the nineteenth-century and later which are not adumbrated in the writings of the Enlightenment.

[1] *Esprit des Lois*, VII, v.   [2] Ibid., XIII, vii.   [3] Ibid., XXIII, xxix.   [4] Ibid., XXVI, vi.

Such views seem to be incompatible with the stricter economic thought of the eighteenth century, which culminated in the laissez-faire theories of Adam Smith in Great Britain and the Physiocrats in France; but the practical influence of the Physiocrats has been much exaggerated, and their relation to the Enlightenment misconceived. Their abstract theorizing belongs to the Cartesian tradition of a priori deduction and their views were shared by few, or none, of the *philosophes*. On the other hand Adam Smith, in so far as he reached similar conclusions, did so as an historian and by the observation of empirical facts. The *Wealth of Nations* belongs to the Enlightenment both in its empirical basis and its utilitarian ends.

The utilitarian ideal had its limitations, but one unavoidable implication was that the end of social organization was the general welfare, in the broadest sense, of all individuals in society. The optimistic faith in the natural identification of economic interests, therefore, was subject to the test of experience in so far as utilitarian ideas prevailed, as they did in Great Britain. French thought, on the other hand, towards the end of the eighteenth century was beginning to flow in different channels, and the Revolution and Napoleonic Empire were to complete the process of diversion. Although the idea of social utility was strongly present in the opening stages of the Revolution, non-utilitarian ideals were to swamp it. With d'Holbach the current of utilitarianism in French thought draws, at least temporarily, to a close, just at the time when in England it was to find its greatest and most influential exponent in Jeremy Bentham.

XV

Hume and Philosophic Scepticism

I F intellectual history followed a neat, logical course, it should
be possible to trace successive stages in the Enlightenment, from
the establishment of its basic ideas in the seventeenth century,
through their growth and elaboration in the eighteenth to their
undermining and final decay. The facts of chronology do not permit
such a simple pattern to be adopted. The development of philosophical thought in particular is out of step with changes in other
fields perhaps because it depends so much upon the accident of
individual genius. Moreover this survey of the thought of the
Enlightenment must disregard what would be unavoidable chapters
if it were a history of philosophy. After Descartes, only one other
of the greater philosophers of Europe makes an appearance in these
pages. Spinoza, Leibniz, Berkeley would dominate a history of the
philosophical thought of the seventeenth and eighteenth centuries,
and they were not lacking in influence at the time, even if it was most
often the influence of a misconception of their ideas. They are
omitted here simply because they do not seem to me to belong to
the history of the Enlightenment, any more than, say, Wesley or
William Law, Fénelon, Vico or Burke. A case might be made out for
the inclusion of Berkeley as a successor to Locke, but he was a
successor who shifted the train of thought on to very different lines.
The philosopher, par excellence, of the Enlightenement is another
heir of Locke, David Hume, whose most important philosophical
work, published when he was still a young man, in 1739-40, was his
Treatise of Human Nature. That this belongs in the main stream of
the Enlightenment can be seen simply from its subtitle – 'Being an
attempt to introduce the experimental method into Moral Subjects.'

Hume begins by asking what we can know by experience. His
answer is: only impressions, which are sensations, passions and
emotions, and ideas, which are fainter images of these. Impressions
are divided into those of sensation and those of reflection. Some
impressions and ideas are simple and some are complex. All this is
apparently an innocuous restatement, and to some extent modification, of Lockian ideas. Then comes the bombshell. We know, Hume

says placidly, our own ideas and impressions – and then adds ruth-lessly, they are just all we do know:

> Let us chace our imagination to the heavens, or to the utmost limits of the universe; we never really advance a step beyond ourselves, nor can conceive any kind of existence, but those perceptions, which have appear'd in that narrow compass.[1]

Ideas and impressions, certainly, are connected with one another in various ways, and particularly by the relation of cause and effect, which is the basis of our discourse about the world of practice. But here again Hume pushes the sceptical trend much farther than his predecessors. From what, he asks, is our reasoning concerning cause and effect derived? His answer is that it is a result of custom or habit; it is nothing but the effect of the liveliness of certain combinations of impressions in our minds. In other words, the belief in causal relations is based on repeated experience; but repetition, even to infinity, cannot establish a necessary connection, it can merely create a belief in an habitual connection. It follows that, since all our practical reasoning involves the principle of causation, it is based only on a belief established by custom, and the strength of our conviction depends on and varies with the strength of that belief. What seems to us necessity is simply the determination of thought to pass from cause to effect and vice versa, 'according to their ex-perienced union'; yet this relation of cause and effect is the only one which enables us to reason beyond immediate impressions. The con-clusion is that all human opinions are prejudices.

What, it may be asked, then, is the function of reason? All we positively know about it, says Hume, is what we deduce from human conduct; and since animals obviously act in the same way and base their behaviour, like man, on the expectation that similar causes will be followed by similar results, if on this ground we attribute reason to man, then we must do the same with animals. The result is the equation of reason and instinct: 'Reason is nothing but a wonderful and unintelligible instinct in our souls, which carries us along a certain train of ideas.'[2]

This is not the end of Hume's scepticism. The very coherence of the human mind does not survive his disintegrating criticism:

[1] *A Treatise of Human Nature*, ed. L. A. Selby-Bigge, 2nd ed. 1896, pp. 67-8.
[2] Ibid., p. 179.

What we call a *mind*, is nothing but a heap or collection of different perceptions, united together by certain relations, and suppos'd, tho' falsely, to be endow'd with a perfect simplicity and identity.[1]

Similarly, on physical objects he follows Berkeley in treating them as nothing but a collection or succession in time of sensible qualities. Their unity is to be explained only in psychological terms. Universals, according to Hume, depend on the fallacy that whatever is separately distinguishable is capable of separate existence. Take solidity – that favourite of the physicists – as an example. It is, he says, the quality which is supposed to be possessed by a body which is solid. Exclude colour, sound and all secondary qualities from the idea of such a body, as Galileo and other seventeenth-century thinkers did, and we are left, as the only other identifying quality of a solid body with the fact that it is capable of motion. Now motion depends on extension, and extension on solidity. It follows that a solid body is a body which is solid, a mere tautology:

When we reason from cause and effect, we conclude, that neither colour, sound, taste, nor smell have a continu'd and independent existence. When we exclude these sensible qualities there remains nothing in the universe, which has such an existence.[2]

Thus there is no mind and no matter. The sensible moderate young Scottish philosopher represented an intellectual force far more explosive and devastating than any of the terrible French materialists.

When the *Treatise on Human Nature* was published, Hume said, it 'fell stillborn from the press'. Even the author perhaps did not realize how devastating was his own logic; but he had put a time-bomb under Western philosophy, and it has never been the same again. This, however, was only the begining. If reason is merely a prejudice, it cannot be treated as a motive of action. Hume's arguments were consequently bound to have far-reaching consequences for moral philosophy. The alleged 'rationalism' of the Enlightenment does not seem quite so unqualified when we read, in the words of its greatest philosopher: 'Reason is, and ought only to be the slave of the passions, and can never pretend to any other office than to serve and obey them.'[3] We return to a more familiar idea when Hume

[1] Ibid., p. 207.   [2] Ibid., p. 231.   [3] Ibid., p. 415.

tells us that the passions are founded on pain and pleasure, the presence or prospect of which causes our aversion or propensity to any object. But he again shakes our trust in eighteenth-century rationalism when he adds:

> Besides good and evil, or in other words, pain and pleasure, the direct passions frequently arise from a natural impulse or instinct, which is perfectly unaccountable.[1]

The consequence of Hume's chain of argument is to eliminate the possibility of the deductive morality that had been upheld by Locke. He is quite uncompromising on this point:

> As long as it is allow'd that reason has no influence on our passions and actions, 'tis in vain to pretend, that morality is discover'd only by a deduction of reason ... Moral distinctions, therefore, are not the offspring of reason. Reason is wholly inactive, and can never be the source of so active a principle as conscience, or a sense of morals.[2]

His refusal to hypothesize the existence of entities for which he has no empirical evidence naturally leads to the rejection of the ideas of vice and virtue: like sounds and colours, they have no existence but in the mind. Moral distinctions are simply the reflection of the impression of pain or pleasure that actions or characters make upon us, and this is the only meaning which can be given to the moral sense. However, he makes one concession: since the minds of all men are similar, affections in one beget corresponding affections in another. This is called sympathy and it is the chief source of social morality.

At about the age of thirty-five, reversing the mental development of Descartes, Hume abandoned, for the most part, philosophy for history. He had, in a way, rehabilitated history from its Cartesian discredit, not by establishing the certainty of history but by destroying the certainties of all other forms of knowledge. We believe the evidence for historical accounts, he says, on the same grounds as we believe all our other impressions. History is no better and no worse than any other form of knowledge. There may be many links in a chain of historical knowledge, but they are all the same kind, and if we accept one we can accept the rest. Finally, history has the virtue

---

[1] *A Treatise of Human Nature*, p. 439.
[2] Ibid., pp. 457-8.

of not depending on metaphysical suppositions. It is not essentially different from the knowledge given us by our everyday experience, which is the best kind of knowledge. We must accept it, just as we should follow prejudices, because they are all we have to follow. Only we should not imagine in either case that we are dealing with rational certainties.

Hume's uncompromising scepticism thus leads him to the defence of prejudice. There was no divine discontent in him, he was quite satisfied with things as they were and had no particular desire to reform anything. This is perhaps why he has always seemed a more respectable figure than the French *philosophes*, who because they believed in something therefore wanted to change things. Hume showed that utilitarianism was not inconsistent with a completely conservative outlook. As Bentham put it, Hume sought for that which is; whereas, he adds, most moralists 'by a strange *petitio principii*' become engaged in defining *that which ought to be*.[1]

In the last resort Hume's scepticism is only destructive philosophically. In other respects common sense reasserts itself. The conclusion can be given in his own words:

I have already shewn, that the understanding, when it acts alone, and according to its most general principles, entirely subverts itself, and leaves not the lowest degree of evidence in any proposition, either in philosophy or common life ... Shall we, then, establish it for a general maxim, that no refin'd or elaborate reasoning is ever to be receiv'd? Consider well the consequences of such a principle. By this means you cut off entirely all science and philosophy: You proceed upon one singular quality of the imagination, and by a parity of reason must embrace all of them: And you expressly contradict yourself; since this maxim must be built on the preceding reasoning ... If we embrace this principle, and condemn all refin'd reasoning, we run into the most manifest absurdities. If we reject it in favour of these reasonings, we subvert entirely the human understanding. We have, therefore, no choice left but betwixt a false reason and none at all ... The *intense* view of these manifold contradictions and imperfections in human reason has so wrought upon me, and heated my brain, that I am ready to reject all belief and reasoning, and can look upon no opinion even as more probable or likely than another.

[1] E. Halévy, *La formation du radicalisme philosophique*, 1901, i, 12.

Where am I, or what? From what causes do I derive my existence, and to what condition shall I return? Whose favour shall I court and whose anger must I dread? What beings surround me? and on whom have I any influence, or who have any influence on me? I am confounded with all these questions, and begin to fancy myself in the most deplorable condition imaginaable, inviron'd with the deepest darkness, and utterly depriv'd of the use of every member and faculty.

Most fortunately it happens, that since reason is incapable of dispelling these clouds, nature herself suffices to that purpose, and cures me of this philosophical melancholy and delirium either by relaxing this bent of mind, or by some avocation, and lively impression of my senses, which obliterate all these chimeras. I dine, I play a game of backgammon, I converse, and am merry with my friends; and when, after three or four hours' amusement, I wou'd return to these speculations, they appear so cold, and strain'd, and ridiculous, that I cannot find in my heart to enter into them any farther.[1]

We should not let this be the last word, however. Hume cannot thus repudiate responsibility for the consequences of his own genius. If the Enlightenment had a worm in the bud, its name was 'le bon David'. On the whole it was as well for enlightened self-confidence that the *Treatise of Human Nature* was not read. Even if it had been, one doubts if its implications would have been understood. The philosophy of Hume is relevant to this discussion of the Enlightenment not because of any influence it exercised but as an indication of the range of the scepticism latent in its ideas.

[1] *A Treatise of Human Nature*, pp. 267-9.

XVI

Diderot: Science and Morals

HUME, for all his broader significance, represented a by-path in relation to the main highway of the Enlightenment. The eighteenth century was more interested in science than in philosophy, though it was an age of consolidation and popularization rather than one of fundamental discovery. General intellectual interest had shifted from mathematics to the natural sciences, in particular chemistry and botany, but the basic steps which were necessary to initiate greater advances in these sciences had not yet been taken. Chemistry, only recently emancipated from alchemy, was enmeshed in the toils of the phlogiston theory — the belief that there is an inflammable principle which is released into the air in the process of burning — which dominated chemical thought until the time of Priestley and Lavoisier, in spite of its irreconcilability with some known empirical facts, such as the gain of weight in combustion. In botany this was an age of collectors. Linnaeus performed an invaluable service in providing a system for the classification of the host of new species that were being discovered, but at the same time helped to consolidate the idea of the immutability of species. The work which seemed to contemporaries the greatest scientific achievement of the age was Buffon's *Histoire naturelle*, of which the first volume appeared in 1749. It was a literary triumph; but Buffon, by inclination a system builder, tended to premature generalization and to substitute a classificatory system for scientific empiricism.

The scientific developments which had most influence on the general thought of the eighteenth-century Enlightenment were in the field of biology. A famous experiment by Needham in 1748 seemed to demonstrate the spontaneous generation of life from inorganic matter. Needham's 'little eels' were satirized by Voltaire, who had a genius for seeing through most forms of humbug, and the validity of the experiment was discredited by Spallanzani; but this was twenty years later, and in the meantime it had exercised considerable influence. On a more serious scientific level were studies of the polyp, which seemed to provide a link between vegetable and animal nature, and of the phenomenon of parthogenesis.

Wild speculations of no scientific value were set off by the new discoveries in biology. Such was the *Telliamed* (1748) of De Maillet, a hodge-podge of pseudo-scientific ideas. This work begins with Cartesian original motion, and harks back to the Gassendists and to Fontenelle. De Maillet suggests, as Buffon also does, that the earth was originally all covered with water; but his own contribution is the suggestion that the human race may be descended from mermen and mermaids, about whose fishy termination he exhibits a certain scientific doubt.[1] One can see that in his writings, in a fantastic way, the old idea of the Chain of Being was passing from the conception of fixed species into a vague evolutionary theory. The gaps between man and animal, and between organic and inorganic nature, seemed for a short period to have been bridged.

Science thus reinforced the philosophic trend towards materialism which the Lucretian tradition had promoted, but which also was a development from Cartesianism, as the Cambridge Platonists had foreseen. The dualism between mind and matter which Descartes had predicated was not to be a permanent solution of the problem of their relations; nor did Malebranche's occasional causes, Leibniz's pre-established harmony, or Spinoza's pantheism prove more satisfactory. Locke was aware of the problem but attempted no answer. Voltaire was shrewd enough to see that Cartesianism was ultimately dangerous to his ideas and stubbornly clung to the Newtonian compromise, uniting a mechanistic physics with deism. As soon as one says, with Descartes, 'Give me movement and matter and I will make a world', Voltaire declared, the idea of a God is excluded. The other *philosophes* remained more under the influence of Cartesian ways of thought; and Cartesian deductive reasoning led them in the direction of broad, sweeping generalizations. Voltaire was the only *philosophe* with any serious pretensions in the field of experimental science. The others were popularizers and literary men, given to speculation, not to observation and experiment.

Both the strength and the weakness of the *philosophes* in the field of science are revealed in Diderot, who was the most practically minded and scientifically curious of them all. In the opening paragraph of his *Lettre sur les Aveugles* (1749), he makes a slighting reference to Réaumer, who had observed the reactions of a child,

[1] De Maillet, *Telliamed ou Entretiens d'un philosophe indien*, 1748, ii, 196-8.

born blind, and given sight as the result of an operation. How much less valuable, Diderot thought, were these petty observations of what actually happened, than would be the reflections of a philosopher on what ought to have happened. But perhaps this was merely the reaction of pique at being excluded from the operation.[1]

The son of a Langres master cutler, educated by the Jesuits in Paris, Diderot dismissed in turn the ideas of a career in the Church and in law, and instead became an inhabitant of the Paris Grub Street. His first writings were unimportant. He published a translation from Shaftesbury, with added notes,[2] and a deistic essay, *Pensées philosophiques* (1746), which was condemned by the Parlement. The *Lettre sur les Aveugles* of 1749, to which reference has already been made, was his first important work. It purported to be an account of a Cambridge mathematician named Saunderson, who had been born blind. Diderot's object was to reverse the method of ordinary sensational psychology, and to consider the effect of the deprivation of a sense, as an illustration of the dependence of the mind and its ideas on bodily functions. He writes:

I have never doubted that the conditions of our organs and our senses have great influence on our philosophy and morals, and that our most purely intellectual ideas, if I may speak thus, are intimately dependent on the conformation of our body.[3]

A man blind from birth will have, he suggests, no idea of normal modesty or shame. His sympathy will be aroused by sounds and not by sight:

How different the moral ideas of the blind are from ours! How those of the deaf would differ again from those of the blind, and how imperfect, not to say worse, a being with one more sense than us would find our moral ideas.[4]

From this philosophical or moral relativism, Diderot passes on to speculate about the variability of living organisms, an idea he was to push much further in later writings. The possibilities seem so limitless than he is led into a glancing stroke against the argument from design:

O philosophers! transport yourselves with me to the limits

[1] *Lettre sur les Aveugles*, 1749, *Œuvres*, 1875, i, 279.
[2] *Essai sur le Mérite et la Vertu*, 1745.
[3] Diderot, *Œuvres*, i, 288.   [4] Ibid., i, 289.

of this universe, beyond the point where I touch [this is put in the mouth of the blind Saunderson], and you see organized beings; travel across this new ocean and search amidst its wild agitation for some traces of that intelligent being whose wisdom you admire in this world.[1]

He takes another step with his *Pensées sur l'interprétation de la nature*, in 1754. He distinguishes here between thinkers who have 'beaucoup d'instruments et peu d'idées' and those who have 'beaucoup d'idées et n'ont point d'instruments',[2] in other words between experimental and rational thinkers. His view is that the two should work hand in hand, but the bias of his own mind was clearly towards speculation rather than experiment. I think that one must interpret in a philosophical rather than a scientific sense his hope that all phenomena will ultimately be reduced to aspects of a single principle.[3] It was perhaps this which led him beyond the traditional theory of the Chain of Being to a more general evolutionary view. He asks:

> Would not one willingly believe that there was never but one initial animal, a prototype of all animals, which nature has lengthened, shortened, transformed, multiplied, deprived of certain organs?[4]

Or again, with an ironic beginning:

> If faith did not teach us that animals came from the hand of the Creator just as we see them; and if it were permitted to have the least uncertainty about their origin and their end, might not the philosopher, abandoned to his own conjectures, suspect that the animal world had from all eternity its particular elements, scattered and mixed up in the general mass of matter; that these elements happened to combine, because it was possible that they might; that the embryo formed of these elements may have passed through an infinity of organisms and developments; that it gained, successively, movement, sensation, ideas, thought, reflection, conscience, sentiments, passions, signs, gestures, sounds, articulate sounds, a language, laws, sciences and arts; that millions of years elapsed between each of these developments; that it has perhaps yet other transformations to pass

---

[1] Diderot, *Œuvres*, i, 310.
[2] Ibid. *De l'interprétation de la nature*, *Œuvres*, ii, 9.
[3] Ibid., ii, 42. [4] Ibid., ii, 15-16.

through, and other developments to achieve, which are hidden from us.[1]

These views were, of course, in violent conflict with those of orthodox religion, which taught that species were immutable in the shape in which they were created. A simple but not wholly unfair reaction to the new ideas of evolution was:

> If men were once fish, if there are still in the sea fish destined to become human beings, one of two things follows: either man does not have a spiritual and immortal soul, or else fishes have the same soul — two equally impious suggestions.[2]

Diderot, combining materialist with evolutionary views, goes even further and — under the influence of Needham's experiment — questions the apparent distinction between living and dead matter, organic and inorganic.[3] In his later writings, such as the *Rêve de d'Alembert*, which is an amazing medley of wild but sometimes prophetic speculation, Diderot produces a full-scale scheme of transformism; but these last works were all left in manuscript and only printed many years later.

The scientific naturalism of Diderot led to a moral naturalism, which went far beyond the simple hedonistic view that self-interest is the essence of virtue and that there is no other justice or injustice — a paradox which he describes, in a criticism of Helvétius, as both false and dangerous. In man's physical organism, sensibility, and natural needs, says Diderot, are to be found a permanent basis of morality.[4] Whereas Helvétius attributes everything to the influence of environment and education, Diderot sees the importance of natural character.[5] Criticizing Helvétius, he addresses him thus:

> Thinking you were writing the history of the human race, you have at most only written your own. Because woman was your only desire, you have supposed that it was the same with everyone else.[6]

He agrees that pleasure and pain are the principles that motivate the actions of men, but charges Helvétius with recognizing only

---

[1] Ibid., ii, 57-8.
[2] A. Vartanian, *Diderot and Descartes: a Study of Scientific Naturalism in the Enlightenment*, 1953, p. 313.
[3] Diderot, *De l'interprétation de la nature, Œuvres*, ii, 58.
[4] *Réflexions sur le livre de l'Esprit*, ibid., ii, 270.
[5] *Réfutation de l'ouvrage d'Helvétius intitulé l'Homme*, ibid., ii, 277.   [6] Ibid., ii, 308.

physical pleasures and pains, and adds, somewhat bitterly: 'j'en ai éprouvé d'autres'.[1]

The final contribution of Diderot to the problem of scientific morality was in his manuscript *Supplément au Voyage de Bougainville*, in which he propounded a high-minded sexual promiscuity. It is difficult to know how seriously he meant this to be taken, or how far it merely represented wishful thinking. The *philosophes* did not reach a high intellectual level when they were dealing with the relations of the sexes; it was hardly possible that they should. Their personal conduct naturally followed the contemporary pattern, but this did not solve the theoretical problem. They had abandoned the principles laid down by revealed religion but did not know what to put in their place. This would not have worried them if, like the earlier French libertines, they had been content with moral indifferentism, but on the contrary, the whole bias of their thought was moralistic. Their attempt to derive moral principles from scientific naturalism was doomed to failure; while a psychological theory which recognized only the conscious mind could not be expected to achieve much understanding of the motives of human action. Diderot's criticism of Helvétius is an indication of his awareness of the inadequacy of current psychological theories, but he made no systematic attempt to put anything in their place. He presented the problem as he saw it in the form of a parable:

> Would you know the short history of almost all our misery? Here it is. There was once a natural man; an artificial man was introduced into this man; and within him a civil war has broken out which will last all his life ... The unhappy monster is torn apart, pinched, tormented, stretched on the wheel.[2]

At least he was aware of the psychological conflict, though he could find no means of resolving it.

To appreciate the direction which Diderot's thoughts were taking we have to turn to the *contes* which he produced in his later years. Deservedly famous among these is *Le Neveu de Rameau*, first known in a German translation by Goethe, who greatly admired it. In striking contrast with the assemblage of types or puppets whose strings are pulled by Voltaire in his stories, it is a work of subtle characterization. In essence a dialogue between a moralist and a

[1] *Réfutation de l'ouvrage d'Helvétius*, Œuvres, ii, 310.
[2] *Supplément au voyage de Bougainville*, ibid., ii, 246.

cynic, the participants are well individualized. In particular the *neveu* is seen in the round. He could so easily have been a mere rating cynic. Instead, he is a man of considerable artistic sensibilities, with ideals which he is never been able to realize and ambitions which have been frustrated. As society has rejected him, so he rejects society. He could be regarded as a natural product of a decadent order of society. 'I do not degrade myself', he protests, 'in behaving like everyone else.' When Diderot tries to urge the case for a moral order the *neveu* refuses to agree. He sees selfishness as the universal motive. His attack — and this is rather unexpected — is not against a society based on caste, but against one in which distinctions are founded on wealth: this is evidently Diderot's own verdict on the France of the *ancien régime*. The *neveu* is aggrieved because wealth is no real standard of merit and because it covers all sins; but he covets it and would use it no better himself. He despises his own character, yet cannot quite swallow other people's contempt, and with a last flicker of optimism he ends: 'He laughs best who laughs last.'

In the course of the conversation Diderot is compelled to admit the force of many of the arguments used against him, and is even driven to agree that the only quality of the average man of his time which the *neveu* lacks is hypocrisy. But though Diderot recognizes how far the existing society is from an ideal one, he leaves the *neveu* to his cynicism and for his part keeps his ideals. It may in conclusion be asked what are these ideals, and what is the right of Diderot to have any.

The answer may be found if we remember that Diderot's first work was a translation from Shaftesbury. He never abandoned the idea that man has a moral sense which he cannot repudiate without doing violence to his own nature. This belief does not emerge in Diderot's philosophical writings so much as in his *comédies larmoyantes* well characterized by their titles, *Le Père de famille* and *Le Fils naturelle*, and in the art criticism, the *Salons*, which he contributed to Grimm's *Correspondance littéraire*. The author of the *Supplément* and of *Les Bijoux indiscrets*, one of the few moderately successful works of near-pornography in literature, in his art criticism exhibits a puritanical disapproval of Boucher's little nymphs, who obviously have only one function in life.[1] He admired Chardin, which did credit to his artistic taste, but perhaps mainly for the high moral principles that could be read into his paintings. But the painter who

---

[1] Cf. Diderot, *Salon de 1765, Œuvres*, x, 256–7.

appealed most to him was Greuze, perhaps not so much for his artistic merits as for his sentimental subject-matter.

This should not be the last word on Diderot. For all the many-sided genius which made him, more than any other of the *philosophes*, in the words of Sainte-Beuve, 'the spokesman of the century', he is to be remembered in the last resort, and above all, as the man who planned, inspired and carried to a triumphant conclusion against many odds, the *Encyclopédie*. Conceived in the first place by a French printer as a simple translation of Chambers's *Cyclopaedia*, it was transformed by Diderot into a great compendium of the ideas of the Enlightenment. The conditions under which it was put together, often by worthy but second-rate collaborators, prevent much of the great work from being more than a scissors-and-paste compilation. The pressure of censorship and the ever-present menace of suppression led to a good deal of veiled language and pretence of orthodoxy, especially in articles on specifically religious subjects. The *Encyclopédie* is more written about than read. It was deliberately conceived as a work of propaganda, and propaganda is usually not a lasting commodity; but for such a large and expensive work its circulation was remarkable, and its influence must have been great. Its most remarkable feature is possibly the eleven volumes of plates, for these reflect an aspect of the Enlightenment that is too often forgotten. They bring us back to the point from which this chapter on Diderot started, and to the scientific interests of the Enlightenment – not in the sense of original creative research, but in the form in which science particularly, though not exclusively, appealed to the utilitarian eighteenth century, that of technology. Here, too, Diderot was in advance of his age or at least his country. The inventive spirit and the interest in machines were not lacking in France, but it was in England that they were to be turned to effective industrial purposes. The lack of practical results of the age of invention in France is to be attributed to many causes but one at least was the decline of the spirit of the Enlightenment before other influences, in the last years of the eighteenth century. And these influences, too, can be detected in Diderot, the most many-sided man of his age.

XVII

Rousseau

WITH Diderot one can see the boundaries of enlightened thought being extended in all directions, but still remaining within the same tradition. When we pass on to Rousseau it is a matter for dispute whether we have the last – not chronologically but logically – of the great French writers of the Enlightenment, or the first of a new and different dispensation. Perhaps the fairest verdict, and one which ensures that the debate will never be concluded, is to say that he was both.

It is significant that while, for most of the other figures who appear in this history, biographical details though of interest are only incidentally of importance in a study of ideas such as this, a knowledge of Rousseau's life, character and even physical condition is essential to the understanding of his thought, though the tale is too well known, and has been told too many times, for more than a brief sketch to be needed here.

Jean-Jacques Rousseau differs from his friends – and enemies – the *philosophes* not least because of his place of birth. They were bred in the schools of Catholic France; he was a child of sternly Calvinist Geneva, even if an errant one. His mother died at his birth. His father, a watch-maker, was a fiery patriot, quarrelsome, irregular in his life and work, who educated his son in a very uncalvinist way by the reading of innumerable romances, and disappeared from Geneva and Rousseau's life when Jean-Jacques was only ten years old. After a couple of years in the house of a pastor, and apprenticeship to a master engraver, at the age of sixteen he ran away. A local curé befriended him and put him on the Catholic 'underground railway' which existed to transfer potential converts to Italy. One of the stopping-places on the route was the house of a young widow, Mme de Warens, a minor Circe with a mission from the Church for taking in young men, assisting their conversion, and passing them on to a religious house at Turin. Jean-Jacques went that way. After four months' instruction in the convent he professed himself converted, and was then found a job as a lackey in a noble household. This was presumably not quite what he had expected. Perhaps the convent had not done its work well enough, or Mme de Warens hers too well. At any rate, he rapidly took the road back to Savoy and the enchantress. In 1778 she appears on the last page Rousseau ever wrote, in sentences that are more significant for what they leave unsaid than for what they say. He wrote simply: 'Today, Palm Sunday, it is exactly fifty years since my first acquaintance with Mme de Warens. She was then twenty-eight, having been born with the century. I was not yet seventeen.'[1] He lived at Les Charmettes with Mme de Warens for ten years, worked a little in the bureau at Chambéry, learnt music and gave a few lessons, and the years slipped by in a rosy mist of sentiment with his *petite Maman*.

What perhaps made the most lasting impression on a still fallow mind was the setting – the gentle hills and lakes of the Savoy scene, in which nature was kind and lovely. Rousseau also read widely and deeply, especially in the later years when he had been to some extent replaced in Mme de Warens' affections. This substitute for formal education gave him some of the defects of the autodidact, and might have completed his ruin if his genius had been less. In 1740 the wandering fit took him again. After a series of false starts in different places and professions, he found himself in Paris at the age of thirty, with a plan for a new musical notation, for he knew himself so little that he imagined he was to achieve fame and fortune as a musical genius. As throughout his life, he found friends and patrons, but settled down, like Diderot, as a natural inhabitant of the Paris Grub Street, living in a 'wretched room, in a wretched hotel, in a wretched street' of the Latin Quarter, and taking a servant-girl, Thérèse le Vasseur, as his mistress. She was neither particularly pretty, nor intelligent, nor good-natured. She lived in her parents' sordid dwelling and he in his lodging-house, and the five children allegedly born of the liaison were put down at the Enfants Trouvés, which probably killed them off rapidly. Mixing with the *philosophes*, though on a lower social level than most of them, Rousseau naturally shared their ideas; and in the school of 'sense, sensibility and sensuality' which was eighteenth-century literary Paris he was a promising graduate.

By 1749, Rousseau was thirty-seven and apparently past hope of redemption from a worthless life, with nothing to his credit but a few trivial writings, principally on music. The revolution in his life,

<hr />

[1] *Les Rêveries d'un promeneur solitaire*, x^e.

if it was doubtless long prepared under the surface, was sudden and violent when it came. According to Rousseau himself it occurred on the road to Vincennes, whither he was going to visit his friend Diderot, incarcerated there, and while he was contemplating the subject proposed by the Academy of Dijon for a prize essay – 'Has the restoration of the Arts and Sciences had a purifying effect upon morals?' What, according to him, happened, is best described in his own words:

> All of a sudden I felt my mind dazzled with a thousand inspirations ... A violent palpitation overcame me and my breast heaved; unable to breathe while walking, I let myself fall under one of the trees in the avenue and spent a half-hour in such agitation that when I came to I found all the front of my coat soaked with my tears, though I had not known I had shed any. Oh, Monsieur, if I had ever been able to write a quarter of what I saw and felt under that tree, how clearly would I have explained all the contradictions of the social system, with what power I would have exposed all the abuses of our institutions, how simply I would have shown that man is good by nature and that only institutions have made men evil.[1]

All this might be dismissed as a mere literary gesture, if it had not been reflected so dramatically in Rousseau's own life. His social ambitions, soon after this, were put behind him; the gold braid, sword, white stockings and fashionable peruke with which he had aped the gentleman given up, and he adopted a petit-bourgeois style of dress. He renounced the sinecure his influential friends had procured for him, became difficult about accepting presents, and took to working at copying music, the only craft he knew. He took Thérèse to live with him, later went through a form of marriage with her, and paid a visit to Geneva for the purpose of resuming his citizenship.

The significance for the history of thought of the psychological experience through which Rousseau had passed is to be found in the writings which followed it. Admittedly the first, the *Discourse on the Moral Effects of the Arts and Sciences*, was a jejune piece of rhetoric, hardly worth the experience on the road to Vincennes. Rousseau himself frankly says so in his *Confessions*: 'Of all my works it is the weakest ... But whatever gifts a man may be born with, he

[1] Rousseau, *Lettres à M. de Malesherbes*, ii, 12 janvier 1762.

cannot learn the art of writing in an instant.' A few anticipations of his later thought may be picked out here and there in the first *Discourse*, but on the whole it is no more than flashy paradox. Of course, it won the prize of the Academy at Dijon and put Rousseau on the literary map. It also produced the foolish stereotype of him as an advocate of crude primitivism, a literary Tarzan. He was to be pictured in Palissot's *Les philosophes* crawling about on all fours in the woods, which was a fair enough caricature of the first Discourse, and would be a reasonable interpretation of the theme of 'back to nature' for historians to adopt if they had never read anything else that Rousseau wrote.

An attempt to win a later competition at Dijon with *A dissertation on the Origin and Foundation of the Inequality of Mankind* (1755), failed to gain the prize, but it was the first of Rousseau's major works. Although written in the form of an historical account, as Rousseau warns the reader:

> The inquiries into which we may enter on this subject should not be taken for historical truths, but only for hypothetical and conditional arguments, proper to throw light on the nature of things, rather than to show their true origins.[1]

The essay begins with the assumption that there are two kinds of inequality – natural, which is derived from differences in bodily strength, mental ability or character, and conventional, based on such institutions as property, social status or political authority. The subject of his discourse is the latter, which he calls moral or political inequality. In accordance with the normal method of argument of the Natural Law school, he begins with a state of nature. He admits that this state 'no longer exists, perhaps never existed, and probably never will exist',[2] but it is a useful hypothetical starting-point. It is a state of equality but not a social state; man in the state of nature is isolated from other men. Being non-social, Rousseau argues, he is therefore non-moral, though he has a natural virtue – *bonté naturelle* – which can be interpreted as a natural capacity for compassion or sympathy.

However, this supposed state of nature has to come to an end. Concrete pressures, such as the growth of population, prevent the non-social condition from continuing; but life in society demands moral qualities which natural man is not capable of, and the result

---

[1] Rousseau, *Discours sur l'inégalité, Works*, ed. Vaughan, 1915, i, 141.   [2] Ibid., i, 136.

is a period of bloody barbarism, in which inequalities of power are the only law:

> Usurpations on the part of the rich, robbery by the poor, and the frantic passions of all, stifling natural compassion and the still feeble voice of justice, made men avaricious, ambitious and evil. Between the right of the strongest and that of the first occupier, there arose a perpetual conflict, which never ended but in battles and bloodshed. The new-born state of society thus gave place to the most horrible state of war.[1]

This condition, however, was not a permanent one. Those who, in this Hobbesian war of all against all, which must not be confused with the state of nature which preceded it, have acquired more possessions than others, now have the idea of making allies of the rest. Let us join, they say, 'to guarantee the weak against oppression, to restrain the ambitious, and secure to everyone the possession of what belongs to him: let us set up rules of justice and peace'.[2] In other words, they propose the recognition of a right of property, and a system of law and government to protect it. Rousseau concludes:

> Such was, or must have been, the origin of society and laws, which bound new fetters on the poor, and gave new powers to the rich; which *irretrievably* destroyed natural liberty, *for ever* established the law of property and inequality, converted clever usurpation into *irrevocable* right, and, for the advantage of a few ambitious individuals, subjected henceforth all mankind to labour, slavery and wretchedness.[3]

The reiteration of irretrievably, for ever, irrevocable, is not accidental. Rousseau is anxious to emphasize that this is an irreversible process. Caught in its own trap, humanity falls increasingly victim to the arbitrary power of despotism, 'raising by degrees its hideous head'.[4]

This is the last stage of inequality, the extreme point that closes the circle, and meets that from which we set out. Here it is that all private persons return to equality, because they are nothing; and that subjects having no other law than the will

[1] Ibid., i, 180.   [2] Ibid., i, 181.
[3] Ibid. The italics are mine.   [4] Ibid., i, 193.

of their master, and their master no other rule than his passions, all notions of good and all principles of equity again vanish.[1]

The last words of the second *Discourse* should be sufficient to prevent us from supposing that it was a mere literary gesture, for Rousseau ends, with an obvious reference to his own day:

> It is manifestly contrary to the law of nature, however defined, that a child should command an old man, a fool a wise man, and that a handful of individuals should gorge themselves with superfluities, while the starving multitude are in want of the bare necessities.[2]

The *Discours de l'inégalité*, unlike the *Contrat social*, was fairly widely read; yet, in spite of its revolutionary social criticism it aroused little or no opposition on this score. Perhaps the explanation is that the economic structure and great inequalities of property were so completely taken for granted that no criticism of them was regarded as serious. Yet, as has been suggested above,[3] the literature of eighteenth-century France is not lacking in such criticism. In the seventeenth century the Levellers and Diggers of the Commonwealth had gone further in the direction of social revolution than most of their successors, but they only represent an episode. As always, the writer whose influence crystallized the vague trends of his time was Locke, who begins with a magisterial assumption of human equality. Though he proceeds to justify great inequalities of property, and even slavery, the effect of his basic revolutionary principles was not entirely dissipated by his more conservative practical conclusions.

The utopian communism to be found in some eighteenth-century writers, which has already been mentioned, is not to be taken too seriously. If we wish to find a work that is revolutionary in its implications, apart from the *Discours de l'inégalité* of Rousseau, we have to turn to the obscure and unimportant pamphlet, *Le Code de la Nature* (1754), by Morelly, an author of whom practically nothing is known. The theme of Morelly is similar to that of Rousseau, but he ends with a plea for a kind of primitive communism. Rousseau, on the other hand, does not wish to abolish property – the inviolability of other people's property is one of the earliest lessons taught

---

[1] Rousseau, *Discours sur l'inégalité*, i, 194.
[2] Ibid., i, 196. [3] pp. 130–2.

to the young Emile – but to render its distribution more equal.[1]

Apart from its implicit belief in the necessity of a system of individual property, there was another reason why the eighteenth century did not envisage economic changes as a means, though it could envisage them as an end, of social reform. In general, it thought in political and not in economic terms. This is why Rousseau's answer to the social ills he had denounced in·the *Discours de l'inégalité* was framed in terms of moral and political philosophy, not of economics. It would be premature to assume that he was wrong in this. The problem, as he saw it, was that 'man is born free and everywhere he is in chains', which incidentally is not the first sentence of the *Contrat social*. His aim was not to abolish the chains – the bonds of society – but to make them legitimate, and the answer he gave will have to be treated when we come to a final discussion of the political thinking of the Enlightenment.

Before the *Contrat social* appeared, Rousseau's genius had at last borne fruit in a series of great works. In 1756 he had retired to the Hermitage, a little country cottage on her estate lent to him by Mme d'Epinay. There he spent his mornings copying music, and the rest of the day in country walks, meditation or composition. There also he met Mme d'Epinay's sister-in-law, the young countess Sophie d'Houdetot, who became the daily companion of his walks and botanizing and with whom he fell hopelessly in love. This might have ended, in the way it began, as a happy and innocent episode, and an unspoiled inspiration to the writer whose genius was so belatedly burgeoning, had it not been for the machinations of the young German baron, Grimm, who had fastened himself as a literary parasite on Diderot, and as a lover on Mme d'Epinay, and who, either from simple malice, or from a determination to have no rivals in their affections, set to work to destroy their friendship with Rousseau. Assisted, of course, by Rousseau's own unhappy temperament, Grimm's plan was a complete success. Rousseau, who later said that at the Hermitage he had passed 'les derniers beaux jours qui lui avaient été comptés sur la terre', after an emotional outburst which affected both himself and his friends deeply, fled, or was driven away. He flung himself into the task – which was perhaps a kind of feverish self-justification, of pouring out his long-pent-up ideas in print.

Rousseau began his quarrel with the *philosophes* by the *Lettre à*

[1] *Economie politique, Works,* i, 254 ff.

d'Alembert sur les spectacles in 1758. There had already been signs of the coming breach. In a *Lettre sur la Providence* (1756), he had attacked the pessimism of Voltaire's poem on the disaster at Lisbon. The new and much more violent onslaught was stimulated by an article on Geneva in the *Encyclopédie*, in which d'Alembert had advocated the opening of a theatre there – for this was a form of vice which the strict Calvinist morals of the city excluded. In his excited condition Rousseau chose to regard the proposal as the spearhead of some kind of diabolical plot against the morals of his native city, to which he replied with an almost Platonic denuciation of the art of the theatre. It was practically a declaration of war against the *philosophes,* and Rousseau should not have been surprised that they retaliated. Voltaire had no forgiving disposition, especially to a literary enemy, but the full fury of his wrath was only to burst forth a few years later, after the publication of *Emile.*

Before this there had appeared, in 1761, a by-product – if one can so describe a work of major influence in the history of literature – of Rousseau's devotion to Mme d'Houdetot. With the *Nouvelle Héloïse* a new voice was heard in eighteenth-century France. It is almost impossible now to conceive or understand the reception of this account, in the form of letters, of a long drawn-out and mostly frustrated love affair. The seductiveness of the portrayal of virtue triumphing over all conceivable temptations and surviving in the midst of constant peril, had already been exploited in Richardson's *Pamela.* But though the *Nouvelle Héloïse* shared some of the same maudlin sentimentality, it would be grossly unfair to dismiss Rousseau as a mere vendor of the kind of moralizing eroticism that has been the modus operandi of innumerable novelists ever since. What makes the *Nouvelle Héloïse* a great, even if it is now an almost unreadable, book, is the fact that it is the work of a genuine moralist, who had something new to say to his generation. It represents, among many other things, the rehabilitation of love as more than a pleasant physical exercise, and motherhood as more than an unfortunate female weakness. Rousseau made virtue seem more attractive than vice, and the indulgences of the mind more alluring than those of the body. Compared with the Shakespeare of the plays, he may be called morbid, unhealthy; but then we should not compare him with Shakespeare, but with his contemporaries. It is difficult to exclude enthusiasm from religion, and even more difficult to exclude passion from sex, but the eighteenth century had done its

best to do both, not without a measure of success. Rousseau rehabilitated emotion as a creditable element in the literary description of
the relations of the sexes, just as he was to reinfuse it into religion.

With the teachings of revealed religion rejected, along with their
miraculous foundations, and the deistic proof of goodness in nature
broken down, the moralizing eighteenth century had found itself
without any justification for its morals. This was the problem that
faced Rousseau, as it did Diderot, and his answer also was to appeal
to an innate principle of justice and virtue in the individual conscience. Morality, being the operation of this principle, therefore
depends on the intention, not the act; and this intention is not a
coldly calculated decision but a general direction of the whole
personality, fused together by emotion and inspired by an elevated
enthusiasm. It would be easy to treat the *Nouvelle Héloïse* as embody-
ing a rejection of the ideals of the Enlightenemnt, if we only looked,
say, at Helvétius or La Mettrie. But to do so would be to ignore all the
contrary indications. If we regard Rousseau as standing quite apart
from his contemporaries, what are we to make of the revolt in the
harem at the end of the *Lettres persanes*, the self-sacrifice of Roxane
and her passionate plea for at least certain rights of woman? What
of the moral sense of Shaftesbury and his followers? How are we to
fit the emotional Diderot into the picture of a coldly intellectualist
Enlightenment? Indeed, were the views of Locke so very different,
save that they lacked, what was all important, expression in the new
style that Rousseau's literary genius created, and which more than
anything else was the secret of his influence?

The other great innovation in the *Nouvelle Héloïse* was the discovery of the country. Again, here, one may say that it had never
been really lost to English literature; but the civilization of France
was much more urban. One supposes that Voltaire, at Ferney, lived
in the country, but it does not seem to have left much mark on his
writings. Otherwise, Rousseau was the only one among the *philosophes* to have spent an important part of his life in rural surround-
ings. It was natural that the scene of his novel should be laid in the
Savoyard countryside that he knew so well. Not the least revolutionary of his ideas was the revelation that one could actually go for
a walk in the country for its own sake. This is perhaps not Enlightened with a capital letter, but it is not unenlightened and it
should not be interpreted as a primitivist cult of 'back to nature'.
With Rousseau, Nature, which had been the key-word of the

Enlightenment, took a new form; but this was a development and not a rejection of enlightened ideals. Nor did Rousseau stand alone. Diderot, and others, were also moving towards a new conception of nature.

After the *Nouvelle Héloïse* there followed in rapid succession the *Contrat social* – some of the leading ideas of which had been anticipated in his article on *Economie Politique* for the *Encyclopédie* – and *Emile*, both in 1762. *Emile* is the basic treatise of modern education. Kant says that Rousseau was attempting to deal with the most difficult problem of the moral life – how to educate man as a moral being, and resolve the conflict between his moral ends and his physical nature with its amoral passions. When Rousseau speaks of education – and this is true of the whole Enlightenment – it is more than simple school instruction that he means. In a famous phrase, he wrote, 'L'éducation de l'homme commence à sa naissance', for he was really continuing one of the basic themes of the eighteenth century – the dependence of man on his environment and the problem of adapting it to the task of bringing out the best in human nature. The discussion is unavoidably complicated by the ambivalence, which we have already seen in Montesquieu and Diderot, of the idea of nature. Rousseau's are not the naturalistic morals sometimes suggested by Diderot. He is closer to the tradition of intuitive ethics, founded on the moral sense, or what was beginning to be called the conscience; but at the same time he also follows the rationalist moral theory of Locke.[1]

On the whole problem of education and environment, *Emile* may be regarded as the culmination of enlightened thought, as well as the basic treatise from which modern educational practice stems. Its immediate influence was to be seen in changes in social custom – in the abandonment of tight swaddling clothes and the introduction of a degree of freedom into the life of the child, in mothers nursing their babies, a vulgar habit which the upper classes had abandoned, in an awareness of the value of home life and maternal affection for the young child – did Rousseau reflect that he had never known this? – in physical exercise and the learning of a manual art. These are far from exhausting the long list of suggestions, nearly all of which are now commonplaces, which were in spite of some anticipations, for instance by Locke, a revelation to the eighteenth century.

Even those who did not accept Rousseau's educational theories

[1] Cf. R. Derathé, *Le rationalisme de J.-J. Rousseau*, 1948.

would have found it difficult to criticize them except as being unduly
idealistic. Yet the period of greatest personal disaster was opened
for him by the publication of *Emile*. This was the result not of his
educational views but of the inclusion of a long religious section
called the *Profession de foi d'un vicaire savoyard*. The argument is
attributed to a simple country pastor, the embodiment of all virtue,
which may be regarded as a way of prejudicing the issue. Rousseau
begins with an explicit rejection of libertine scepticism. There
follows a rather ingenuous statement of the traditional case for deism:
the general character of all existence is motion; from my own
motions I infer my will, from the motions of nature a greater will;
since the world obeys laws this must be an intelligent will; and since
I am aware of goodness, in the universe and in myself, it is a good
will. Thus we have a benevolent, all-powerful deity. Secondly, from
man's will, and it is self-evident that this is a free will, Rousseau
deduces the presence of an immaterial soul, which can survive the
body and suffer reward and punishment, which he takes to assume
the form of the memory of good and evil deeds. The injustices of
this world are thus redressed in the hereafter, Providence is justified
and the goodness of God upheld. This is not quite the optimism that
Voltaire had criticized. Rousseau is as aware as Voltaire or Dr Johnson that the attempt at a rational demonstration of the goodness of
God had broken down before the fact of evil. His solution, like the
latter's, is not to reject it, but to abandon the attempt to prove it.
'J'anéantis ma faible raison devant ta justice.'[1]

The arguments of the Savoyard vicar hardly amount to more than
an old-fashioned deism. What Rousseau adds is the element of
emotion that had been lacking, and a prejudice in favour of instead
of against religion. The history of the religious influence of Rousseau,
says P.-M. Masson, shows once again that the influence of a popular
writer always goes far beyond the limits of his own ideas.[2] Rousseau
himself, Masson argues, hardly appreciated the full purport of his
ideas, or saw that 'more than once, what he believed to be the
religion of nature was only the religion of his fathers'.[3] This may be
a little exaggerated, but that the influence of Rousseau, manifest in
such writers as Bernardin de St Pierre, Châteaubriand and de Maistre,
worked in the direction of religious revival cannot seriously be
denied. Voltaire, with his usual penetration, saw the danger in

[1] *Profession de foi du vicaire savoyard.*
[2] P.-M. Masson, *La Religion de J.-J. Rousseau*, 1916, iii, 3.   [3] Ibid., ii, 293.

advance. 'It is because Jean-Jacques still has partisans', he wrote in
1765, 'that the true philosophers have enemies.'[1] The fury of the
high-priest of infidelity against 'ce sombre énergumène', 'cet ennemi
de la nature humaine', was unbounded. He even wrote, in the guise
of a citizen of Geneva defending religion:

> A madman may be pitied, but when the madness becomes fury
> he has to be bound ... He has dared to publish a new slander in
> which he wildly outrages the Christian religion ... He must be
> taught that if an impious novelist is punished lightly, vile sedition
> is a capital offence.[2]

This is not Voltaire at his highest, but Rousseau did not fare any
better on the more orthodox side. To discuss religion seriously and
in language which appealed to men's emotions, and yet neither in
terms of religious nor anti-religious orthodoxy, was his innovation,
and his crime, for both Christians and unbelievers.

The Parlement of Paris proscribed Rousseau. He was censored
by the Sorbonne. The Council of Geneva and the Papacy issued
decrees against him. The Government of Holland and the Archbishop of Paris condemned him. In the little village of Motiers in the
Jura, where he had been accepted as a harmless eccentric, the pastor
stirred up the populace to stone the house where he was staying. His
devoted friend, Maréchal Keith, gave him refuge for a time;
Frederick II protected him despite the efforts of Voltaire; but
Rousseau was expelled by the authorities of Berne. Then came the
unhappy visit, in 1766, at the benevolent invitation of Hume, to
England, whither he was still pursued by the malice of Grimm and
Voltaire. Back in France in 1767, he resumed his frantic wandering
from place to place. That Rousseau was most of this time suffering
from persecution mania is indubitable, and the physical cause has
been shown by the chronological association between his worst
periods and the attacks of uraemia from which he suffered and
probably died, which also account for the long Armenian robe he
wore.[3] This is not to say that he was not also a victim of persecution:
a worse fate can hardly be conceived than to suffer from persecution
mania and to be actually persecuted, and the combination is enough
to explain the episodes of wild panic and not always entirely causeless
flight.

[1] Masson, *La Religion de J.-J. Rousseau*, iii, 38.
[2] Voltaire, *Sentiment des citoyens*, *Œuvres*, xxv, 310, 314.
[3] Cf. F. C. Green, *Jean-Jacques Rousseau*, 1955, pp. 82, 317, 330, 358.

After a tormented decade, in Rousseau's last years, from 1770 to 1778, the hue and cry against him died down. Indeed, he had already won the battle. The baron Grimm would have made a first-class journalist for a weekly literary and political gossip-sheet, but who now reads him? Influential as Voltaire was, can it be believed that he changed much that would not have been changed in the same way, a little later perhaps, without him? But if Rousseau were to be expunged from the pages of history it would be necessary to invent him. In his last years the man who was now the most famous literary figure in Europe was living in obscurity in a modest Parisian apartment, sought out by many, but receiving only a few old friends and younger disciples. A calm settles over his tormented figure. One wonders if the fact that Thérèse was never happy outside Paris, and that now at last Rousseau had returned to what for her was home, had anything to do with it.

The period, if quiet, was not unproductive. A series of political writings on Corsica, Poland and Geneva were not published until after Rousseau's death. His *Confessions*, from which he gave readings to small groups, produced panic among some of his former friends, who set on foot a campaign to discredit them in advance if possible. Finally, the *Rêveries d'un promeneur solitaire* created a new literary form.

In 1778 Rousseau accepted a little house on the estate of a friend at Ermenonville, and there, a few months later, he died. He was already a legend in his lifetime, and his grave, in a romantic spot on the île des Peupliers, became a place of pilgrimage. Lytton Strachey is far from being the most reliable of historians, even in his judgment of individual character, but he said one thing about Rousseau that needed to be said, and has been put better by nobody:

As we see him now, in that long vista, Rousseau was not a wicked man; he was an unfortunate, a distracted, a deeply sensitive, a strangely complex, creature; and, above all else, he possessed one quality which cut him off from his contemporaries, which set an immense gulf betwixt him and them: he was modern. Among those quick, strong, fiery people of the eighteenth century, he belonged to another world — to the new world of self-consciousness, and doubt, and hesitation, of mysterious melancholy and quiet intimate delights, of long reflexions amid the solitudes of Nature, of infinite introspections amid the solitudes of the heart. Who can wonder that he was misunderstood, and buffeted, and driven mad?[1]

It is impossible to say that he was only a man of the Enlightenment, but equally difficult to say that he was not a man of the Enlightenment.

[1] Lytton Strachey, 'The Rousseau Affair', *Books and Characters*, 1922, p. 174.

XVIII

The Politics of the Enlightenment

WITH Diderot and Rousseau, though it would be impossible to separate them from the main stream of the Enlightenment, there are signs that we are moving into a new intellectual climate; but before concluding even this short survey of the Enlightenment there is one major aspect which remains to be discussed. This is its political thinking, which may be regarded as its culminating feature. The *philosophes*, as has been noted above, took as their end the happiness of individuals. This they believed to be largely dependent on environment and education, and these in turn on social institutions and government, which therefore held the key to a happier society. The neglect of the political thinking of the Enlightenment can be attributed to various causes. The history of thought, because of the political historian's general lack of interest in ideas, has tended to be left to students of literature, who are naturally less interested in politics. It is also true that, so long as the explanation is kept on a fairly superficial level, a consistent account can be provided of the political history of Western Europe in the eighteenth century, up to 1789, without introducing any consideration of political ideas. Thirdly, between Locke and Burke and Bentham there are no outstanding names in the history of British political thought; while in France, Montesquieu does not fit easily into the accepted pattern and Rousseau has often been taken as belonging to the subsequent period. Finally, it has been assumed, ever since the 'enlightened despots' was invented as a text-book category, that the political thought of the Enlightenment must be summed up as a justification of their despotism. This last, since it is the most common prejudice, is perhaps the best point from which to start a discussion of the politics of the Enlightenment.

The rise of contractual and Natural Law thought, and its culmination in the work of Locke, have already been described, as well as the decline of the influence of these ideas in the practical politics of Europe. As has been said above, the period from the sixteenth to the eighteenth century, which saw the triumph of the great European monarchies, witnessed the culmination of ideas of divine right and absolutism. The Natural Law school of thought itself, with Grotius assimilating the rights of government to property, and Pufendorf preserving the forms of the natural law–social contract pattern but abandoning the right of resistance, seemed to be moving towards a justification of absolute sovereignty.

To set against these great names of European political thought there was only the translation of Locke's *Second Treatise* into French, but it was enough. The clue to French eighteenth-century ideas on politics is provided, in the absence of genius, which cannot be made to order, by second-hand and second-rate writers such as Barbeyrac and Burlamaqui, who were not the less influential at the time for lacking the originality of their greater predecessors and successors. Barbeyrac's translations into French of Pufendorf and Grotius, which went through many editions, might easily be supposed to have spread the absolutist tendencies of these writers; but in fact, the effect of the text is largely counteracted by the translator's notes, in which are given long extracts from Locke, opposing his views to those of Pufendorf. Barbeyrac claims that there is always a tacit right of resistance, which comes into operation when the prince abuses his power or uses it against the people's interest. Obedience may be refused on moral grounds, even by state officers. For example, the Parlements of France may refuse to register a law; again, there is a right to refuse to bear arms in an unjust war. Unlike Pufendorf, Barbeyrac favours the division of powers. He admires the English constitution. He criticizes Grotius' equation of sovereignty with the right of property.

Burlamaqui was an able Swiss popularizer. His *Principes du droit naturel* (1747) and *Principes du droit politique* (1751), with little or no original thought in them, became standard treatises in the eighteenth century. He followed Montesquieu in praising the balance of powers and mixed government, either in the form of limited monarchy as in England, or of aristocracy tempered by democracy as in Geneva. Like Montesquieu he insisted that there were limitations on the rightful authority even of absolute monarchy. He declared:

> We must not confound an absolute power with an arbitrary, despotic, and unlimited authority. For, from what we have now said concerning the original and nature of absolute sovereignty, it manifestly follows, that it is limited, from its

very nature, by the intention of those who conferred it on the sovereign, and by the very laws of God.[1]

This is an assertion of fundamental law, and that it is not an appeal to an abstract, unenforceable platitude is shown by what follows:

> The fundamental laws, which limit the sovereign authority, are nothing else but the means which the people use to assure themselves that the prince will not recede from the general law of the public good.[2]

The significant point, of course, is not the recognition of the general good as the end of sovereignty, but of the right of the people to enforce it. A similar assertion of the right of resistance to tyranny is to be found in the Genevan Vattel, one of the greatest of the successors of Grotius in the field of international law.[3]

Geneva and England were the chief sources of constitutional ideas in eighteenth-century Europe. Montesquieu in particular was responsible for the general admiration of the English constitution. The view that such admiration came to an end about 1760 has been shown to be mistaken:[4] the change came rather with the American War. It was partly a result of Whig attacks on the corruption of the House of Commons and the despotism of George III, partly of the propaganda of the American colonists, and partly of the prestige resulting from their victorious revolt. They offered an alternative ideal, and one which, it might be argued, was closer to true Lockian ideals and at the same time more in line with the literary cult of republicanism.

This cult should not be misunderstood. By a republic was understood a country ruled by laws and not arbitrary will; it was not necessarily incompatible with limited monarchy. Classical education, and the classical revival in the second half of the century, contributed to the growing favour of the republican ideal, which is reflected in the definitions in the Dictionary of the French Academy. In 1694 republican equals seditious; in 1718 this unfavourable definition is suppressed; and from 1740 favourable examples of the term appear. Voltaire was a good monarchist, but he could write *Brutus*, a republican tragedy, as early as 1730, and even in his later years did not abandon his admiration for the English constitution.

---

[1] *The Principles of Politic Law*, trans. 1752, vii, 2, p. 50.
[2] Ibid., vii, 4, pp. 59-60.   [3] Vattel, *Le Droit des Gens*, 1758.
[4] Cf. G. Bonno, *La Constitution britannique devant l'opinion française de Montesquieu à Bonaparte*, 1932.

Since Voltaire is often taken as a representative of the supposed bias of the *philosophes* in favour of enlightened despotism, it will be useful to examine in a little more detail his political ideas. They are not the less significant for being unsystematic and incidental, expressed in works which for the most part are not primarily concerned with politics. His praise of Catherine of Russia and Frederick II should not be forgotten, nor his contempt for the masses – the people 'sera toujours sot et barbare'.[1] 'Quand la populace se mêle de raisonner, tout est perdu.'[2] Faced with the question whether a republican government is preferable to that of a king, he concludes, with characteristic political Pyrrhonism, 'la dispute finit toujours par convenir qu'il est fort difficile de gouverner les hommes'.[3] On the other hand, he can write, 'La liberté consiste à ne dépendre que des lois'.[4] When Voltaire says, 'I will admit to you that I would adapt myself well enough to a democratic government ... I like to see free men themselves making the laws under which they live,'[5] he puts this in the mouth of a citizen of the Dutch Republic. Such pious sentiments do not take us very far, and on the other hand Voltaire criticized Montesquieu's definition of republics; they were founded, he said, not on virtue but on pride and ambition, and were suited only to small States. He opposed intermediate powers in the State, such as the Parlements, and was almost the only *philosophe* who understood the real political needs of France well enough to defend the suppression of these courts by Maupeou and Louis XV. He was more interested in practical reforms than in constitutional safeguards, and he saw the Parlements for the obscurantist defenders of vested interests that they were. From all this no consistent picture or systematic political view emerges. On the whole we must conclude that Voltaire was not very politically minded. He was intensely liberal, but hardly appreciated how much personal liberties depend on political forms. In spite of this, to take him as an advocate of despotism would be to do violence to his thought.[6]

For more developed political ideas we must look elsewhere. The political articles in the *Encyclopédie* were largely compiled by the chevalier de Jaucourt out of the works of Locke and Montesquieu, and express a contractual theory of government. Diderot himself

[1] Lettre à M. Taboreau, 3 février 1769, *Œuvres*, xlvi, 251.
[2] Lettre à M. Damilaville, 1 avril 1766, *Œuvres*, xliv, 256.
[3] *Dictionnaire philosophique*, art. 'Démocratie', *Œuvres*, xxiii, 335.
[4] *Pensées sur le gouvernement*, *Œuvres*, xxiii, 526.   [5] *L'A.B.C.*, xxvii, 347.
[6] See also P. Gay, *Voltaire's Politics, the Poet as Realist*, 1959.

argues that man being made for society, the common good should be his supreme law. By nature men are equal, and for the establishment of government there is needed either a formal or a tacit contract between them and their rulers. Government is necessary for society, but it is only legitimate in so far as it promotes the general happiness.[1] While condemning democracy as chimerical, or at best only possible in tiny States, he is bitter against despotism. It is sometimes claimed, he says, that the best government is that of a just and enlightened despot. This is to forget that, 'on peut abuser de son pouvoir pour faire le bien comme pour faire le mal'. A man is never entitled to treat his fellow beings as a troop of cattle.[2] If a legislator does not consult and respect the general will, he destroys the bonds of society.[3] Although Diderot wrote no political treatise, an anthology of such apophthegms could be selected from his works.

The most systematic political theorist among the *philosophes*, apart from Montesquieu and Rousseau, is d'Holbach, in whom can be traced the same development that was occurring in English political thinking. This was the almost complete substitution of the principle of utility for the idea of the contract. It is not difficult to trace in d'Holbach the main stages in the eighteenth-century progress to utilitarianism. It begins from the generally accepted view that the function of politics is to put moral principles into practice.'[4] Since 'nature makes men neither good nor bad',[5] it is the task of parents, teachers, rulers to do that. Thus politics is 'the art of regulating the passions of men and directing them to the good of society',[6] which d'Holbach defines in strictly utilitarian terms:

Laws, to be just, must have as their invariable end the general interest of society, that is to say, to ensure to the greatest number of citizens the advantages for which they are associated together. These advantages are liberty, property and security. *Liberty* is the capacity of doing for one's own happiness whatever does not injure the happiness of others ... *Property* is the ability of each member of the society to enjoy the advantages which his labour and industry have obtained for him ... Justice ... prevents members of a society from using against one another the inequality in strength, which nature or industry may have created.'[7]

[1] Diderot, *Œuvres complètes*, 1875-6, xvii, 134-7. *Encyclopédie*, art. 'Société'.
[2] Ibid., vi, 448.   [3] Ibid., xv, 431. *Encyclopédie*, art. 'Législateur'.
[4] D'Holbach, *Système social*, i, 8.   [5] D'Holbach, *Système de la nature*, i, 148.
[6] Ibid., i, 140.   [7] Ibid., i, 142-3.

Like Bentham later, d'Holbach, having decided that it is the function of government to reconcile the self-interest of individuals with the good of society, is faced with the problem of ensuring that it shall want to do so. At this point, where the thought of Bentham passes over into democracy, d'Holbach falls back on the traditional Lockian argument of a negative control over government: 'Since government only derives its authority from society, and is only established for the good of society, it is evident that society can revoke this authority when its interest so demands.'[1]

Like Locke, he has a profound suspicion of political power. He writes, in Actonian language: 'The experience of all ages will convince nations that man is always tempted to abuse power.'[2] From this emerges a full-scale onslaught on despotism. D'Holbach argues in Lockian fashion that the despot is the true revolutionary. The evils of despotism he sees equally in the state of national and international affairs.[3] In their relations with one another, rulers are in that Hobbesian state of nature which is simple anarchy:

> Do not their continual wars; their quarrels, often unjust and puerile; the unconsidered passions and caprices to which these sovereigns sacrifice so lightly both their own happiness and that of their subjects, declare that they are still for the most part Caribs or true cannibals?[4]

From his attack on despotism, d'Holbach passes on, in a spirit not dissimilar from that of Diderot and Rousseau, to a general denunciation of the whole existing order of things. His references in this vein are brief and scattered, but they are violent. Are nations made, he asks, 'to work without respite to satisfy the vanity, the luxury, the greed of a pack of useless and corrupt blood-suckers'?[5]

What hope is there then? His answer brings us back to what was the panacea of the *philosophes* -- enlightenment or education. D'Holbach's faith is in the power of truth, which nothing, he says, can destroy.[6] 'The love of truth is only the love of the human race.'[7] The power of truth is greater than that of any armed rebellion. Nor is this a mere forlorn hope: there are signs that enlightenment is spreading.[8] Everywhere can be seen the effects of the 'progrès des lumières', he believes.

[1] D'Holbach, *Système de la nature*, i, 141. [2] Ibid., i, 145.
[3] *Système social*, i, 194-5.   [4] Ibid., i, 194.   [5] Ibid., ii, 151.
[6] Ibid., iii, 159.   [7] Ibid., iii, 153.   [8] Ibid., iii, 160.

If error and ignorance have forged the chains of the peoples, if prejudice perpetuates them, science, reason, truth will one day break them. The human mind, benumbed for a long succession of centuries by superstition and cruelty, has at last reawakened.[1]

D'Holbach's political views may be excessively optimistic, they are not ignoble. Nor is the advocacy of despotism or governmental tyranny of any kind to be drawn from his writings.

For even a plausible attribution of a theory of benevolent despotism there is only one group of thinkers to be found in eighteenth-century France. This is the Physiocratic school, who were economists rather than political theorists. Their thought was basically Cartesian. They were rationalists who believed in a natural order of things. Evil is the result of breaking this order, which, if it is allowed to operate freely, ensures the maximum degree of welfare. In economic matters laissez-faire was the corollary of this faith in natural laws. On the other hand, politically they took obsolute monarchy to be the best form of government, being that in which the interests of the ruler in the maximization of the wealth of his State is identical with those of his subjects. His power has nothing arbitrary about it because his function is simply to proclaim and enforce natural laws. The result is a combination of total economic liberty for the individual with total political power for the ruler. That this added up to simple nonsense became evident even to the second generation of Physiocrats themselves, such as Mercier de la Rivière, and they abandoned the idea of enlightened despotism.

The greatest name, after that of Montesquieu, in the history of French political thought during the eighteenth century is that of Rousseau. Whether he belongs to the pattern of enlightened thought that has been sketched, or anticipates the ideas of the Romantic and Idealist thinkers of the following century, is a matter of dispute. Sir Ernest Barker declares:

We may almost say that the vogue of Rousseau depends on the fact that a great master of style gave to the world of letters, and the general reader, a system of thought which had hitherto been expressed mainly in Latin, and written by lawyers for lawyers.[2]

There are two defects in this analysis of the importance of Rousseau

[1] Ibid., i, 159.   [2] E. Barker in Gierke, *Natural Law*, p. 324 note.

as a political writer. The first is that the works of the great authors of the Natural Law school were either written in English or French, or else translated into those languages; and that, as the number of editions they went through shows, some of these works were widely read. The second point is that far from popularizing their ideas, the *Contrat social* was, of all the works of Rousseau, that which received the least notice, at least up to 1789. This was suggested long ago by Mornet's analysis of a large number of eighteenth-century libraries. Whereas he found, for example, 165 copies of the *Nouvelle Héloïse*, and even eighty-two of such a bulky and expensive work as the *Encyclopédie*, of the *Contrat social* he found only one.[1] Stories such as that of Marat reading the *Contrat social* to admiring crowds at the street corner are such patent nonsense that it is a wonder that any reputable historian should ever have troubled to repeat them. Whatever political influence Rousseau had is a result of the Revolution, and then it is to be found in the beginning as much, if not more, on the counter-revolutionary as on the revolutionary side.[2] In spite of these qualifications, however, Sir Ernest Barker is right in associating Rousseau with the Natural Law school of thought. He asks the same questions and he uses the same language. It might almost be held that the whole school culminates in the work of Rousseau, which, it has been said, crowns 'the struggle against royal absolutism and enfranchisement from the traditional doctrines of the Catholic Church on the divine origin of civil authority'.[3]

The basis of Rousseau's political theory is the essentially individualist conception of the State of Nature, to which he gives his own particular interpretation in the *Discourse on Inequality*. It follows that for him the State cannot be more than an 'être moral' or 'corps artificiel' – a body, that is, with only an 'abstract and collective existence'. Wherever Rousseau uses what appears to be organic language in dealing with the State, it is clearly only as an analogy.[4]

It would be a mistake, however, to suppose that for Rousseau man in society is still the isolated, atomistic individual of his hypothetical State of Nature: the creation of society has involved a psychological revolution:

[1] D. Mornet, 'Les Enseignements des Bibliothèques privées, 1750–80', *Revue d'histoire littéraire de la France*, 1910, xvii, 449–96.

[2] The justification for this statement is to be found in a forthcoming book by Dr Joan Macdonald (née Bedale) on the influence of Rousseau on the Revolution.

[3] R. Derathé, *Jean-Jacques Rousseau et la science politique de son temps*, 1950, p. 62.

[4] Ibid., appendix iv, pp. 410–13.

This passage from the state of nature to the civil state produces in man a very remarkable change, substituting in his conduct justice for instinct, giving to his actions the morality which was lacking in them hitherto. It is then only that, the voice of duty succeeding to physical impulse, and justice to desire, man, who up to this point had only considered himself, sees himself compelled to act on other principles and to consult his reason before listening to his desires.[1]

In other words, once he has entered into society man has become a moral and political animal, with possibilities for good and evil which he did not previously possess. This is the basic fact of the situation. Quite early Rousseau had written that the vices of man 'do not belong so much to man as to man badly ruled'.[2] In other words, the key to the good life is in politics. In the *Confessions* he put down as one of the discoveries that had most influenced his thinking that of the basic importance of politics, that 'tout tenait radicalement à la politique'.[3] It was indeed only in the eighteenth century, with the rise of the idea of absolute sovereignty and the emancipation of government from the restraints that had formerly bound it, that this began to be true. The sovereign State was at last becoming a fact and Rousseau's political theory was an attempt to come to grips with the problem it presented. His theory of the General Will represents an attempt to reconcile liberty with sovereignty and he demonstrates his affiliation with his century in regarding this as fundamentally a moral issue.

As Rousseau states it, the problem is that the natural goodness, or compassion, of man, his *bonté naturelle*, is not adequate to resist the temptations which arise out of social life. These are the result of the moral crisis which comes with the passage from the isolated individualism of the State of Nature to life in society, which brings with it also the change in motivation from natural self-preservation – *amour de soi* – to *amour propre*, which one might call, in Hobbesian language, pride. To all the innocent if amoral passions, *amour propre* adds an element of perversion, to cope with which man's individual *bonté naturelle* has to be supplemented by *vertu*, which is the triumph of reason over the passions. In the individual this is the moral and rational conscience; in society the General Will, which, like the conscience in the individual, is always present, even when its voice

---

[1] *Contrat social*, I, viii.   [2] *Préface de Narcisse*.   [3] *Confessions*, Part II, livre ix.

is not heard. For the laws of the State to be legitimate, Rousseau holds, the General Will must find expression in them.

The General Will is reconcilable with liberty, first because it is the exteriorization in politics of the moral will of the individual; and secondly, because of the limitations Rousseau introduces, which may also possibly be taken as evidence of his appreciation of the dangers implicit in the idea. It must be emphasized that the idea of a sovereignty which is both absolute and limited is a commonplace of the Natural Law school of thought; there is nothing paradoxical in the title Rousseau gives to one of his chapters – 'On the limits of the sovereign power'. Thus his General Will has only the function of laying down and maintaining the laws of society, by which he means fundamental, constitutional laws, not day-to-day regulations. It cannot take any particular decision affecting individual persons or acts. Secondly, a clear distinction is drawn between the General Will, which operates only by general laws and is sovereign, and the Government, which exercises all the usual executive powers but has no sovereign authority. Thirdly, the General Will is not the will of all: it is the will which is inspired by good motives and directed only to the common interest. It is indeed an ideal of perfection, which Rousseau expects to see realized on earth rarely if ever.

These are all safeguards against the use of the idea of the General Will to justify tyrannical power, but they also carry Rousseau far beyond his starting-point. If he began with all the normal presuppositions of the school of Natural Law, he has now moved away from them. The particular quality of Natural Law thought, as represented, for example, by its most influential exponent in this period, Locke, had been that it rigorously limited the scope of politics and therefore of political power. The criteria by which political action was judged were outside politics. The real problem was to discover what they were. After those laid down by revealed religion had been seen as patently unsatisfactory, theorists fell back on the rational and moral judgment of the individual; and while the State was restricted to more or less utilitarian ends, they could be measured satisfactorily by utilitarian standards. Rousseau reintroduced an ideal of perfection into politics, the effect of which was to bring back dangers similar to those of religious politics, which the Enlightenment believed it had eliminated. Voltaire, however unfair and worse he was to Rousseau, saw truly that there was something alarming in his genius, even if he did not understand what it was.

But in the last resort Rousseau still belongs to the world of the Enlightenment and shares its liberal ideals. Defending himself against Genevan critics, he declared that Locke had treated the same subjects in exactly the same manner as himself;[1] and if this seems a little exaggerated, we may agree that Locke, along with Montesquieu, certainly exercised the greatest influence over his political thinking.[2] Rousseau's later political writings, the *Lettres écrites de la montagne,* dealing with the Genevan constitution, his *Project pour la Corse* and *Considérations sur le gouvernement de Pologne,* are proof of this. If the *Contrat social* points in a different direction, it stands alone. But it shows that while Rousseau did not follow where his genius led, he was conscious, like Diderot, of coming changes.

The immediate influence of the *Contrat social* was negligible. To attribute to Rousseau the intention of revolutionizing political life, or even of promoting an actual revolution, is moreover to misunderstand him and his thought. Of course, he *was* misunderstood, even at the time. As he complained, men persisted in seeing a revolutionary 'in the man of the world who has the truest respect for national laws and constitutions, and the greatest aversion for revolutions'.[3]

A change was coming over political thinking in the last quarter of the eighteenth century. Anticipations of it may be detected in such writers as Diderot, Rousseau, Mably and even d'Holbach; but they still belong essentially to the Enlightenment. For the continuation and culmination of its political thinking, however, we shall have to recross the Channel and see what had been happening to the tradition of Locke in his own country. For England, in the eighteenth century, was not immune from the growing influence of the idea of sovereignty, though it was parliamentary and not monarchical sovereignty as on the Continent. The temper of the age can be detected in Blackstone, when he writes: 'There is and must be [in every state] a supreme, irresistible, absolute uncontrolled authority, in which the *jura summa imperii,* or the rights of sovereignty, reside.'[4]

In the second half of the eighteenth century this idea of sovereignty was to come into rough conflict with the still surviving influence of the Lockian tradition, in such episodes as the Middlesex election of 1768, General Warrants, and above all the dispute with the

[1] *Lettres de la Montagne, Works,* ed. Vaughan, ii, 206.
[2] Cf. *Du contrat social,* ed. G. Beaulavon, 3rd ed. 1922, p. 71.
[3] *Rousseau juge de Jean-Jacques,* troisième dialogue.
[4] *Commentaries on the Laws of England,* 1765, Intro. §2.

American colonies, where the pure milk of Lockian doctrine was still undefiled. In America, ideas of social contract, natural rights, government as trusteeship, and so on, continued to dominate political thinking. The writers of the American Revolution, it has been said, had a theory of society, a theory of government, and a theory of the relation of the one to the other: but of the State in the modern sense they knew little.[1] If a summary of the ideas of the revolutionary pamphleteers, of greater figures like Jefferson, and of the Declaration of Independence are not recited here as illustrative of the political thought of the Enlightenment, it is only because to do so would be merely to repeat what has already been said in treating of Locke and the political thinking of the seventeenth century.

In England, too, the dispute with the colonies provided the occasion for protests against the assertion of parliamentary sovereignty. Thus the great lawyer, Lord Camden, declared: 'Taxation and representation are inseparable; this position is founded on the laws of nature.' And, quoting Locke: 'The supreme power cannot take from any man any part of his property without his own consent.'[2] Among British writers on politics also the ideas of Natural Law survived. This has only been forgotten because, in the absence of great names, these writers, like Barbeyrac and Burlamaqui in France, have dropped out of text-book currency. But Thomas Rutherford upheld the right of resistance in his *Institutes of Natural Law* (1754–6). The Swiss Delolme, in his widely read eulogy of the British constitution, described resistance as 'the ultimate and lawful recourse against the violences of Power', and attributed the 'freedom of the Constitution' to 'an equilibrium between the ruling Powers of the State'.[3] Similar ideas are to be found in Adam Ferguson's *Essay on the History of Civil Society* (1782), and many other works.

Again, Richard Price, in *Observations on the Nature of Civil Liberty* (1776), which went through eight editions in ten years, declared: 'Government ... is in the very nature of it, a trust; and all its powers a delegation for gaining particular ends.'[4] Price, however, and the English democrats such as Priestley, Cartwright, Paine, tend to drop the formal social contract out of their theory; and though retaining and emphasizing natural rights, they give them a more patently

---

[1] R. G. Adams, *Political Ideas of the American Revolution*, 1922, p. 175.
[2] *Parliamentary History*, xvi, 178, 180. Cf. G. H. Guttridge, *English Whiggism and the American Revolution*, 1942.
[3] J. L. de Lolme, *The Constitution of England*, 4th ed. 1784, pp. 315.
[4] Price, *Civil Liberty*, p. 15.

utilitarian turn. This development may be explained in terms of the general eighteenth-century bias away from the abstract, rationalist, a priori thinking of the previous age, and towards a more historical and empirical attitude. The contract now comes under criticism as unhistorical. Soame Jenyns, denying the State of Nature and the original contract, writes, in Burkian language: 'The natural state of man is by no means a state of solitude and independence, but of society and subordination; all the effects of human art are part of his nature.'[1]

The most devastating, though not necessarily the most influential criticism of the contractual argument was that of Hume. He put the case in both philosophical and pragmatic terms. To be valid, he said, a contract implies a preceding agreement that contracts should be kept. In other words, it requires as a necessary preliminary the conditions that it is supposed to create. The result is to plunge us into an infinite regress. Secondly, in practice men do not, Hume points out, obey government because of some hypothetical contractual obligation to do so; their real motive is utility 'because otherwise society could not subsist'[2] and this is enough by itself. This verdict is the only one compatible with Hume's philosophy, with his refusal to accept hypothetical constructions, or fictions masquerading as truth, to account for what can be explained much more directly by the plain facts of observation. As he puts it:

> If the sense of common interest were not our original motive to obedience, I wou'd fain ask, what other principle is there in human nature capable of subduing the natural ambition of men, and forcing them to such a submission?[3]

Adam Smith and Bentham accept Hume's arguments on the contractual theory as decisive, and whether we attribute it to the effect of Hume's criticism or not, this was the end of the contract.

The consequence of its abandonment, however, was not to set up an absolute right of sovereignty. On the contrary, even for the conservative Hume, resistance to government, when it is a case of self-preservation or of defending the public good, is more than a right, it is an inescapable fact.[4] Although political thinking in Great Britain in the second half of the eighteenth century bifurcated into two

---

[1] *Disquisitions on Several Subjects*, 1782, p. 136.
[2] 'Of the Original Contract', in *Essays Moral, Political and Literary*, 1741–2.
[3] *Treatise of Human Nature*, p. 553.   [4] Ibid.

streams – the democratic, natural right, and the conservative, utilitarian trends – they both retained essential marks of their origin. And just as they had already been largely fused into a single theory by d'Holbach in France, so ultimately they were to come together in the political ideas of Bentham in England.

Meanwhile, we find with Burke, as with Rousseau, the limits of enlightened thought stretched to the point at which new ideas are clearly breaking through. Burke follows Hume in abandoning the State of Nature and the Lockian contract. 'Art', he says, 'is man's nature.' To the idea of the abstract natural rights of man he opposes that of practical utility, in the form of concrete, attainable interests. He retains the idea of government as trusteeship, and allows a right of resistance. This is not merely in theory, for while regretting the causes of revolution, Burke justified it in America and India, and only condemned it in Ireland on the practical ground that it was bound to fail. The French Revolution he regarded as falling into a different category: he saw it not as a defence of the interests of the people but as an attempt on the part of one section of the nation to acquire dominance over the rest. It was a struggle for sovereignty, not liberty. It took the form of the assertion of theoretical principles against practical interests, and consequently was unjustifiable on utilitarian grounds.

Burke follows Hume in the conservative interpretation of utilitarianism. His might be described as an historical utilitarianism. The fact that an institution has survived for many centuries is the best proof of its utility. It may have been set up for a purpose which it no longer serves, but this is no ground for condemning it; if it survives, that is evidence that it still serves some other, perhaps even fortuitously acquired, useful end. For this reason, rational calculation cannot reveal all the purposes of social institutions, to say nothing of the fundamental ends of society. What we call prejudice is a deeper kind of wisdom. 'The individual is foolish … but the species is wise.'[1] And so, starting from sound eighteenth-century beginnings, we find outselves with Burke, and much more drastically than with Rousseau plunged into a new intellectual climate. In Burke, though the interests of individuals remain the basic factor in social ethics, political society has regained the emotional aura which Locke had deliberately excluded. Social value` begin to challenge individual ones. The past is reinstated in the name of historical tradition.

[1] Burke, *Works*, 1869, vi, 147.

Natural Law reacquires its medieval religious connections, because religion is for Burke the oldest and greatest of social institutions, the most universal of prejudices. It is the basis of morality and of the whole social order. But at this point we must stop, for Burke, much more than Rousseau, straddles the old age and the new.

It would be a mistake to conclude the history of the political thought of the Enlightenment at this point. Even if it was drawing to an end, or being transformed into something different with Rousseau and Burke, the greatest and most influential, after Locke, of enlightened political thinkers was only to appear towards the end of the century, and not to achieve recognition until the nineteenth century, when his ideas were to exercise by far the greatest single influence that British social and political institutions have ever experienced.

Jeremy Bentham's importance for the history of the nineteenth century is such that one is sometimes tempted to forget how thoroughly by birth and education he belonged to the eighteenth. He was born in 1748 and bred on a diet of French *philosophes*, to whom he subsequently acknowledged his indebtedness for his basic utilitarian ideas. His first work, an onslaught on Blackstone's *Commentaries*, begins with an invocation to the true spirit of the Enlightenment:

> The age we live in is a busy age; in which knowledge is rapidly advancing towards perfection. In the natural world, in particular, every thing teems with discovery and with improvement. The most distant and recondite regions of the earth traversed and explored – the all-vivifying and subtle element of the air so recently analysed and made known to us, – are striking evidences, were all others wanting, of this pleasing truth.
>
> Correspondent to *discovery* and *improvement* in the natural world, is *reformation* in the moral.[1]

He proceeds to abandon all the familiar presuppositions of the Natural Law school. The 'chimera' of the Original Contract, he says, has been 'effectually demolished by Mr Hume': 'I think we hear not so much of it now as formerly. The indestructible prerogatives of mankind have no need to be supported upon the sandy foundation of a fiction.'[2] The Law of Nature is 'nothing but a

[1] *A Fragment on Government*, 1776, Preface §§1, 2.   [2] Ibid., ch. i, §36.

phrase'.[1] The State of Nature, or natural society, in which there is no government, is an imaginary extreme at one end of the scale, just as a 'perfectly political' state is at the other.[2] Government is based not on such hypotheses as the contract, but on the habit of obedience.[3]

Before proceeding to discuss Bentham's more positive political ideas, it will be helpful to try to place him in the general setting of eighteenth-century moral philosophy. As we have seen, the Enlightenment approached the problem of morals from two angles, which were not always mutually exclusive. Locke believed that moral truths, like mathematical truths, could be discovered with certainty by the deductive reason. He failed to demonstrate this by deducing any system of moral truths himself, and it might be held that this cannot be done. In particular, it may be said that moral judgments are always practical – that is, they are intended to eventuate in action, or in judgments about action. If moral are to be equated with mathematical truths, on the other hand, while a beautiful, self-contained system, such as that of Descartes, may be created, we can have no proof that it has any relation to the actual world. The appreciation of this difficulty is one reason why the eighteenth century preferred to speak of reason in the field of moral philosophy as 'practical reason', but the failure to deduce a system of moral truths by any kind of reason led in due course to the abandonment of this line of approach.

Secondly, instead of deductive reason, appeal was made to a 'moral sense', by which, it was argued, moral truths were recognized. The difficulty here was to attribute any positive and stable content to this supposed sense. Historical and geographical discoveries seemed to indicate the relativity of all moral codes. The eighteenth-century Enlightenment therefore found itself driven back, as a third line of defence of morality, on utilitarianism. The moral value of actions was to be judged by their consequences on the happiness of individuals, or of society as a collection of individuals. The problem of the nature of happiness, and its relation to the pleasure-pain motivation was, on the whole, side-stepped; and it was possible to reach agreement on a good many practical issues before it presented itself in an acute form. In the last resort, of course, the appeal to expediency is not quite satisfactory, but generally, in the eighteenth century, the last resort was not reached.

[1] *A Fragment on Government*, ch. iv, §19.   [2] Ibid., ch. i, §§11-13.   [3] Ibid., §10.

These different trends in moral philosophy produced similarly divergent trends in political thinking. Intuitionists, like Price, supported policies of political and social reform; while utilitarians, like Hume, were more conservative in their political views. This, however, is only a very loose generalization. Utilitarianism had its reforming side from the beginning. The influential Italian advocate of reform of the criminal law, Beccaria, wrote, in 1764:

> It is better to prevent crimes, than to punish them. This is the fundamental principle of good legislation, which is the art of conducting men to the *maximum* of happiness and to the *minimum* of misery, if we may apply this mathematical expression to the good and evil of life.[1]

The object of legislation said Beccaria, before Bentham, should be 'the greatest happiness of the greatest number'.[2] For d'Holbach in France utilitarianism was associated with social amelioration in a broad sense; while for Bentham it became a specifically reforming system of thought, the effects of which penetrated into every corner of the political and social system.

With Bentham the object of political thinking undergoes a major change. The aim ceases to be to justify the existence of society and government; their necessity is taken for granted. Instead, Bentham, assuming that government is justifiable only in terms of its consequences, wants to find out how to improve these consequences. He begins with a classic statement of the pleasure-pain motivation.

> Nature has placed mankind under the governance of two sovereign masters, *pain* and *pleasure*. It is for them alone to point out what we ought to do, as well as to determine what we shall do. On the one hand the standard of right and wrong, on the other the chain of causes and effects, are fastened to their throne.[3]

This hedonistic analysis is translated, on the first page of his first book, into the formula which has been identified with Bentham's name, though it was not a new one in eighteenth-century thought, of the greatest happiness: 'It is the greatest happiness of the greatest number that is the measure of right and wrong.'[4] This is, in other words, the

---

[1] *Essay on Crimes and Punishments*, ch. xli.   [2] Ibid., Intro.
[3] *An Introduction to the Principles of Morals and Legislation*, 1789, ch. i, §1.
[4] *A Fragment on Government*, Preface, §2.

principle of utility, and Bentham regards it as self-evident. It is 'the principle which furnishes us with that *reason*, which alone depends not upon any higher reason, but which is itself the sole and all-sufficient reason for every point of practice whatsoever.'[1] There follows a simple statement of the problem of government: 'The business of government is to promote the happiness of the society, by punishing and rewarding.'[2] It may be said that this is far too simple, that, like Locke, Bentham narrows the scope of politics and excludes from it much of what makes life worth living. In a general system of moral values this might be a defect, in a political theory it is an advantage. If we criticize Bentham for holding that 'push-pin is as good as poetry', at least it saved him from the danger of trying to make men poetical by Act of Parliament.

The utilitarian doctrine also safeguards Bentham from an easy acceptance of the rising idea of sovereignty. He condemns Blackstone's assertion of the principle of absolute sovereignty.[3] Political authority, if it is not limited by an express agreement, he admits to be indefinite, but it is not infinite.[4] There is an echo of Montesquieu when Bentham says that the difference between a free and a despotic government depends on the manner in which political power is distributed in the State, on the frequent interchange of position between rulers and ruled, on the blending of their interests, on the responsibility of those who exercise the government, and on such liberties as those of the Press, of association, and of peaceful opposition. In the last resort there is a point at which active resistance becomes 'commendable':

It is *then* ... when, according to the best calculation he is able to make, *the probable mischiefs of resistance* (speaking with respect to the community in general) *appear less to him than the probable mischiefs of submission*. This then is to him, that is to each man in particular, the *juncture for resistance*.[5]

It is not necessary to pursue further the development of Bentham's thought, to trace the manifold developments to which his simple, primary ideas, were subject, or the realizations, stretching through

---

[1] *A Fragment on Government*, ch. i, §48.
[2] *Principles of Morals and Legislation*, ch. vii, §1.
[3] *A Fragment on Government*, ch. iv.
[4] Ibid., ch. iv, §23.
[5] Ibid., ch. iv, §20. Cf. ch. i, §43; ch. iv, §16.

the next century and a half to the present day, of the plans his immensely fertile and benevolent mind produced for bettering the lot of his fellow beings. It is sufficient to say that Bentham's is the last great name in the history of the political thinking of the Enlightenment. Through him it legislated for posterity.

PART FOUR

THE FRUSTRATION OF THE ENLIGHTENMENT

XIX

The Wars of the French Revolution

THE century of the Enlightenment ended in a blaze, if not of glory at any rate a blaze. The struggles of the French Revolution and the Napoleonic Empire opened a new age of wars and revolution which was to reach, so far, its culmination in the twentieth century, and to bring back with it, in peace as well as war, massacres, terrorism, tortures, persecutions, witch-hunting, superstition, and a general cult of violence and irrationality – in short all the things that the Enlightenment fondly imagined it had expelled, or was on the point of expelling, from the civilized world. There is danger of a misunderstanding here, which must be guarded against. I am not suggesting that actual conditions in the eighteenth century were in any way 'better' than they became in the following century, or that its humanitarian ideals have disappeared or have ceased to influence social life; but merely that while civilization in the eighteenth century seemed to be moving in one direction, there are at least grounds for thinking that in some respects since then it has been moving in the opposite direction. What we have to explain, if this is true, is at least the partial failure of the Enlightenment. But there is another and even more serious charge to be considered first. It has been suggested that the horrors of the modern world are to be attributed not to its failure but to its success – that the Enlightenment is in fact responsible for them. This is a paradox that is to be found mostly in the writings of publicists and propagandists; but one or two scholars of distinction have also lent their support to it, and their views cannot be passed over without discussion.

The thesis which identifies the French Revolution with the triumph of the powers of evil, and attributes this to the influence of the *philosophes*, goes back, of course, as far as Burke and the abbé

Barruel. It found its most powerful exponent in Taine. Of the various subsequent attempts to interpret the Enlightenment in these terms only two are of a sufficiently scholarly nature to require attention. The brilliant essay by Carl Becker on *The Heavenly City of the Eighteenth-century Philosophers* analyses the thought and, by implication, the influence of the Enlightenment. Becker writes: 'I shall attempt to show that the *Philosophes* demolished the Heavenly City of St Augustine only to rebuild it with more up-to-date materials.'[1] His thesis is that they tried to bring down the Kingdom of God from heaven to earth, to postulate the possibility of mundane perfectibility, to posit an Earthly Paradise within man's grasp. To substantiate their hypotheses, he says, they used the methods of deductive reasoning. This is to identify the Enlightenment with Cartesianism, as indeed Taine also did; and this book will have been written to no purpose if the error of such an interpretation needs to be emphasized. As, however, Becker's thesis has already been subjected to a thorough and to my mind decisive criticism, I will not repeat the arguments against it here.[2]

More recently, another powerful and far-ranging indictment of the thought of the eighteenth century has been produced in *The Origins of Totalitarian Democracy* by Professor J. L. Talmon. His thesis is ingenious and important. Put briefly, it starts with the contemporary judgment that there are two kinds of democracy – empirical liberal and totalitarian Messianic. The latter, which has produced such striking consequences in our own time, originated, he holds, in the thought of the eighteenth century. Its line of development is from eighteenth-century rationalism, by way of social determinism, to belief in a single valid system of society based on faith. The thought of the Enlightenment, Talmon agrees with Becker, amounts in fact to a secular religion; and it has led by an 'inner logic' to political and social Messianism. The theoretical postulates of the eighteenth century, he argues, became political fact in the course of the French Revolution, first in the 'Jacobin improvisation' and then in the 'Babœuvist crystallization'. These are seen as an anticipation of modern totalitarian communism, which is their logical and also their historical sequel. The clue to the understanding of this process, which can be traced in the evolution of

[1] C. Becker, *The Heavenly City of the Eighteenth-century Philosophers*, 1932, p. 31.
[2] In *Carl Becker's Heavenly City Revisited*, edited by Raymond O. Rockwood, 1958, and particularly in the contribution to this symposium by Peter Gay, 'Carl Becker's Heavenly City', pp. 27-51.

practical politics, he finds in the theoretical pattern which unites eighteenth-century enlightened thought with twentieth-century totalitarianism. It may be summed up as the assumption that there is a sole and exclusive truth in politics; it postulates a preordained, harmonious, perfect plan of society; and recognizes only one, all-inclusive sphere of human action, which is the political. According to this doctrine, to summarize Talmon, politics is the art of applying an all-embracing philosophy to the organization of society.

It may be held that this neat bifurcation between liberal and totalitarian democracy is an over-simplification — as Bentham pointed out, total government and total anarchy are both imaginary extremes — but this does not destroy the basic validity of Talmon's analysis of the contemporary situation. What needs to be challenged is not this, but his discussion of totalitarian sources. In the first place, it must be pointed out that the game of chasing origins can easily lead to very peculiar conclusions, as Voltaire indicated when he wrote that all children have parents, but not all possible parents have children. Tracing a line of descent backwards is bound to produce positive results, and then by a simple process of reversion we can create the illusion of a necessary catena of cause and effect. Thus one could trace a train of influence leading from Stalin back through Lenin, Marx, Hegel, Kant, Rousseau, Locke and Hooker to Aquinas. Each link in the chain is valid, yet it must be confessed that, though there are common features and affinities in the ideas of Aquinas and Stalin, the whole has distinctly less value than the parts.

Another possible source of historical error in the study of ideas is an arbitrary and unduly narrow selection of sources, and it may be thought that Professor Talmon has not escaped this danger. He takes his examples of eighteenth-century enlightened thought only from France, and even there excludes most of the major thinkers of the century from his canon. There are only incidental references to Montesquieu and Voltaire, none to the articles in the *Encyclopédie*, none to Turgot, only one to Diderot. The thinkers he relies on, and whom he describes as those who 'do deserve, in our opinion, to be considered as speaking for the eighteenth century',[1] are a very small group, and not all of these are in fact appealed to seriously. Con-dorcet is mentioned, and his superficial sketch of the progress of the human race might seem to make him a profitable candidate for a role in the history of political Messianism. Unfortunately, since he

[1] J. L. Talmon, *The Origins of Totalitarian Democracy*, 1952, p. 261.

was also the principal author of the 'Girondin' Constitution of 1793, which pushed liberal political ideas beyond the bounds of common sense, he cannot easily be treated as a prophet of totalitarianism, and Professor Talmon makes little use of him. D'Holbach was a much more serious political and social thinker, but as has been sugested above, his ideas are profoundly liberal and he also affords little support to the thesis. He is thrown in, occasionally, to make weight with Helvétius, whose crude and immature utilitarianism is indeed sometimes stated in more or less totalitarian terms. However, the strongest support for Talmon's thesis to be found in Helvétius comes in the letters published in 1788, which are now known to be a propaganda publication of that date and falsely attributed to him.[1] Moverover, before allowing that Helvétius is typical of the En-lightenment it would be necessary to take into consideration the severe criticism which Voltaire and Diderot, among others, directed against his ideas.

We are left with three more serious candidates – Morelly, Mably and Rousseau. Morelly's pamphlet, the *Code de la Nature*, has had to bear a weight of argumentation, from both left- and right-wing writers, far beyond what such a slight source can support. Mably's voluminous works are a rag-bag of eighteenth-century ideas. He is capable of expressing the most extreme views, and then limiting and qualifying them in so many ways that they practically lose all significance. He wants to see a free society, but believes that in modern States, and particularly in France, the people are incapable of liberty. Professor Talmon himself truly says of Mably's thought that it is 'entangled in the gravest incongruities and contradictions'.[2] Finally, there is Rousseau, on whom in the last resort the gravamen of the argument rests. The extent to which totalitarian views can be attributed to Rousseau is a much disputed question but one which need not delay us here. Even if one were to agree – which I do not – that Rousseau's political thought is totalitarian, this would only serve to show that he had broken with the liberal, individualist ideas of the Enlightenment, and that the *philosophes* were right in regarding him as their greatest enemy.[3]

There is one last point which must be made. We may agree that

<hr />

[1] R. Koebner, 'The Authenticity of the letters on the *Esprit des Lois* attributed to Helvétius', in *Bulletin of the Institute of Historical Research*, xxiv, 19-43.

[2] Talmon, *Totalitarian Democracy*, p. 56.

[3] I have discussed this problem, on the basis of the excellent works of M. Robert Derathé, in 'New Light on the Political Thought of Rousseau', in *Political Science Quarterly*, lxvi, 272-84.

Professor Talmon's analysis of the idea of totalitarian democracy is a significant contribution to political thinking; and we may agree with him in deploring the practical consequences of the idea. But such a condemnation requires some standard of values, or some other political system, by comparison with which to make such a judgment. This can only be the alternative system of liberal democracy. Now when we ask where the ideas of liberal democracy come from, we find ourselves thrown back precisely on the Enlightenment, which Talmon has indicted as the *fons et origo* of totalitarianism. In earlier chapters I endeavoured to present as comprehensive a picture of the political ideas of the Enlightenment as space allowed, without schematizing a many-sided movement into a simple pattern; and I think it will be difficult to deny that in it can be seen the roots of modern liberalism. Of course, the same intellectual movement might conceivably be responsible for both liberalism and totalitarianism, but to establish this would require rather more evidence of the supposed totalitarian element in the Enlightenment than we have been given. Before falling back on such an explanation we should see if there is not a less paradoxical one. It would be generally agreed that the turning-point came towards the end of the eighteenth century, and it is consequently reasonable to consider whether we can, or cannot, detect in the Revolutionary and Napoleonic era new trends which may provide a clue to the failure of the high hopes of the Enlightenment, instead of hypothesizing such a basic self-contradiction in its ideas.

We must not, of course, idealize the eighteenth century. If persecution, torture, superstition were declining in Western Europe, there still remained much to deplore. The age of the Enlightenment was not immune from wars and revolutions: yet it is surely not an illusion to think that those of our own day are of a different kind from the dynastic struggles, wars of succession or partition, or coups d'état that can be seen in the eighteenth century, at least until we reach the French Revolution. In 1789, however, a new force seems to appear on the historic stage. To sum up the French Revolution simply is impossible. It is a great ocean into which many rivers poured their waters. It defies generalization. For an attempt to discover what new forces were at work in the last years of the eighteenth century, an easier approach is offered by the Revolutionary War, because it is a more restricted, though crucial, subject of inquiry, and because, whatever improvement had been secured, or adumbrated, in other respects, the ideals of the eighteenth century had little effect on international relations.

When the French Revolution burst on an astonished world it came with the promise of liberty and peace. The rulers of the other States of Europe did not exactly welcome it, but they had no intention of interfering in the affairs of France. The government of Great Britain, which was to prove the most enduring enemy of revolutionary France, was profoundly pacific. The Younger Pitt, in his budget speech of 1792, uttered the famous prophecy that 'There never was a time in the history of this country when from the situation of Europe we might more reasonably expect fifteen years of peace than at the present moment'.[1] Why were these hopes of peace disappointed? Why did such a deep-seated opposition develop between the other powers and revolutionary France that instead of fifteen years of peace, over twenty years of war followed? The question may be put in more general terms – why was the revolutionary State unable to live at peace with the rest of Europe?

It is worth pointing out, because the fact is often overlooked, that however much the other powers disliked the Revolution, the declarations of war did not come from them: it was France which declared war in turn on Austria, Prussia, Great Britain, Holland, Spain. But the question of responsibility for the beginning of the war is not the essential issue. The important question is not even whether there was any factor in the Revolution which was likely to lead to war – there are always plenty of causes of war – but whether there was anything which made peace impossible in a way in which it had not been impossible in earlier international conflicts. Those who lived at the time thought there was. The first point that strikes one, in considering the causes of the long continuance, rather than the origins, of the Revolutionary War, is the fear of propaganda. The revolutionaries aimed at establishing direct relations with all peoples over the heads of their governments. In those who sympathized with their principles they had a Fifth Column everywhere. 'The genius of the French Revolution marched forth,' said Pitt, 'the terror and dismay of the world.'[2] Its aim was to bring liberty to all nations. But to quote Pitt once again,

They will not accept, under the name of Liberty, any model of government, but that which is conformable to their own

[1] *Parliamentary History*, xxix, 826.   [2] Ibid., xxxiv, 1327 (February 3rd, 1800).

opinions and ideas; and all men must learn from the mouth of their cannon the propagation of their system in every part of the world.[1]

While such a combination of ideas and policies prevailed in the Revolution, the other powers saw no security in peace with France.

Even at the time, however, it was realized that revolutionary propaganda by itself was not a sufficient motive for war. The other countries of Europe, if left to themselves, were quite capable of suppressing their own Jacobins without undue difficulty. To Fox's charge that he was making war on opinion, Pitt replied: 'It is not so. We are not in arms against the opinions of the closet, nor the speculations of the school. We are at war with *armed* opinions.'[2] The power of French armies was what made revolutionary opinions dangerous; and though we must not underestimate the great wave of genuine idealism with which the Revolution began, those who controlled the actions of the revolutionary armies, even at the beginning, were not moved exclusively by idealistic motives. When, early in the Revolution, the French Assembly passed a decree repudiating all conquests, it was undoubtedly sincere. But this idealistic frame of mind did not remain undiluted for long. Revolutionary dynamism was not to be confined within the narrow limits of a single State. The revolutionaries soon learned to rationalize their aggressive instincts, and imagined that they had thereby moralized self-interest.

With the military genius released by the Revolution, with military tactics adapted to make use of the enthusiasm of the early volunteers, and with the solid weight of man-power provided by the *levée en masse* — the first time that the whole manpower of a nation had been mobilized for war — it was not long before war meant victory. As it went on, annexation followed occupation, and the plebiscites which at first accompanied liberation by the revolutionary armies soon came to be omitted as an unnecessary formality. The frontiers of France swelled, satellite States formed excrescences on the new boundaries, and the pretence of liberation wore thinner and thinner. The French armies brought many good things in their train: they brought a more humane and rational legal system, more efficient administration, opportunities for the unprivileged to rise to places of power and prestige. But the conquered countries had to pay a heavy price in government by small pro-French cliques, whose

[1] Ibid., xxx, 278 (February 1st, 1793).   [2] Ibid., xxxiv, 1051 (June 7th, 1799).

authority rested on French bayonets and political police, and in furnishing continual supplies of men and money for the French armies. By 1795 the dominant aims of French foreign policy, which can be traced without any disguise in the records of the Ministry of Foreign Affairs as early as 1792, were reduced to two: first, to obtain strategic frontiers, and a glacis of dependent territories in front of them to protect the gains of France from counter-attack and provide a jumping-off ground for further aggression. Secondly, France required economic advantages – money, corn, cattle, clothing, boots – requisitioned by the generals or legally obtained by treaties of peace and friendship. Bonaparte had nothing to teach the Republic in the arts of aggression and confiscation. The Revolution was aggressive abroad even before it became tyrannical at home, and Pitt was right in believing that the only limit on French conquests was the strength of the resistance opposed to them.

Of course, we must not exaggerate the novelty of much of this. Sorel has pointed out that practically every crime in international relations with which the Revolution has been charged could be found in the repertoire of the ancien régime, only the Revolution did on principle what the ancien régime had done from lack of principle. Herein lies the crucial problem. Is this just the normal decline in the idealism of a political movement under the temptations of power? 'Tout commence en mystique', wrote Péguy, 'tout finit en politique.' We might believe this to be the explanation, if it were not that the Revolution turned into something which went far beyond the normal aggressions of international politics. It developed into a bid for universal empire and changed war from a limited struggle between governments into an almost unlimited struggle between nations. The French Assembly early passed a decree – not put into practice – that no British or Hanoverian prisoners should be taken. The speeches and propaganda of the revolutionary leaders, denouncing their enemies as nations of cannibals, inhuman beasts of prey and so on, have a very modern ring. Their opponents retaliated in kind and the result was the first draft – admittedly a very imperfect one – of totalitarian war, war without restriction in its methods and without limit in its ends.

Such a war could not arise merely out of the customary rivalries of power politics; it presupposes the introduction of a new factor. This new factor was the development of an ardent opposition of ideas. Such an opposition played little part in international conflicts during the eighteenth century: they were simple clashes of material interests, with which principles had nothing to do. More recently, the reaction produced by the exaggerated propaganda of the First World War increased the disposition, particularly among historians, to look with suspicion on the alleged role of ideas, or principles, in the struggles of the past. War was a mere conflict of interests, and polititics a glorified intrigue; ideas had nothing to do with either of them. In the course of the last thirty years Communists and Nazis have taught us, at a heavy price, that ideas do matter in history. We could have learnt the same lesson more cheaply from a study of the French Revolution.

I hope I will not be suspected of attempting to sum up a great and complex movement in terms of a simple formula. The Revolution was many things. It was an attempt to reform the government of France, a revolt against well-known abuses, a struggle to displace the privileged classes, and much more. But it was also, and this is what concerns us here, the embodiment of a great idea, the idea of the sovereignty of the people, or nation. For a statement of the meaning of the principle of popular or national sovereignty, we do not have to go to the writings of the Enlightenment, and if we did we should not find it there. We need to look no further than to the little abbé who in 1789 was the oracle of the *tiers état* in France, Sieyes.

> The Nation [Sieyes wrote,] exists before all things and is the origin of all things. It is sufficient that its will is manifested for all positive law to vanish before it. In whatever manner a Nation wills, it is sufficient that it does will: all forms are good, and its will is always the supreme law.[1]

This was the essence of the revolutionary creed, and this was what turned the political conflict into a major war of ideas.

The theory of popular sovereignty is different in one particular from every other theory of government. It is a theory according to which those who exercise power, and those over whom it is exercised, are one and the same. The People rules — whom does it rule? — it rules itself. Popular sovereignty, according to its exponents, is self-government, and therefore freedom. The argument is plausible. I think it is fair to say that many, asked to define democracy, would define it in some such way, and would refuse to believe that the definition differs from normal democratic practice. But it *does*

[1] Sieyes, *Qu'est-ce que le tiers état?*

differ, and differ fundamentally. Can anyone in his senses really believe that the people actually, concretely, rule this or any other country? Are *we* the Government? Do *we*, the people, impose the taxes on ourselves and decide how to spend them? Do *we* pass and carry out the laws on military service or tariffs or capital punishment? Do *we* appoint our Secretaries and Ministers, or any of the Civil Servants who manage our affairs? Of course we do not. What we mean by saying that we are a democracy is not that we *are* the Government, but that through the process of election and representation we can *influence* or change the Government. This is quite a different thing, as Burke saw when he was confronted with the revolutionary theory. 'The people', he said, 'are the natural control on authority; but to exercise and to control together is contradictory and impossible.'[1] The identification of the Government with the people, Burke realized, was the new thing in revolutionary theory. The Revolution ended many evils and introduced many reforms, but in letting loose this principle on the world, it released a spirit perhaps more potent for evil than even those that it had exorcized.

The idea that the rulers can be identified with the ruled, the Government with the people, and that this is the meaning of democracy, was, is and must be fatal to liberty and peace. That may seem a sweeping statement, but it will hardly seem exaggerated if we consider for a moment the implications of the belief that Government and people can be one and the same. The identification is, as I have said, in practice impossible; but the mere *belief* in such an identification makes any constitutional device for attempting to control or limit government unnecessary and irrelevant. A Government has only to assert that it is the Government of the people to be automatically emancipated from all restraints. Whoever lifts a finger against it, or utters a word of criticism, is an enemy of the people. He is guilty not of lèse-majesty, but, in the words of Robespierre, of lèse-nation or lèse-peuple. Even under the most despotic pre-revolutionary regimes, at any rate in Western Europe, it was admitted that the individual had some rights. Before the new theory of sovereignty those rights faded away like snow in summer. Whatever the Government had the power to do, it had the right to do: any crime was permissible because if it was done in the name of the people it was not a crime.

Internally the theory was a justification of tyranny, externally of

[1] Burke, *An Appeal from the New to the Old Whigs, Works*, iii, 78.

aggression, for popular sovereignty inevitably meant the assertion of the claims of the nation, if necessary by force, against those of all other nations. It was because he saw this consequence in the French Revolution that Burke opposed it so bitterly. He had no doubt what the theory of popular sovereignty would come to mean in the end.

> What now stands as government in France [he wrote,] is struck out at a heat ... The will, the wish, the want, the liberty, the toil, the blood of individuals, is as nothing. Individuality is left out of their scheme of government. The state is all in all. Everything is referred to the production of force; afterwards, everything is trusted to the use of it. It is military in its principle, in its maxims, in its spirit, and in all its movements. The state has dominion and conquest for its sole objects; dominion over minds by proselytism, over bodies by arms.[1]

And who exercises this vast power in the name of the people? The common sense of the Younger Pitt saw the answer as clearly as the more theoretical mind of Burke.

> In what is called the government of the multitude, [he said] they are not the many who govern the few, but the few who govern the many. It is a species of tyranny, which adds insult to the wretchedness of its subjects, by styling its own arbitrary decrees the voice of the people, and sanctioning its acts of oppression and cruelty under the pretence of the national will.[2]

The justification for this excursus into revolutionary history will now, I hope, be apparent. Change a few of the circumstances and we have a picture of the world in the last four decades. Modern revolutions, promising peace, have similaarly brought about a climate of war. Neighbouring States have been swallowed up, or puppet governments established in them. Revolutionary propaganda has created Fifth Columns throughout the world. Wherever, by arms or propaganda, a revolutionary creed has been able to seize power, a government on its own model has been set up. The expansive pressure has been continuous, for like the Napoleonic Empire the modern revolutionary State has no principle of limitation within itself. Its dynamism demands a continual forward movement. Held

---

[1] Burke, *Reflections, Works*, v, 255.
[2] *Parliamentary History*, xxx, 901-2 (May 6–7th, 1793).

back in one quarter it breaks out in another, for it lives on the political, economic and psychological conditions of expansion.

The cleavage, as a century and a half ago, much more than between opposed social systems, is between opposed conceptions of government – the one, as then, based on the principle of the sovereignty of the people, which in practice means the government, whether Fascist, Nazi or Communist, and the other recognizing the rights and interests of the individual. In both, government is in the hands of the few, as it always is, but in liberal democracy it is subject to free criticism and periodic revision. In popular democracy criticism is ruthlessly suppressed and the machine of government is organized to prevent control over it from being exercised from any quarter outside the governing circle. Of course, though both interpretations of democracy may be sincere – attributions of insincerity, such as are usual when two sides to an argument use the same term in contradictory senses, seem to me out of place here – they cannot be equally valid. The test of political liberty, as much as anything else, is whether the people, if they are dissatisfied with those who rule them, can freely and peacefully cause their government to change its policy, or themselves change their government. The answer, in the modern totalitarian States as in revolutionary France, is that they cannot. And one reason why they cannot is, ironically, the operation of the principle of popular sovereignty.

There is a conclusion of great practical importance to be drawn from this parallel. It suggests that a single historic force has been at work in all the great revolutions of the modern period. It has been assumed too easily that the cause of the contemporary cleavage is to be sought in the economic theories and practices of communism. The example of the French Revolution suggests that the principle of popular sovereignty, pushed to the extreme limit, is by itself capable of producing an unbridgeable gap between a State and the rest of the world. Soviet Russia has undoubtedly been to school to Marx and derived much from him. But if what is called communism in Russia were a faithful expression of the principles of the author of *Das Kapital*, it would be the first time in history that an idea has been translated into an ideology without suffering a radical change. In fact, one of the ironies of the modern world is that in the name of Marx, whose theoretical pattern was fashioned with a view to the ultimate 'withering away' of the State, the State should have reached its apogee.

Paradoxically, however, if the argument so far has any validity, it follows that the world is not quite so clearly divided ideologically as we have been apt to think. For all modern States have been influenced by the theories of the French Revolution, and all, to a greater or less degree, assert the principle of popular sovereignty and base on it the claim of their governments to embody the will of the people. The conflict, therefore, is not one of absolute opposites, and the assertion of a total antithesis between the Communist States and the rest is an artificial simplification. Undoubtedly, the State, being, as Marx saw, the embodiment of power, if it has complete sovereignty, tyranny at home and conquest abroad will be unrestrained. The result of freeing the State from control, by pretending that the people can themselves be the Government, was shown between 1789 and 1815. The same experiment has been made in our own day, with similar results. Leviathan lives and moves before our eyes, all the more dangerous because in infancy he was called liberty.

Such an indictment, however, rather states our problem than solves it. If we agree that a prima facie case can be made out for the idea of popular sovereignty as the tap-root of totalitarianism, we still have to examine the origins of this idea, and discover what connection it has, or does not have, with the Enlightenment.

XX

The Rise of Nationalism

TYRANNY at home and aggression abroad were the logical
and historical consequences of the attempt to put the theory
of popular sovereignty into practice. Yet the belief that the
people should have some say in their own government was not
absent from the political thinking of the Enlightenment and it is
surely not an illiberal idea. To turn the idea of democratic representative institutions into the basis of an aggressive and authoritarian
regime something more was needed than the application of a mere
theory, and not even a new one, such as popular sovereignty. Some
form of political alchemy or conceptual legerdemain must be
postulated, and it was not lacking in practice. It can be detected without difficulty in the opening phases of the French Revolution, when
perhaps the political conjurors were less experienced and could not
keep their cards up their sleeves as skilfully as they learnt to do later.
Indeed, one may say that subsequently democratic fraud became so
much second nature to politicians that they perpetrated it by instinct
and almost without giving conscious thought to what they were
doing.

The secret of this transmutation, a political philosopher's stone in
reverse, by means of which democratic gold was changed into totalitarian dross, is revealed by Sieyes, who in appealing to the principle
of popular sovereignty, whether consciously or not, rapidly substitutes the term 'Nation' for that of the 'People'. The effect of this
is to do away with the individualism formerly implicit in the idea
of the people. The nation is 'one and indivisible'. Its sovereignty does
not need, and indeed is not consistent with, a counting of heads.
Moreover, as the nation it has an emotional quality which the
people, as a community of individuals living under one government, lacks. And the idea of the nation was also a new invention in
European political thought.

This last statement doubtless may be thought to require some
justification, for surely it will be said, nations are older than a century
and a half. It must be premised that since we are talking of

sovereignty, the subject under discussion is rather the nation state than the nation. The assumption is sometimes made that the modern nation dates from the sixteenth century and symbolizes the breakdown of the medieval world. Whatever interpretation we give to the term, this view is untenable. In one sense it attributes to the sixteenth century what was really the work of the Middle Ages; in another it presupposes developments that only came about in the nineteenth century. It may be said that this is a matter of interpretation, and that before we can say anything about the nation state we should define what is meant by the term. But historical phenomena are not abstractions to be neatly tied up in the academist's definitions. They are changing things, and their real meaning is apparent in their history. All we need assume, to begin with, is that the term nation state corresponds to some concrete political reality, and that we are not using meaningless jargon when we describe, say, France, Norway or the United States as nation states. What such States have in common might, of course, be decided by a purely contemporary analysis, but a more instructive approach is to attempt to trace the historical origins of such nation states, as fact and idea, and discover how they came to be what they are today.

As a political unit the nation state is normally larger than the tribe or the city state, and smaller than the empire; but it must not be supposed that any necessary historical development is implied in this comparison, for if we examine the sequence – tribe, nation state, empire – we find that the middle term is often left out. Society, when it progresses beyond the tribal stage, may crystallize in the city state form, and from this pass directly into empire. This was in the main the line of development followed by the classical world. Taking the whole course of history, it will be found that the nation state is by no means a common phenomenon. Pre-European Africa and America never really developed beyond the tribal stage, except in so far as conquering tribes such as the Aztecs or the Incas subjected neighbouring peoples to their rule. The Arab peoples passed directly from tribe to empire. In Asia, until very recent times, nation states developed only in a few areas where geographical isolation provided favourable conditions, as they did, for example, in Persia, Burma, Siam and Japan. Only in Europe has the development of the nation state been the rule rather than the exception.

It has been maintained that many of the States of the pre-classical world – those of the Egyptians, Sumerians and Assyrians, for example – possessed the essential characteristics of the nation state;[1] and certainly it is true that by the continual wars in which they engaged these states destroyed or weakened one another just as more recent nation States have done. Subsequently the political conceptions of the city-state civilization of the Greeks and Romans triumphed throughout the Mediterranean, and during the classical period there were no nation states, though the Latin term 'natio' was applied to the barbarian tribes outside the Roman world. It is often assumed that there is an established historical connection between these tribal 'nations' of the barbarian world as the Romans knew them, and the nation states of modern times. Far older than the nation state, it has been said, 'reaching back into the misty dawn of pre-history, is the national community which, founded on the personal life of the nation, yet exercised most of the functions of the State'.[2]

In this interpretation there seems to be an assumption of permanence in the tribal 'nations' which may hardly be justifiable. Even a superficial study of the American Indian, as well as of other tribal societies, says an American ethnologist, 'will quickly dispel the idea that they are simple or permanent units'.[3] There are two other considerations which make the thesis of the tribal origin of the modern nation state unacceptable. In the first place, the differences between the primitive tribe and the State are so great that they are not to be overcome merely by including them both in a single category. In primitive tribal conditions some of the raw materials of statehood may have existed, but for the study of what Aristotle called politics, to include a congeries of related tribes, or a transient and partial military confederacy such as the Gauls under Vercingetorix, the Germans at the time of Arminius, or the Angles, Saxons and Jutes when they invaded Britain, under the same heading as modern France or Germany, is to introduce an element of hopeless confusion. The existence of linguistic and cultural affiliations between a number of tribal communities is a fact of importance for the student of language and culture: until it has some permanent institutional embodiment it cannot be regarded as a political fact, or as belonging

[1] M. T. Walek-Czernecki, 'Le rôle de la nat' onalité dans l'histoire de l'Antiquité' in *Bulletin of the International Committee of Historical Sciences*, 1929.
[2] C. A. Macartney, *National States and National Minorities*, 1934, p. 21.
[3] J. R. Swanton, *The Evolution of Nations*, 1942, p. 1.

to the same order of things as the nation state. The second implication which we cannot accept is that the modern nation state is the descendant of earlier tribal nations. Primitive tribalism has been described as a 'small-scale nationalism',[1] but this seems to me a gross over-simplification; for the creation of nation states the importance of a tribal inheritance of common language and culture can easily be exaggerated. In the development of nation states a common language and culture have more often been a result than a cause. The nation states of today rarely correspond to any former anthropological, linguistic or ethnographical unity.[2]

In the making of nation states, non-tribal elements, such as the semi-Latinized population of Gaul, or the Norman conquerors of England, often played a leading part. The process was sometimes a ruthless one, as in the conquest of southern France by the feudal barons of the north. Groups of related or unrelated peoples were welded into political unity during the medieval period by the force of feudal overlords. Where no single military supremacy was established, nation states were late in developing or never developed at all. Where such supremacies approached or overlapped one another, lands of uncertain allegiance appeared. Thus during the Middle Ages powerful dynasties laid the foundations of the English and French nations, while lesser ones, such as the Ramon Berenguer dynasty, were creating smaller nationalities like the Catalan. The constituents of practically all the medieval nations are diversified and without any common tribal or cultural background. The Catalan nation, which developed a clearly marked identity earlier than the larger nations of the West, has been described as 'above all an historical product ... On to the old Iberian stem have been grafted stocks that were Greek, Roman, Goth, Arab and Gaul ... It is the Catalan tradition which counts, not the descent of the Catalan race'.[3]

It was long before the medieval monarchies acquired names of their own; usually they were known by the title of their chief province. Thus France was so called from the Ile de France, Saxony or Franconia equalled Germany, Polonia gave its name to Poland. However, by the twelfth century in Western, and the thirteenth century in Eastern Europe, a number of nations existed. 'The formation of a State nationality', it has been said, 'marks, properly speaking,

[1] C. H. J. Hayes, *The Historical Evolution of Modern Nationalism*, 1937, pp. 1-2.
[2] Cf. A. van Gennep, *Traité comparatif des nationalités*, 1922, i, 211.
[3] J. B. Trend, *A Picture of Modern Spain*, 1921, pp. 90-5.

the end of the Middle Ages.' For many nations the fourteenth century is the climax of this age of nation-making.[1]

It must be emphasized that throughout this period the word 'nation' continued to be understood in a non-political and mainly linguistic sense. It was thus that it was employed in the medieval universities. The advocacy by Dante of the Tuscan vernacular as a literary language for all Italy might be looked on as a manifestation of national feeling, as perhaps in one sense it was. But the arguments with which he supported his case were almost exclusively linguistic and literary, and his political ideals, as exhibited in the *De Monarchia*, far wider than anything that could be included under the concept of the nation.

The growth of nations during the Middle Ages was a purely practical development. Medieval States were dynastic and political entities, and there was no belief in any necessary connection between cultural and political ties. At the same time, although the work of the great medieval monarchies was primarily one of political consolidation, the development of political unity naturally stimulated the growth of a common language and culture, and the assimilation of alien cultural elements. There are possibly indications that language was beginning to be thought of to a certain extent as a factor in politics by the fifteenth century, but in the present state of our knowledge we cannot say more.

During the Middle Ages the political divisions of Europe were constantly changing, some centres of power rising, while others were declining or even disappearing. Provincial sentiment remained strong. The French distinguished themselves from Normans, Lorrainers or Burgundians, Gascons from French, Bretons from Normans. But the feeling of loyalty to broader political unities was increasing, and by the sixteenth century a number of recognizable nation states existed in Western Europe. The trend towards the formation of nation states had in most cases been arrested at an earlier stage in Central and Eastern Europe. Many factors contributed to this. The absence of suitable geographical barriers,[2] an excessive intermingling of alien elements; the existence of wide

---

[1] In this paragraph I have followed the interpretation of M. Handelsman, 'Le rôle de la nationalité dans l'histoire du Moyen Age', in the *Bulletin of the International Committee of Historical Sciences*, 1929, cf. pp. 237-40, 242, 247.

[2] It is to be noted that the two countries in Central Europe which were the most like geographical regions, Bohemia and Hungary, were also those in which medieval monarchies came the nearest to success in building up nation States.

divergencies in cultural level; the failure to produce a succession of strong rulers such as medieval England enjoyed, or a long and unbroken hereditary succession such as that of the French Crown; the complications resulting from the ambitions and rivalries of the Papacy and the Holy Roman Empire; the undue extent of Germanic territory, which, along with the persistence of tribalism well into the Middle Ages and the strength of centrifugal authorities, made it an impossible task, under medieval conditions, to establish an effective government for Germany as a whole; the survival of the cities in Italy – these were some of the causes of the weakness of the nation state in Central Europe. In some countries the process of building up the nation state was checked, before it had reached completion, as a result of foreign attacks. Such was the fate of Hungary and Bohemia. The Balkans, which had not been behind Western Europe in their political development during the earlier Middle Ages, suffered severely from the Ottoman conquest, which destroyed the material bases of their civilization, wiped out their old aristocracies and middle classes, and even in some cases obliterated their traditional frontiers. On the other hand, Poland fell into a condition of arrested development for internal reasons, because of the power retained by her nobles, which prevented the monarchy from completing the task of political unification.

In spite of such failures, from what has been said it may reasonably be concluded that the nations of Europe developed in, and were adapted to, a medieval political environment. This environment was rapidly changing during the fifteenth and sixteenth centuries, when the basic conditions of political life were profoundly modified both in practice and in theory. The States of the Middle Ages had not been sovereign States in the modern sense of the word; in so far as sovereignty existed, it was in the Papal claim to *plenitudo potestatis*. It has been said, with some justice if the term is used in its modern connotation, that the only State in the Middle Ages was the Church. The idea of secular sovereignty reappeared when the Middle Ages were drawing to their close. As was to be expected, the influence of the new political ideas was first felt in Italy. There, in a society of small independent States, the least medieval of medieval countries, was a situation to which they were eminently applicable. From Italy they spread over the rest of Europe, and though their influence varied from country to country, it was sufficiently widespread to constitute a real political renaissance. And since the idea of sovereignty was revived in a society in which the nation State had become the strongest form of political organization, out of this combination the new political ideal of the sovereign nation State ultimately emerged.

The rise of sovereignty was not altogether favourable to the continued growth of nation states, however. It emphasized the rights of government, and so intensified the process of unification in nation states which were already set in that path; but it militated against the development of the process where different political entities prevailed, as in the petty States of Germany and Italy, or the great dynastic empire of the Habsburgs, to which Czechs and Magyars now became subject. It also proved fatal to the smaller nations in Western Europe. Wales was absorbed politically by England, and Ireland was subjugated. Brittany came under the French Crown. Aragon was amalgamated with Castile. The sixteenth century might indeed be called the age of the breaking, rather than of the making, of nations.

The formation of nation states therefore experienced a setback at the end of the Middle Ages from which it did not recover until the nineteenth century. During the early modern period also the word 'nation' changed its significance: it lost its linguistic and acquired an almost exclusively political meaning. The possession of a separate government came to be the criterion of nationhood, and though the smaller independent states were not commonly termed nations, Vattel, in the very first sentence of his treatise on international law, assumes that State and nation are synonymous. By the eighteenth century, in fact, most of the cultural and linguistic significance had been emptied out of the word 'nation'. It merely meant the State considered in respect of the ruled rather than the ruler. The Dictionary of the Académie Française as late as 1878 was still giving as its primary definition of the nation, 'the totality of persons born or naturalized in a country and living under a single government'.

Already, however, by the end of the Middle Ages, there existed a number of nation states in which political unity was combined with a greater or less degree of cultural unity. The history of Europe is unique in that nowhere else, and at no other time, has such a considerable group of nation states survived in geographical contiguity and close association with one another over a period of many centuries. This persistence of the political divisions of Europe is to be explained primarily by the absence of any power capable of uniting the whole Continent under its military dominion. Lacking such a unifying force, the peoples of Europe, instead of being assimilated to one another, grew more distinct. The unifying forces of Latin Christendom became weaker after the Reformation and the shifting of the focus of European society from the Mediterranean to the Atlantic coastline; while a further source of political cleavage was to be found in the division into Latin, German and Slav, three large groups none of which was strong enough to conquer and absorb the others.

The consequence was that European politics were kept in a perpetually unstable equilibrium on the system of balance of power. Such a result is inevitable wherever a number of independent States, none of them strong enough to establish a permanent dominion over the rest, are in continuous contact with one another. The relations of the city states of ancient Greece presented a similar situation and a similar consequence. If any State grew powerful enough to threaten the balance, sooner or later it drew on itself the enmity of a more powerful coalition. The island State of Great Britain played an essential part in the maintenance of this balance. Too small and too separate to aim at continental empire, it was at the same time protected from conquest by its naval power. In every century since the decline of the Middle Ages British power has intervened to prevent the establishment or consolidation of European hegemony by a dominant military power. The advantages and disadvantages of this system of balance, and of the survival in Europe of so many independent States, are both obviously great, but need not be discussed here.

Out of this division of Europe into a large number of independent States there gradually evolved the idea of a right of independence on the part of these States. Grotius and his successors in the development of international law upheld this principle, which found its most striking expression, towards the end of the eighteenth century, in the reaction against the partitions of Poland. A new factor appeared in the protests against the extinction of the Polish state, as it had in those provoked, a little earlier, by the sale of Corsica by the Genoese to the French. 'Thus', it was said of the latter, 'was a nation disposed of without its consent, like the trees on an estate.'[1]

---

[1] *Annual Register*, 1768, Historical Section, i, p. 2. It is possible that Burke wrote this; if he did not, at least it was written under his close supervision.

'It is making fools of people', wrote Rousseau of the same episode, 'to tell them seriously that one can at one's pleasure transfer peoples from master to master, like herds of cattle, without consulting their interests or their wishes.'[1] We can see in such quotations the beginning of a new association between the idea of the political State and that of the national community, in consequence of which the idea of the nation state was at last to appear in its modern form. But to understand the significance of the development we must turn to what was a necessary concomitant to the new stage in its history, the assertion of the right of popular sovereignty, which has already entered our analysis in a different context.

The long history of representative institutions, which, like the nations themselves, are a product of the Middle Ages, may seem to contradict the attribution of a recent origin to democracy. But medieval representative institutions were extinguished in many countries, and declined in importance in practically all, when the New Monarchy of the sixteenth century appeared, and with it the later medieval or renaissance conception of sovereignty. Although in one or two States, such as England, the history of representative institutions forms an unbroken chain from the Middle Ages to the present day, their revival and extension throughout Europe in the nineteenth century was not a direct consequence of these survivals, but of the attempt at the end of the eighteenth century to create a democratic government of a new type in France. The French Revolution, as has already been suggested, must not be thought of as no more than a struggle to establish in France principles of government that already existed, although perhaps in an imperfect form, in those countries where medieval representative institutions survived. It was a revolution of a far wider compass than this would imply, a revolution not only in the institutions, but in the political ideas of the Western world. By proclaiming the principle of popular sovereignty, the French revolutionaries fundamentally altered the prevailing conception of the State. And it was through the combination of the revolutionary idea of popular sovereignty with the new importance attached to the national community that the nation state ceased to be a simple historical fact and became the subject of a theory.

The nation states of the Middle Ages, as I have said, had been the creation of the medieval monarchies, but it was also held that

[1] Rousseau, *Political Writings*, ed. C. E. Vaughan 1915, i, 340-1.

the people was an active participant in the State. This attitude of
mind, inherited by the contractual school of thought, was generally
accepted in the seventeenth and eighteenth centuries. It was maintained, in the words of Locke, that, 'Wherever, therefore, any
number of men so unite into one society, as to quit every one his
executive power of the law of nature, and to resign it to the public,
there, and there only, is a political, or civil society.'[1] The belief that
the agreement to establish a common legislature and government was
the factor which made a collection of individuals into a State was
still the prevailing view on the eve of the French Revolution, when
Sieyes defined the nation as 'a body of associates living under one
common law and represented by the same legislature'.[2] There was
then a fundamental change, however. The great achievement of
revolutionary political thought, for good or evil, was, as I have
already said, the conception of government as a manifestation of
the democratic will, and the identification of the State as sovereign
with the people. This was the meaning of Sieyes when he said that
the *tiers état* was nothing and ought to be everything; and it was
what the Constituent Assembly meant when it declared, 'Sovereignty
is one, indivisible, inalienable and imprescriptible: it belongs to the
nation'. The result was a great *translatio imperii* in reverse.

During the last century and a half, beginning with the revolt of
the American colonies, there has been a renewed wave of nation-
state making, but in place of a feudal monarchy the unifying power
has been the will of the people, or rather of the politically conscious
classes, though a major part was also played in this movement by
the military power of monarchies such as Piedmont and Prussia.
Both in the medieval and the modern periods of the formation of
nation states, the process has been mainly a political one, initial
differences of language, race or culture being of comparatively minor
account. The Americas provide many modern examples of this
fact. Belgium and South Africa belong to the same class of political
nations, of which the classic example is Switzerland.

As I have already said, however, the modern conception of the
nation did not remain purely political. A new meaning was given
it during the latter years of the eighteenth century, and one which
has affiliations with the early romantic movement and the medieval
revival. Among the manifestations of a new attitude towards the
nation were: the writing of the first national hymn of Norway and

---

[1] *Second Treatise on Civil Government*, §89.   [2] *Qu'est-ce que le tiers état?*

the first history of Norway inspired by the idea of Norwegian independence, both in 1772; the development of national ideas in the Austrian Netherlands and the adoption of the ancient name of 'Belges' to describe their inhabitants; the writing of a Finnish national poem; the demand for Parliamentary independence for Ireland, and so on.[1] Many other examples might be found of the increased significance of the idea of the nation in this period, which was also that in which Herder, the best-known and the most influential of the prophets of nationality, was writing. Herder had absorbed the humanitarian and liberal ideas of the Enlightenment, and he saw no contradiction between these and the idea of a world divided into cultural entities held together by a common language, that is, nations. But as the nation came increasingly to be conceived as the real unit, it became gradually the sole possessor of rights, and the individual and *his* rights began to fade away.

There is no need to summarize here the well-known history of the nationalist movement. The point to be emphasized is that whereas before the French Revolution there had been no necessary connection between the State as a political unit and the idea of a nationality as a cultural one, these two elements were combined as a single conception in the phase that now opened in the history of the nation state.

Although nation states had existed for centuries, before the nineteenth century no specific relationship had been posited between culture or language and the political State. Some States were more or less culturally united, others were composed of culturally disparate elements. The matter was not one that was regarded as of fundamental importance. It did not occur to anyone to criticize the Habsburg Empire on the ground that its peoples spoke different languages, had different cultures, and were only united by their allegiance to a common dynasty. For the ancien régime one State was as good as another. In the definition of the State, communal ties, and all aspects of social life that were not narrowly and directly governmental, played no part. The State was a juristic and territorial concept. It was the land and its ruler the lord of the land. The new idea of the nation changed all this: in October 1789 the 'roi de France et de Navarre' became 'roi des Français', and during the next half-century the nation state entered on a new stage in its history.

[1] Cf. Halvdan Koht, 'L'esprit national et l'idée de la souveraineté du peuple', in *Bulletin of the International Committee of Historical Sciences*, 1929.

Hitherto it had been an historical fact: now it became the embodiment of the theory of nationalism, which assumed the identification of cultural and political communities in a universal system of nation states.

As an agency of destruction the theory of nationalism proved one of the most potent that even modern society has known. Empires or States that were not homogeneous in culture and language were undermined from within or assaulted from without; nation after nation broke away from its traditional allegiance. There was less success in the task of rebuilding a stable system of States on the ruins of older political structures.

An illuminating example of the consequences of the attempt to fuse together the political and cultural ideas of the nation is provided by Hungary, which was by the end of the nineteenth century the solitary survivor in Central Europe of the medieval nation states of the type of England and France. Her tragedy was that, as a result of Turkish and Habsburg domination, she had never been able to push the process of nation-making to completion throughout her territories, and her unassimilated peoples were consequently caught up in the nationalist movement of the nineteenth century. In place of the slow but successful assimilation that had gone on in previous centuries a desperate policy of compulsory Magyarization was now adopted, which only accelerated the onset of disaster. The fatal conflict of two different ideas of the nation comes to the surface in the Hungarian Law of Nationalities of 1868, which declares: 'All citizens of Hungary ... form a single nation – the indivisible unitary Magyar nation – to which all citizens of the country irrespective of nationality, belong.'[1] At a time when the other peoples of Central Europe were struggling to convert their cultural nationalities into politically independent States, Hungary was still attempting to force her way in the opposite direction, from political to cultural unity.

During the nineteenth century the belief in the necessary identification of cultural or linguistic nation and political state obtained widespread acceptance, though among the voices raised in protest against the new nationalist gospel were those of Proudhon, Le Play, Bakunin, Lecky and Acton. The conception of the nation State which was embodied in nineteenth-century nationalism reached its highest point in Europe in 1919 and the following years, and already it was spreading to Asia and Africa. Only in the area dominated by the

[1] C. A. Macartney, *National States and National Minorities*, p. 119.

Soviet Empire has the tide of nationalism been dammed; and this may prove only a temporary setback.

At different times different institutions have embodied the political ideals of men. We need not here pass judgment on the historic process which has at one time fixed men's hearts on the city or the nation, at another on a civilization or an empire. The truth is that while loyalty to the community in which for the time being are enshrined the highest aspirations of social organization is a perennial quality in human nature, the object of that loyalty has varied widely from age to age. There is no reason to believe that the combination of cultural and political unity in the idea of the nation state is the last, or that it is the highest, of those mortal gods to which men have sometimes paid undue adoration. That it is still the dominant one there can be no doubt.

To the democratic idea of popular sovereignty, which emerged with such startling suddenness into practical politics in the second half of the eighteenth century, was thus added the emotional force of nationalism. In the cause of national sovereignty, individual liberty and all the other interests of the individual were to be ruthlessly sacrificed. Here was a new force, which had not entered into the calculations of the men of the Enlightenment, and before which their liberal ideals were to struggle for existence and often to struggle unavailingly.

XXI

The Idea of Sovereignty

To treat democracy and nationalism as major causes of the decay of the ideals of the Enlightenment, and of what from that point of view would seem an ethical recession, may at first sight seem paradoxical. It will probably be agreed without difficulty that, however far back we may trace their antecedents, they emerge as leading influences in European society only at the end of the eighteenth century; and also that, if they are judged by the immediate and later historical developments associated with them, their practical consequences involve a decline from the standards of the Enlightenment. On the other hand, what could be more reasonable than that a nation should be free from what it regards as alien domination, or that a people should choose its own government and change that government if it has serious grounds for dissatisfaction? Are not such views, it may be said, rather a natural development from, than a contradiction of, the political ideas inherent in the Enlightenment? This is a fair argument, and it leads to the conclusion that the trouble was not in the ideas themselves so much as in the fact that they were put into practice in the setting provided by the great sovereign States of Europe. Here, it may be suggested, was the reason why the Enlightenment, which had won its tactical battle by 1789, was to be defeated in the grand strategy of the campaign. What seemed like victory over the despotic monarchies of old Europe – a victory beginning in France and gradually, in the course of the nineteenth century, extending to all the other nations of Europe – was in another sense a disguised defeat; for monarchical despotism was to be replaced by a Leviathan of far more formidable proportions and fatal consequences.

The turning-point can be detected in the period of the French Revolution. The consequences of the Revolution were so momentous for Europe at the time, and for the whole world subsequently, that it has cast a shadow over the whole of modern history. It split the nations vertically and forced men to declare themselves for or against it, and so acquired in their minds a unity and a personality which even historians have taken for granted. A more detailed study of the

Revolution has revealed its multifarious variety, but even writers of monographs on revolutionary history have most often been unable to resist the temptation to speak of it as if it were essentially a unity, the expression, fundamentally, of one great principle. As to what that principle was, of course, there has been much disagreement.

Yet an inherent contradiction in the ideas of the revolutionaries can be detected from the beginning, and in its fundamental document. The *Declaration of the Rights of Man and the Citizen* is, by and large, an expression of the ideals of the Enlightenment. Like the *philosophes* it combines natural rights with utility, as can be seen in the very first article:

> Men are born and remain free and equal in rights. Social distinctions can only be based on general utility.

Again, the *Declaration* asserts the Lockian natural rights of 'liberty, property, security, and resistance to oppression', and it defines liberty as —

> consisting in being able to do anything that does not harm others; thus the exercise of the natural rights of each man has for its only limits those that ensure to other members of society the enjoyment of the same rights.

Such liberal rights as freedom from arbitrary imprisonment, freedom of opinion 'even religious', no taxation without representation, and so on, are asserted. All this is the pure milk of the Enlightenment. Only one clause reveals to us the presence of a different tradition: this is article 3:

> The source of all sovereignty resides essentially in the nation, no body and no individual can possess authority that does not clearly derive from it.

> Sovereignty is one, indivisible, inalienable and imprescriptible: it belongs to the nation.

The greatest of all the revolutionary pamphleteers, Sieyes, won his success not by any appeal to the ideals of the Enlightenment but because he grasped firmly what was to be the new gospel, and proclaimed the sovereignty of the nation.

In simple terms this meant the transference to the people or nation of the rights of sovereignty that had formerly been claimed on behalf of the king. To see what these were we need not look to the despotisms of Central and Eastern Europe. The weak monarchy of Louis XV was as capable of proclaiming the principle in uncompromising language, even at the nadir of its actual political power. In the famous 'séance de la flagellation' of 1766, Louis XV thus addressed his parlements:

> It is in my person alone that the sovereign power resides ... It is from me alone that my courts derive their existence and authority; and the plenitude of this authority, which they exercise only in my name, remains always with me ... It is to me alone that the legislative power appertains without any dependence and without any division ... The whole public order emanates from me ...[1]

By the last quarter of the eighteenth century this idea of absolute sovereignty, despite the criticisms of enlightened thought, was too firmly rooted in the States of continental Europe — and also too valuable a bulwark for any government, established or revolutionary — to be abandoned: it could merely be transferred, and this is what the Revolution did. From a practical point of view, also, there were reasons why a reforming party would not wish to abandon the idea of sovereignty. The enemy that the Third Estate in France saw before it was not the monarchy, but the noblesse, the Church, the parlements and other selfish, sectional corporations. The contractual theory of government was lacking in appeal to the Third Estate, for it had been adopted, in support of their claims to the revival of a long-lost authority, by the noblesse and parlements. The officials and professional men, whose chief desire was practical reform and the improvement of their own status, and who constituted the dominant element in the revolutionary movement, looked first to the King to introduce the social changes they desired. When they were disappointed in this hope they proclaimed the reforms they wanted in the name of the people or nation, to which they transferred the idea of sovereignty.

This was a fairly rapid development in the last years of the ancien régime and the opening phase of the Revolution. Its historical causes are easily comprehensible; but the result was incompatible

[1] J. Flammermont et M. Tourneaux (eds.), *Remontrances du Parlement de Paris*, 1895, Séance royale, dite de la flagellation, 3 mars 1766, ii, 557-8.

with both the individualist natural rights and the utilitarianism of the political theory of the Enlightenment, which were embodied in the Declaration of Rights. The Revolution reinstated political authority as an absolute right, though exercised now in the name of the people instead of that of God. But as one of the revolutionaries observed later: 'Quand on fait pour Dieu et pour le peuple, on ne croit jamais faire ni trop ni mal.' The Revolution set up its government on the basis of will, and allowed for only one will in society — that, either individual or collective, which could establish, by whatever means, its claim to represent the nation. All other wills were partial, selfish, evil, and therefore to be suppressed.

One further step was needed. Because sovereignty is an exercise of will, and will is assumed to be indivisible, for its realization something more than an association of individuals under one Government was required; society had to be conceived not merely as a community held together by a combination of individual interests, but as a unity greater than its component parts, which henceforth were to find their fulfilment in, and if necessary be sacrificed to, this greater unity. The idea of nationality provided the emotional bond that was needed to turn popular sovereignty into a practical political force. Popular sovereignty thus became national sovereignty, government was fused with people by the emotional heat of nationalism, and the rational, individualist, utilitarian ideals of the Enlightenment were consumed in the process.

XXII

Idealism and Pessimism

THE crucial period for the development of the new political ideas, which emerged with such startling suddenness in the opening stages of the French Revolution, must have been, one would think, the decade or so immediately preceding the Revolution. Curiously, however, although many books and pamphlets on the problems of government appeared then, those calling for the reform of social evils were much more numerous than those that dealt with the question of government.[1] Even among the political writings, declares Mornet, for one which shows a little independence there are three which are completely loyal and politically orthodox.[2] In none of them do we find a theoretical justification of the idea of national or popular sovereignty; and this is only what should have been expected, because, though the idea of sovereignty has had a long history, popular sovereignty and nationalism have been practical rather than theoretical developments. Attempts to justify either of them, such as the *Qu'est-ce que le Tiers État* of Sieyes, amount to little more than an assertion of a claim to political power without any serious theoretical argument.

That this absence of justification is not accidental can be shown by a rapid survey of possible theoretical positions. Sovereignty based on divine right had been thoroughly discredited, and apart from this it was essentially bound up with the idea of monarchy: short of a return to the tribal religion of the Old Testament (something like this was yet to come) it could not be attributed to a people or nation. Secondly, the assertion of an absolute right to power, such as was implicit in the idea of popular or national sovereignty, was not theoretically compatible with the dominant utilitarianism. Thirdly, the older principle of natural rights was inseparable from individualism and could not be reconciled with any political doctrine which concentrated all rights in society or the State. In so far as popular or national sovereignty was advocated, then, by so much was the attempt at a moral justification of political

[1] D. Mornet, *Origines intellectuelles de la Révolution française*, 1933, p. 249.
[2] Ibid., p. 217.

power abandoned, though it was only in the twentieth century, as was suggested much earlier in this book, that this extreme was finally reached and political theory completely disintegrated. Before this, relics of earlier political ideas survived, however illogically, to provide a semblance of ethical justification for a system of nationalism with which they were essentially inconsistent.

The rise of the idea of national sovereignty, then, must be treated as primarily a practical development. But this is not to say that there was no subsequent attempt to bolster up the ethics of the nation state by substituting a new system of political values for that of the Enlightenment. It took the form of the German Idealist school of philosophy. Anticipations may possibly be found in Rousseau and Burke, but neither of these abandoned the essentially individualist ethics of the eighteenth century. The real transition from the Enlightenment to Idealism was effected by Kant.

The contents of Kant's ethics are the enlightened ideals of the eighteenth century, but their philosophical basis and methodological framework belong to a very different order of ideas. Whereas Rousseau, and even Burke, started with the individual, Kant starts with Reason. Where they envisaged society as existing to promote the interests of its members and founded on this its moral justification, for Kant the basis of society is the principle of disinterested obedience to a moral law. In morals this means obedience to a law which we prescribe ourselves, but in politics, Kant knows, coercion is inevitable; in the State obedience to the moral law therefore means obedience to authority. The division of law into natural and positive is now abandoned: there is for Kant only one law, the check on which is the requirement of its own nature that it shall be assumed to act rationally.[1] Its sanction comes from the State, and the authority of the State must embody the realization of the idea of Right; but this takes into account no utilitarian considerations of the actual consequences to the individual. Kant expressly attacks the idea of the 'welfare State' – i.e. the State directed to the well-being of its members. We are far removed from the political theory of the Enlightenment when it can be said, as it is by Kant:

If, ... under a certain actual state of the law, a people should conclude that the continuance of that law would probably take away their happiness, what would they have to do? Would it

[1] Cf. Gierke, *Development of Political Theory*, p. 321.

not be a duty to resist the law? The answer can only be that the people should do nothing but obey.[1]

This is specifically to exclude all right of resistance to tyranny. To quote Kant's own words again:

All resistance to the Sovereign Legislative Power, every kind of instigation to bring the discontent of the subjects into active form, and rebellion or insurrection of every degree and kind, constitute the highest and most punishable crimes in the commonwealth; for they would destroy its very foundation ... Even if the Supreme Power, or the Sovereign as its agent, were to violate the original contract, and thereby in the judgment of the subject to lose the right of making the laws, yet as the Government has been empowered to proceed even thus tyrannically, no right of resistance can be allowed to the subject as a power antagonistic to the State.[2]

The moral philosophy of Kant is, of course, much more subtle than can be indicated by these brief references, but its political tendency should be sufficiently obvious.

When we move on to Fichte we find a much greater concentration of attention on politics, and an abandonment of most of the cherished ideals of the Enlightenment. For Fichte there can be no law except the law of the State: Natural Law is now not merely dead, but buried.[3] Economics, education, religion, must be controlled by and directed in the exclusive interest of the State. Separation of powers is ruled out. Finally, Fichte concludes:

Looking at the thing as it is in truth we find that the individual does not exist; that he cannot count for anything, but must disappear completely; and that the group alone exists and it alone must be considered as existent.[4]

We take a long pace forward again with what has been called the 'political Protestantism' of Schliermacher, a pastor from a deeply religious family, who carried the national idea to the point at which

[1] *The Principles of Political Right*, 1793; in Kant's *Principles of Politics*, ed. W. Hastie, 1891, pp. 47-8.
[2] Ibid., p. 50.
[3] Cf. R. Aris, *History of Political Thought in Germany from 1789 to 1815*, 1936, ch. iii.
[4] H. C. Engelbrecht, *J. G. Fichte*, 1933, p. 85.

the State could be conceived as an organic unity.[1] And from this we can move on to Hegel and Marx and all the horrors of the nineteenth century. By now the world of the Enlightenment is left far behind, and its optimistic hopes, which still continued to dominate practical politics in Western Europe, were gradually being swamped in the more forward-looking minds by a mounting wave of pessimism. This needs further consideration, for it is closely connected with the decline of the ideals of the Enlightenment.

Underlying the literature, art, ethics, philosophy, in fact the whole practical and theoretical activity of each age or civilization, there is always some world-outlook or philosophy of life, often not present consciously in the minds of those who nevertheless base their whole thought and action on its presuppositions. Such a world-outlook, or *Weltanschauung*, may be classified according to various principles. Among these one of the most fundamental is the distinction between the optimistic and the pessimistic interpretations of the world. On the whole the world-outlook of Western civilization has been optimistic, but it is quite possible for a civilization to take a fundamentally pessimistic view of life. By pessimism I mean, roughly, an attitude of mind which condemns the whole process of human life, regarding it as essentially evil both in its nature and its end. The medieval outlook was conditionally pessimistic, but fundamentally optimistic; for while it regarded this life as a time of trial, and human nature as vitiated by Original Sin, it also took the trials and torments of this wicked world as a necessary stage in the process of salvation. The end, therefore, was in a sense good. After the rise of humanism in the Renaissance the optimistic interpretation came to prevail even for life in this world, and optimism rose to its climax in the eighteenth century. But at the end of the century a contrary current of pessimism made its appearance; it was to become one of the outstanding characteristics of European thought during the next century and a half, until, in more recent times, it developed into a total rejection of the established values of the Enlightenment.

Pessimism was a feature of the development of romantic thought from the end of the eighteenth century. Implicit in romantic writings from Rousseau to Dostoevsky, it became explicit in the world of practice in our own time. The creative spirit of the great romantics turned in the end, like the volcanic glow of the Wagnerian *Nibelun-*

[1] R. Aris, ch. x.

genlied, to a consuming fire; the struggle and torment of *Sturm und Drang* found peace in death.

The unqualified pessimism of many of the greatest writers and thinkers of the nineteenth century is in striking opposition to the qualified optimism of the previous age. It forms an equally remarkable contrast to the concrete achievements of the period. The former of these two contradictions, however, helps to explain the latter. It may be suggested that the practical life of one age tends to reflect the theoretical achievements of the previous age. Such theorists as Locke and Montesquieu, Diderot, Voltaire, Adam Smith, Bentham, anticipated and laid the foundations of nineteenth-century progress, by the extent of which their achievement can be judged. Voltaire's optimism is admittedly restricted to 'Il faut cultiver notre jardin': but the nineteenth century took him literally and followed his advice, not without success.

The intellectual roots of the twentieth century are very different. The modern mind is essentially the romantic mind, and it begins with the first man in whom the romantic spirit shines through clearly, Jean-Jacques Rousseau. In Rousseau, although the infectious optimism of his age was continually asserting itself, there was a more personal strain of pessimism, which provided the model for romantic gloom and foreshadowed the deeper and more tragic outlook of some of the greatest minds of the nineteenth century.

The first stage of the pessimistic movement, however, we may pass over rapidly. The pessimism of Rousseau is mainly important for the history of literature. Romantic melancholy had no great significance. *The Castle of Otranto* is doubtless an ancestor of the American horror comic, but neither is more than a symptom. *Sturm und Drang,* with its conventions of murder and sudden death, eternal friendships and swift betrayals, of revolt against social bonds, conflict of loyalties and insoluble dilemmas, achieved melodrama rather than tragedy. Byronic lawlessness, the revolt of Cain against judgment, the defiance of the powers of good, remained a pose and never became a philosophy of life. Ossianic thunders were a piece of stage-craft that was soon exposed. The nostalgia of Chateaubriand only led back to the Catholic Church and the Ministère des Affaires Etrangères. The blue flower of romanticism withered in the salons and literary circles of reactionary France and Germany. Victor Hugo was left to proclaim the romantic faith to an unromantic generation, one too concerned with material gain to worry much about spiritual loss. Literary romanticism, in fact, exercised an extensive rather than a profound effect on the European mind.

It was the philosophers and not the poets who brought back the tragic sense of life. To a certain extent the philosopher who began the whole process was the cheerful, common-sense Scotsman, David Hume; for it was Hume, as has been suggested above, who undermined the foundations on which the eighteenth century had built its view of the world. The significance of Hume in the history of European thought is now generally recognized. What he did to it has already been indicated, but may bear a brief repetition. The essence of his philosophy was the conviction that the fundamental beliefs of mankind could not be established intellectually by the methods of philosophy. He did not therefore deny them, but concluded: 'So much the worse for philosophy.' Similarly he overthrew, and with even greater ease, the current Lockian empiricism. Locke had asserted that all our ideas come from the outside world by way of sense data. Hume pertinently asked how in this case we could distinguish a true from a false idea, and answered — only because we can believe it. He concentrated his attention in particular on the difficulties presented by the conception of causality, and gave reasons for holding that although it is essential to coherent thought about the world, it is none the less not susceptible of rational proof. The basic assumptions on which we conduct our lives, he concluded, cannot be established by philosophical argument: they must be based on feeling or belief, not on reason. In the field of morals Hume's critique was equally destructive of accepted ideas. He could find no rational basis for moral action: he did not therefore resort to the moral scepticism of a Mandeville, but concluded that the basis of moral behaviour must lie elsewhere than in the reason.

From Hume it would be possible to pass directly to some of the most important developments of contemporary philosophical thinking. But the European mind failed to see the positive aspects of Hume's scepticism, took it to represent a purely destructive criticism, and sought a way round it. Kant provided one by refusing to admit the validity of Hume's premises. Objective reality, the thing-in-itself, he agreed, lay outside the scope of the human intellect. But the human mind remained. Let it reconcile itself to the limitations imposed by its own nature, accept the inescapable fact that it can only know reality through the medium of its own operations, and seek for truth and goodness therein. Of the relation of our mental processes to ultimate truth and absolute goodness we can know nothing.

Already, it will be seen, the thin edge of pessimism has been inserted, but Kant himself was too much a man of his century to press it home. The structure of his thought was new, but its content was old. When he looked into his mind he discovered therein the values that the optimistic, eighteenth-century world outlook had already implanted, and it did not occur to him that subsequent thinkers might find radically different values.

On the foundations laid by Kant, Hegel created a great and comprehensive philosophical system, taking the form of the dialectical evolution in which all reality was encompassed – all reality past and present, that is, for the future did not enter into Hegel's philosophy. The subjective character of Kantian thought was disguised but not destroyed by Hegel, and from this subjective element it logically followed that the development of reality was bound to come to an end with the mind that thought it. The progress of the dialectic culminated and ended in the Hegelian exposition of the nature of the Absolute. With Hegel history concluded, and it only remained for the philosopher to sit in judgment upon it. 'The owl of Minerva only takes to flight when the shades of twilight have already fallen.'

Hidden under the complacency of Hegelian idealism the principle of pessimism was at work. The decisive step was taken by a professed philosopher of pessimism, Schopenhauer. Starting from the Kantian belief that the thing-in-itself is unknowable, he held:

> However much we investigate, we can never reach anything but images amd names. We are like a man who goes round a castle seeking in vain for an entrance, and sometimes sketching the façades.[1]

But while Kant, living in the eighteenth century, had believed that the world of phenomena that we know is rational and good, Schopenhauer took it to be irrational and evil, because a transient and unreal world:

> Every individual, every human being and his course of life, is but another short dream of the endless spirit of nature, of the persistent will to live; is only another fleeting form, which

[1] Schopenhauer, *Selections*, ed. D. H. Parker, 1928, *The World as Will and Idea*, ii, 17,

it carelessly sketches on its infiite page, space and time: allows to remain for a time so short that it vanishes into nothing in comparison with these, and then obliterates to make new room.[1]

The highest good is to escape for ever from these shadows that surround us:

> How blessed the life of a man must be whose will is silenced, not merely for a moment, as in the enjoyment of the beautiful, but for ever ... Life and its forms now pass before him as a fleeting illusion, as a light morning dream before half-waking eyes, the real world already shining through it so that it can no longer deceive.[2]

At the same time as Schopenhauer was leading philosophy towards absolute pessimism, romantic thought, as we have seen, was moving in the same direction on more purely emotional grounds. Romantic pessimism also finds its most intense development in Germany. Many examples might be given, but the *Hymns to the Night* of Novalis afford as good an illustration as one could wish of the ecstatic cult of pessimism that was growing up in romantic literature. Night, love and death are the constant themes of Novalis, invoked in a mixed spirit of eroticism and religion.

At first, the strong dose of pessimism that had been injected into the Western mind proved ineffective. Gradually, however, its influence began to be felt, spreading wider and deeper until it had profoundly affected the whole structure of Western thought. It is not necessary here to follow the process step by step. Philosophers like Nietzsche and von Hartmann, theology with Kierkegaard, writers like Pushkin, Leopardi, Ibsen, Tolstoy, Dostoevsky, all contributed to the ever-swelling current. Literature, by the end of the century, was submerged under the mounting wave of depression. Baudelaire and Verlaine, Maupassant, Swinburne, Wilde, Chekhov, d'Annunzio, Mann, Wassermann, Gorki, Gide, raise the green sickness of the fin de siècle sometimes to the point of tragedy and carry it on to our own day, while Spengler popularized the pessimistic outlook as a grandiose historical system, which Professor Toynbee continued in a modified form.

Of the existence and scope of the pessimistic movement, which

---

[1] *The World as Will and Idea*, iv, 58, p. 238.
[2] Ibid., iv, 68, p. 276.

sapped the foundations of the optimism of the Enlightenment, there can be no doubt. But what is the explanation of it, for what we have given so far has been a description but not an explanation? Indeed, has it any explanation, or is it merely a great historical movement that the historian must record without attempting to understand its causes? I propose to consider a few possible explanations.

In the modern world the power of the Churches and the general influence of the religious outlook on the world has undoubtedly declined. One explanation of pessimism is that it may be the result of discarding the prop that the human mind had hitherto possessed in religion. Man, it is said, left to himself, and deprived of the hope that religion offers him, becomes the victim of despair. This is a tempting theory: it provides a simple explanation and an easy remedy. It is so facile a solution, in fact, that it arouses one's suspicions.

The first difficulty to be noted in this hypothesis is that the Enlightenment of the eighteenth century, in which the optimistic world view reached its height, was itself marked by a strong hostility to religious institutions, and is certainly not famous for its religious feeling. On the other hand, Hegel in his philosophical theory came very close to erecting a religious system of his own; the inspiration of Schopenhauer was drawn in part from the classics of Hindu religion; and many of the greatest minds of nineteenth-century pessimism were profoundly religious. Bearing such facts in mind it would even be possible to argue that the pessimism of nineteenth-century thought was the result not of the loss but of the recovery of religious feeling. An association between a religious attitude of mind and pessimism would indeed not be unnatural, for the condemning of this life, which is the essence of the pessimistic world-outlook, may arise from a consciousness of its imperfections compared with some other-worldly standard. On the whole, however, we are hardly justified in concluding that the pessimistic trend of modern thought is to be attributed either to the loss or to the recovery of the religious outlook.

The common feature in both hypotheses may have more truth in it: pessimism may arise because of a conflict between the ideal and the actual. Considered in relation to individual psychology, the typical situation which produces an attitude of absolute pessimism is that of feeling in an impasse, caught as it were like a rat in a trap, with inexorable fate slowly closing in and no way of escape, no possibility even of putting up a serious fight. There may have been something like this in the mind of the Western world, to explain why the pessimistic outlook was acceptable to such large sections of its intellectual and literary classes, if an impasse, such as would be the natural result of an apparently insoluble conflict between irreconcilable facts or principles, existed.

Can such a conflict be discovered in nineteenth-century society? The obvious one is that between the optimistic world-view inherited from the eighteenth century, along with the hope of material advance offered by scientific and industrial development and the general spread of liberal and humanitarian ideals, on the one hand, and the actual political and economic realities of reaction, unemployment, class struggle, war and revolution, on the other. This dichotomy certainly helped to bring about the downfall of the optimistic outlook; but it does not solve our problem, for it has to be shown that it was a cause rather than a result, especially since the seeds of the pessimistic outlook had been sown at the end of the eighteenth century, before this particular conflict had developed. In fact, moreover, the nineteenth century was an age of unprecedented material progress.

A more deeply seated cleavage in the modern mind goes back behind the nineteenth century to the very beginnings of the romantic movement. The essential principles of romantic thought can be summed up in the terms, primitivism and subjectivism – back to nature and back to human nature. The most marked features of the development of modern society, on the contrary, have been an increasingly complex and 'artificial' social life, and an increasing reduction of the individual to a mere unit in a vast industrial system. The more Western man sought for nature, the further away his society moved from the natural and the unsophisticated. At the same time, the more intensely subjective his thought became, the more he lost confidence in his individual initiative. There is evidently something in this consideration, though we must not push it too far.

At the same time, a conflict developed not only between the ideal and the actual, but also within the realm of theory itself. The ideals which the nineteenth century inherited from the eighteenth, although influenced by the rise of subjectivism and primitivism, were still essentially rational. The greatest blow to the optimistic world view was delivered by the rise of irrationalism. The eighteenth century was optimistic because its aims were limited and by definition attainable. Pessimism, it may be said, is the logical consequence of unqualified irrationalism. The importance of this consideration arises from the fact that the primitivism and subjectivism of the romantic movement led almost irresistibly away from reason and faith in human nature, and so provided an appropriate setting for a pessimistic philosophy of life. They both tended to produce hostility to reason and a cult of the irrational elements in man and society. The romantic substitution of emotion for reason, along with the philosophy of pessimism, found its fullest expression in German romantic thought, and the religious traditions of Germany provided the anti-rational movement with a peculiarly fertile soil. Catholicism and Calvinism both allowed some part to the rational element in human nature, but in Lutheranism there was a strong strain of mysticism and hostility to reason. For Luther the heart of religion was the personal religious experience, with which Reason — 'diese Hure' — had nothing to do: the foundations of Faith were subjective and non-rational. The natural tendency of Lutheran thought was for the act of believing to become more important than what one believed. As Troeltsch put it, the idea of faith triumphed over the content of faith. In consequence the rational element in religion tended to disappear. The same attitude of mind was reflected in the general tendency to regard reason as negative and destructive, and emotion as positive and creative. Philosophy and religion thus united to undermine the rational world-outlook of the eighteenth century, and therefore its optimism.

This, wrote Ortega y Gasset in the 'thirties of the present century, is the new thing, the 'right not to be reasonable', 'the reason of unreason'.[1] But it was not so new as he thought. The shutters were pulled down on the human mind not in the twentieth century, but when the *fiat lux* of the Enlightenment was repudiated. If the eighteenth century was the age of reason, the nineteenth was the age of old faiths revived and new ones — Jehovah's Witnesses, Christian Science, Communism, Latter-Day Saints and innumerable lesser ones — created. Philosophical idealism was itself a kind of faith in metaphysical clothes. And above all others there was the secular faith of nationalism.

---

[1] Ortega y Gasset, *The Revolt of the Masses*, trans. 1932, p. 80.

PART FIVE

CONCLUSION

XXIII

The Moral Crisis of the Twentieth Century

To attribute prime importance, as the argument of this book implies, to theoretical trends mainly apparent in philosophy, science and literature, will seem to some a distortion of the true proportions of history; and it would be wrong to suggest that there were no other factors involved both in the rise and decline of the Enlightenment. A movement so completely initiated and fashioned by an intellectual élite is hardly conceivable in a society of feudal barons and serfs, for example, or in the absence of a class with sufficient leisure to devote itself to disinterested inquiry. The mutual influence of different States or nations, with differing policies, social patterns, religions and ideals, was a fructifying force which could not have operated in a closed civilization lacking such varieties of behaviour and belief. The subsequent rise of the sovereignty of the State was facilitated, if not made unavoidable, by the pressure of economic problems resulting from the colossal and unprecedented growth of population, beginning in Western Europe, which may well be considered the basic fact in modern history. The ideas of sovereignty and of the nation state became immensely more menacing when they were applied not to the comparatively small, unpopulous, and by modern standards rudimentarily governed, States of the eighteenth century, but to the leviathans of the modern world. It is in these, and above all in the social and political patterns characteristic of Fascist, Nazi and Communist totalitarianisms, that are to be seen the most patent manifestation of the problem of inhumanity, with which this inquiry began.

But these patterns are intimately associated with changes in ideas. To say that they have justified the pessimism which was such a marked trend in nineteenth-century thought, in striking contrast to that of the previous century, would be true; and it would also be fair to observe that the new ideas of the nineteenth century played an important part in bringing about this very justification of their own pessimism. The new trend of ideas, and new social forces arising at the end of the eighteenth century, together swept Western society into a harsher climate, in which the ideals of the Enlightenment could not but wither.

To speak of the strength of the forces which opposed the Enlightenment is, however, to imply the existence of weaknesses and limitations in the Enlightenment itself, and the picture would be incomplete if no mention were made of these. The most obvious is its geographical limitation. The theory of sovereignty may have developed in Western Europe and flowered in the Bourbon monarchy of Louis XIV, but it was never unqualified or unchallenged even there. Farther east, under Habsburg, Hohenzollern and Romanov, uninfluenced, or only superficially influenced, by the moderating tendencies in Western society, more ruthless despotisms prevailed, which remained fundamentally unaffected by such stray beams of enlightened thought as penetrated their darkness. The Enlightenment of the seventeenth and eighteenth centuries, as we have described it, was confined to France, the Low Countries, some of the Swiss cantons, Great Britain and its American colonies, and to a certain extent Scandinavia, with a minor influence on a small educated class in Spain, Italy and Germany. It never really crossed the *limes Germanici* or became translated into German. The Slav world remained almost untouched and the extra-European world completely immune.

On the other hand, within strict geographical limits, and if we judge the Enlightenment by something more modest than world-wide success, we must admit that where it took root its influence was lasting. Its tolerant, liberal, scientific, reforming ideals have survived in those nations of Western Europe, and their overseas extensions, where they first became influential; and the great totalitarian dictatorships which shortly dominated the world now seem less the portentous anticipation of the future than the last monstrous survivals of an earlier age.

Within a limited geographical environment the Enlightenment has been justified of its children. The progress of scientific knowledge and technological invention has vindicated the methods of those who founded modern science and carried discovery far beyond their highest hopes; and as the realm of science has expanded so that of superstition has contracted. Toleration of religious, and even of irreligious, opinion is now an accepted principle, and religion itself has been purged of many of its grosser elements. The zeal for persecuting and burning those of a different faith, if still latent, is not allowed to take practical form. Freedom of thought and expression is subject to increasingly few restrictions. Liberal political ideals are widely accepted and the arbitrary element in government has been greatly reduced. The law is now directed much more to the protection than to the suppression of the individual. It is almost universally accepted that the object of government is utilitarian, to promote the welfare of all members of society. An hereditary system of privilege is much less dominant in society, and what Burke called 'that unbought grace of life' is no longer the monopoly of a caste. Jeremy Bentham, if he could see his country a century and a quarter after his death could take pride in the achievement of his disciples. Voltaire would find the struggle against cruelty an unending one, but the victories of humanitarianism notable. Locke and Rousseau would see education still regarded as the key to a good society.

If this seems an idealized picture, it will be more impressive if we compare it with the realities of the age in which the men of the Enlightenment worked. Yet we must admit that it does not quite carry conviction. The pessimistic spirit still prevails in contemporary society, and not only because of the fact of war and the menace of nuclear destruction. Plague was an equally ever-present menace to an earlier generation, and with the further knowledge that if no human choice could let it loose on society, none could restrain it; but it did not inhibit a basic optimism. The Enlightenment, it may be said, was a greater age than ours, because it was making the effort to create, with great hopes and without overriding fears, the civilization that we seem to be trying to destroy. This is a reason for pessimism. Another explanation offered for the decline of the optimistic spirit is that the ideals developed by an intellectual élite look rather different when they have become the heritage of the masses. But enlightened Europe, even if it despised the canaille, believed in the universal validity of its ideas, and therefore could not have consistently accepted this explanation. It would, I believe, have been pleased to find how many of its aspirations could be adopted by the majority of the population.

The real explanation of the contemporary malaise, I suggest, is none of these. Nor is it a mere survival of Wagnerian gloom. Even the cult of irrationality is not quite adequate to account for it. An explanation of the conflict between enlightened hopes and the realities of practical politics has been offered by the American theologian, Reinhold Niebuhr, which should be considered at this point, since it is one of the few serious and influential discussions of the problem of ethics in our time, and it also offers, I believe, an explanation of the pessimistic spirit. For Niebuhr the conflict between actual political behaviour and the moral consciousness, of which we are uneasily aware, exemplifies that deeper conflict between 'moral man' and 'immoral society' in which, according to him, lies the universal and tragic dilemma of mankind. To use his own words:

> The inevitable hypocrisy, which is associated with all of the collective activities of the human race, springs chiefly from this source: that individuals have a moral code which makes the action of collective man an outrage to their conscience.[1]

The tragedy of the human spirit, he believes, is 'its inability to conform its collective life to its individual ideals': 'Our contemporary culture, he writes, 'fails to realize the power, extent and persistence of group egoism in human relations.'[2]

What Niebuhr argues is that there are three different levels of moral behaviour: the standards we recognize in our relations as individual to individual are attenuated in collective actions within our society, and vanish in relations between societies. He takes this conflict of ethical standards to be – to use current jargon – a universal human predicament, and one from which there is no escape. If his position is a valid one, no other explanation for contemporary pessimism need be sought, and there can be no solution to a universal and insoluble problem.

The first point to be noticed, however, is that it is not universal. There seems no reason to doubt that in tribal society individual morality is normally satisfied by conformity with the social code of the tribe and is conscious of no obligations outside it. If this is so, the conflict of standards between individual and social morality must be an historically conditioned and not a universal phenomenon. It can only appear when the individual, on moral grounds and as more than an isolated event, challenges the validity of the social code.

Ancient Greece provides – at least in the history of the Western

---

[1] Reinhold Niebuhr, *Moral Man and Immoral Society*, 1932, pp. 8-9.
[2] Ibid., pp. xxii-iii.

world – the first recorded major revolt of the individual against the moral code of society. It is associated with the name of Socrates, but the rise of the sophists and the decline of accepted religious ideas had earlier prepared the way for him. Like others later, he was unjustly condemned as a cause of the attack on religious orthodoxy, when he was merely a result. Along with the speculations of the sophists, the development of Greek scientific thought also played its part in undermining the foundations of Olympus. The result was to expose social customs to rational discussion, and out of this came the Socratic appeal to the individual conscience.

A further development followed from the decay of city states and the rise of universal empire. Stoic thought enlarged the ethical community to include all humanity, and replaced local tribal law with the idea of a universal Natural Law. The scientific conception of nature was extended to include the idea of uniformities in the ethical as well as the physical realm. These ethical norms were called Natural Laws, and they were regarded as consistent with, and capable of being discovered by, reason. The ethical content of Natural Law, incorporated in and expanded by way of the Roman *jus gentium* and Christianity, passed on to the medieval peoples without experiencing any further development until the early modern period. There then ensued a renewed wave of ethical discussion. The emergence of the modern State may have been the factor which led to a concentration of attention at this time on the rights of the individual, but it would be mistaken to suppose that this was essentially new, though the specific emphasis may have been. As Gierke wrote: 'A fugitive glance at Medieval Doctrine suffices to perceive how throughout it all ... runs the thought of the absolute and imperishable value of the Individual.'[1]

It is not difficult to identify the new ethical contributions of the Enlightenment. They can be picked out from our earlier pages. Slowly and hesitantly the principle of religious toleration came to be affirmed; torture, taken for granted from time immemorial as a necessary adjunct to civil and religious society, was discredited; war was no longer regarded as a necessary evil; the rule of law was asserted and arbitrary police powers condemned; slavery was denounced; utilitarianism proclaimed that the object of government was the greatest happiness of the greatest number. Such ideas – and the list could be extended – have become the commonly accepted

[1] Gierke, *Political Theories of the Middle Age*, trans. Maitland, 1913, pp. 81-2.

norms of Western civilization. They are the essential ingredients in the 'moral man' of whom Niebuhr speaks.

The social forces which are regarded as 'immoral' are also not difficult to place, for basically there is nothing new about them. They arise out of the survival or re-creation of earlier ethical conceptions. Some nations almost completely, as has already been suggested, and some sections in almost all nations, escaped the influence of the ethical revolution of the eighteenth century; and even where it seemed to have triumphed there has since been a partial withdrawal. The consequent conflict of ethical standards is, I suggest, the real source of what seems to Niebuhr to be a conflict between moral man and immoral society. It appears as such only because the broader ethical norms of the Enlightenment are those that are associated with the idea of an ethical standard applicable to all men; while the narrower morality is a new kind of tribalism, for which the social unity or State is an ethical end in itself, and which excludes from the obligations of ethics all who are outside it. In a sense, therefore, the Enlightenment is correctly identified as the source of the current conflict in ethical values and the consequent pessimism; for without it most of what seems to those still under its influence immoral in the behaviour patterns of the contemporary world would simply be taken for granted.

One solution to this conflict, of course, might be to abandon the ethics of the Enlightenment in toto, and this is what Nazi Germany did. But it is not really a solution, or at least it cannot stop at that, for the Enlightenment is all of a piece and cannot be accepted or rejected in parts. Along with its ethics we must be prepared to jettison its science, utilitarianism and the whole rationality of social life. This is what happened in Nazi Germany and for a time in Stalinist Russia, only the loss of science was concealed by the progress of technology. It is still too early to say that it may not be happening, more slowly and more insidiously, elsewhere.

XXIV

The Restoration of Moral and Political Theory

IT is difficult to deny that there has been an ethical recession from the standards of the Enlightenment in the course of the present century. A detailed analysis of the decline does not fall within the scope of this study, but one feature of it, which has already been singled out, may be regarded as particularly significant. It has been marked from the start by a tendency, which has become increasingly strong, to reject the processes of reason as a means of arriving at valid conclusions about man and society, whereas in both the ethical revolutions of the ancient and the modern world an essential feature was the attempt to set up ethical norms by the use of reason. Natural Law was an appeal to reason as something more permanent than, and ethically superior to, transient volition. As Gierke writes:

> If there is a binding external rule not simply for this or that will, but for the will in itself, this must be rooted in a spiritual faculty independent of the will. This faculty is reason. Hence law is not the common will that something shall be, but the common conviction that something is. Law, whether manifested directly in usage or declared by a social organ appointed for this purpose, is the conviction of a human society that in it there are external rules for the will, that is, limitations of freedom which are externally binding and by hypothesis enforceable.[1]

Some such assumption is a necessary condition of moral philosophy, and is implied in any rational political theory. Its rejection is intimately bound up with that decline of political theory which was described at the beginning of this book. In conclusion we must turn again to this problem, which seems to lie so near the heart of the contemporary crisis. Since this decline was obviously not intended or consciously calculated, an explicit and rational statement of the case against rational political theory, which indeed sounds self-contradictory, is difficult to find; and naturally it appears, if at all, at the end rather than the beginning of the process. The only one

[1] Gierke, *Development of Political Theory*, p. 329.

229

with which I am acquainted is in Mr T. D. Weldon's *The Vocabulary of Politics*, with a preface by Professor A. J. Ayer, and since this is a consistent, significant and influential statement of the case, it may fairly be taken as a basis for discussion.

Mr Weldon begins by repudiating Essentialism, which is the modern term for what used to be called Idealism, and, along with this, Marxism, the democratic stereotypes, and so-called scientific politics. It is not difficult to agree with him so far. But his criticism goes deeper. He objects to political philosophy as a whole, not merely because of the answers that political philosophers give but also because of the questions that they ask, on the ground that they are questions which are not capable of being answered. They represent, he says, attempts to find some basis of justification for the laws of a particular society outside the conditions of that society itself. This, he argues, is the great mistake. The belief that to answer questions of political right we have to discover some real, absolute or fundamental rights, of which legal rights are merely the expression, is the besetting illusion of political philosophers. Political laws, he says, do not come from outside. They are not natural laws to be discovered, but social rules that we make up for ourselves, just as we do the rules of cricket. This is clearly true of many of the rules of society, which evidently belong to the class of by-laws, such as not walking on the grass and not smoking in a railway compartment reserved for non-smokers. It is a matter of expediency which rule we choose, so long as it fits in with the other rules and we do choose one and stick to it.

It has been held that there are other rules, of a more fundamental nature, what we might call moral rules, which are not to the same extent a matter of choice. Mr Weldon denies this distinction. When we say that political rules are derived from moral rules, he translates this statement into: 'The codes of behaviour which influential minorities make for themselves tend to be enforced by law on majorities for whose use they may or may not be suitable.'[1] He does not suggest, of course, that we do not make moral judgments, or to use his term, appraisals. The mistake, according to him, lies in the supposition that such appraisals are based on any kind of objective standard. On the contrary, they are 'empirical judgments made by individuals'. If it is asked why political philosophers have been so unwilling to recognize this and have persisted in the search for

[1] *The Vocabulary of Politics*, 1953, p. 189.

something more fundamental, Mr Weldon's explanation is that the answer is to be found in the bogy called subjectivism, the fear that if we discard political ideologies and abandon the search for foundations we will be reduced to complete political scepticism, and all possibility of distinguishing between right and wrong will disappear. This is an unnecessary fear. It is enough, he suggests, that ordinary people do in fact make such judgments:

> They do not think that when they do so they are just reporting their personal preferences, and they produce reasons in support of their statements. Sometimes they even convince one another without the assistance of the Inquisition and the concentration camp. They manage to do this because they avoid the intellectualist error of pretending that there must be one test and only one test.[1]

I am not sure that political philosophers *have* always suggested that there is only a single test, or that this is necessarily an intellectualist error. At any rate, concludes Mr Weldon:

> The situation is not alarming. Each of us has his own tests, which are no doubt rough and crude, but they will serve their purpose, which is to check and confirm the conclusions of experts based on thorough research.[2]

Here we come to the constructive, positive part of his argument. The statement, he says, 'It was wicked to send people to Belsen or Buchenwald', 'is not the sort of statement which requires or admits of demonstration'.[3] He observes, to people with normal eyesight, observing in a good light, 'it is pointless to ask "How do you know that this pillar-box is red?" It seems to me equally pointless to ask "How do you know that it is wicked to torture human beings or animals?"'[4]

This statement comes so close to our initial problem that it demands further examination. First let us consider the matter of the pillar-box. Is it quite pointless to ask: 'How do you know it is red?' If the questioner happens to be colour-blind it is quite a reasonable question and it would be worth while explaining to him that, when he comes to the next traffic-lights, he would do well, even if he could not see the difference, to accept the fact that the lights were not all

[1] Ibid., pp. 150-1.   [2] Ibid., pp. 175-6.   [3] Ibid., p. 99.
[4] Ibid., p. 16.

of the same colour. This illustration may help us to realize that Mr Weldon has possibly set up an Aunt Sally to demolish. Perhaps it is pointless to ask 'How do I know that this pillar-box is red?'; it is not pointless to believe that we must act in some circumstances on the supposition that red is not the same colour as green, that not everybody is capable of seeing this difference, and that those who are not should be persuaded that there is a difference. This is a practical matter and the persuasion may take the form of appealing both to scientific investigation and to the general consensus of opinion.

When we come to Mr Weldon's other question – 'How do you know that it is wicked to torture human beings?' – we have a question which has no more than a grammatical similarity. If there is such a thing as moral colour-blindness, it is not susceptible of correction by scientific observation. Failing that, can we appeal to general opinion? In some countries, at the present time, there may be a general opinion that torture is wicked, but what is this more than one of Mr Weldon's social rules, perhaps inspired by a dominant minority? At other places and other times the opposite view may have prevailed. Indeed, there is no need to be so modest about this: as we know, it *has* prevailed, and still does, pretty extensively.

I do not mean merely that torture has been practised. As Mr Weldon rightly points out, following Hume, what *is* does not tell us what *ought* to be. But torture has also been justified on various grounds in the past, and the historical fact is that most people at most times have thought that in some circumstances it was a *good* thing. They have said that it is the only way of discovering the truth in a judicial process, that only by torture can enemies of the State be suppressed, that it is better to try to save the souls of heretics by torturing their bodies than to condemn them untortured to eternal damnation, that only by torture can false religions be stamped out, that it is the only safe way of dealing with witches, that it is necessary to education, and so on.

Those who have acquired a prejudice against torture may, as Mr Weldon suggests, endeavour to show, as the enemies of witch-burning and the reformers of the law did, that the arguments by which torture is justified are mistaken. But torturing other people is such a well-established habit of the human race that empirical observation must at least suggest the possibility that the normal appraisal is 'Torture is good', and that the arguments employed to justify it in particular cases are merely rationalizations to explain the selection of victims. In saying that there is nothing odd about the statement 'It is wicked to torture human beings', Mr Weldon is going in flat contradiction of the historical evidence. It is a very odd statement indeed, and one that could hardly have been made, except by a crank, before the seventeenth or eighteenth centuries. When he also says that the statement 'It was wicked to send people to Belsen' is not the sort of statement which requires demonstration, then, either he must believe that normal men will always make such an appraisal, which is obviously untrue, or secondly he is indifferent whether they do or not, which I somehow doubt, or thirdly he may say that personally he would like to demonstrate to other people that torture is wrong, but that unfortunately he knows that such a statement does not admit of demonstration. If people think torture is a good thing, as most of them certainly have done in the past, what can be done about it on Mr Weldon's philosophy? So far as I can see, nothing.

He may say, what can you do about it on any other philosophy? The answer is that, as we have seen, historically something *was* done about it. Clearly therefore something *can* be done. Torture went on being regarded as good and right throughout recorded history, until the seventeenth and eighteenth centuries. At that time there appeared the idea that it was a bad thing and simultaneously there was a marked decline in its actual infliction. This new development was associated with the ideas of the Enlightenment; and the reappearance subsequently of a favourable appraisal of torture, and its revival as a political institution, was accompanied by a rejection of these ideas. I hesitate to say more of them because according to Mr Weldon they are mere abstract theories or illusions. A small minority of the human race may say that torturing people is wrong, and the vast majority that it is right; and behind these opposed appraisals we cannot go. The impasse is complete. Yet seventeenth- and eighteenth-century thinkers tried to show that torture is wrong, and did in fact persuade at least some Western European societies of this, so successfully that Mr Weldon has apparently come to take it for granted. It is, of course, possible that the wrong people, by the wrong methods, managed to arrive by accident at the right answers. But on what ground can they even be said to be the right answers, for they have certainly been given to the wrong questions according to Mr Weldon? His view is that the questions raised by traditional political philosophy are merely 'confused formulations of purely empirical difficulties', and 'writers on political institutions and statesmen, not philosophers, are the proper people to deal with them'.[1]

It is not very helpful to be told that empirical difficulties should be dealt with empirically. Such difficulties are those that can be stated by a question beginning: How. There are plenty of political problems of this type and evidently the statesman or the political scientist is the person to answer them. The mistake lies in the supposition that all political questions are of this type. The questions of political philosophy are of a different kind. Before asking 'How can I cross this river?' I might ask 'Ought I to wish to cross it?' Surely this is a legitimate question. Certainly such questions *are* asked, and we cannot without self-stultification query whether we *ought* to ask them, for the query is itself a question of the same type. But if we ask such questions, it appears from Mr Weldon that we must expect no answers, or none that will be worth listening to. Empirical facts will give us none; the answers of the political philosophers of the past he rejects in toto; and he himself provides none to take their place – quite logically, since he holds that they are mistaken questions. His book is a declaration of the bankruptcy of political philosophy.

However, even Mr Weldon finds it difficult to resist the temptation to give some kind of positive indication of the way in which questions, which are inevitably asked, might be answered. In spite of his earlier statement that 'ought' cannot be derived from 'is', he now argues that by an intensive study of the facts we can reach sound appraisals. This is the basis of his view that political scientists and statesmen, not philosophers, are the proper people to deal with the problems that can legitimately be raised by political philosophy. What is wanted is not the discussion of theories but the discovery of facts. 'If we knew all the probable consequences of our acts', he writes, 'we should very seldom be in any doubt as to what we ought to do.'[2] This is what the utilitarians said, and it was not an unreasonable point of view in the eighteenth century, when a considerable measure of agreement had been reached among the thinkers of the Enlightenment as to the ends of society. Such agreement no longer prevails. Hitler wanted to achieve one set of consequences, I dare say that Mr Weldon would have liked to achieve rather a different set; and if we want to choose between their respective preferences there is no alternative but to enter on a discussion, in the course of

[1] *The Vocabulary of Politics*, p. 192.   [2] Ibid., p. 192.

which most of the questions of traditional political philosophy would arise. But Mr Weldon will not let us do this. He relegates the discussion to writers on political institutions and practical statesmen.

This is his last word; I have examined it in detail because it seems to me the clearest exposition of a common and influential contemporary view. Putting it in more dramatic language, it advises us to burn our books of political philosophy and entrust ourselves to our men of action, aided by their experts in political science. One objection to this advice is that obviously there is no point in discarding the ideologies of the political philosophers and leaving the choice of political objectives to statesmen and political scientists, if the latter are themselves under the influence, perhaps unconsciously or at second or third hand, of political philosophers, as in fact they always are. It is difficult to believe that there is anywhere in this world such a thing as a pure politician, unsullied by any taint of theory. The mind of the ordinary politician is littered with the glacial debris of half a dozen receding political philosophies. The author of *The Vocabulary of Politics* is himself not lacking in liberal ideas. He does not say where he got them, but I suspect they came from those very political philosophers whose completely erroneous conception of the nature of political problems he condemns so severely, and in particular from the theorists of the Enlightenment.

It may be thought that this justification for the decline of political theory, though it expresses pertinently and clearly the prevailing view, does not quite carry conviction; but the fact of the decline remains to be dealt with. If it is to be explained by some inherent misdirection in contemporary thinking about politics, the remedy might appear to be to work out, on abstract grounds, the proper way of thinking. This method has certain attractions. It can be used to justify practically any theory that appeals to us; because the conclusions we arrive at will be determined by the assumptions we start from, and we are not in much danger of starting from assumptions that do not appeal to us. Fortunately, however, we do not have to *invent* political theory; that was invented long ago. If there is a right way of considering its problems, I think we should be modest enough to believe that it might possibly be the way of all the greater political thinkers of the past; that is, if there is a way which so many, and such diverse, theorists have in common. I think there is. In the first place we have the simple, obvious fact that they all wrote with a practical purpose in mind. Their object was to influence actual political behaviour. They wrote to condemn or support existing institutions, to justify a political system or persuade their fellow citizens to change it, because they were concerned with the aims, the purposes of society. Even Machiavelli does not merely describe the way in which things are done, without also indicating the way in which, and to what ends, he thinks they *ought* to be done. At the opposite extreme, Plato's *Republic* may represent an ideal which the human race – perhaps happily – cannot attain, but in his mind it was no mere Cloud-cuckoo-land of fantasy.

Political theory in the past was essentially practical. The political theorist, in his way, was a party man, and party men themselves used not to be afraid to season their practice with the salt of theory. One of the striking differences between political discussion in, say, the eighteenth century and at the present day is that politicians have on the whole ceased to be interested in theoretical discussions. They are not altogether to be blamed for this, because the study of political theory, which was formerly the work of men intensely concerned with practical issues, has become instead an academic discipline, written in various esoteric jargons almost as though for the purpose of preventing it from being understood by those who, if they did understand it, might try to put it into practice. It has entered the high realm of scholarship, and, as Whitehead has pointed out, some modern forms of scholarship, at least, reproduce the limitations which dominated thought in the Hellenistic epoch. 'They canalize thought and observation', he says, 'within pre-determined limits, based upon inadequate metaphysical assumptions dogmatically assumed.'[1]

The view that the connection between political theory and practical politics is a condition of the survival of theory deserves a more elaborate discussion than it can be given here. But if it were to be accepted, then there is an important corollary to be noticed. The implication is that the issues with which political theory has been concerned in the past were not chosen arbitrarily, or as a result of some theoretical argument, and that theory was able to come to grips with the practical world because its discussions were determined by the actual conditions and problems of the day. For example, John Stuart Mill lived in an age when new social problems called for measures of State action which conflicted with established ideals of individual liberty; his thought derives its value from the

[1] A. N. Whitehead, *Adventures of Ideas*, 1933, p. 151.

fact that he devoted himself to the task of attempting to reconcile the two demands. Bentham's lifework was to establish a theoretical basis for the legislative and administrative reforms that were urgently needed in *his* day. Burke, faced in Great Britain, America, Ireland, France, with a challenge to the existing bases of political allegiance, attempted to provide an alternative to the new democratic principle of the sovereignty of the people. Rousseau, conscious of the moral collapse of divine-right monarchy, offered a new justification for political authority. Montesquieu, earlier, had seen the defects of absolutism, and established the case for the limitation of all power by law. Locke provided a political theory for a generation which wanted both to legitimize and restrict revolution. Hobbes and Spinoza, in an age of civil wars, maintained that sovereignty meant all or nothing. And so we might continue, till we reached in the end – or rather the beginning – Plato and Aristotle, attempting to prescribe remedies for the diseases of the city state.

If political theory *has* become generally disengaged from practice, and if this disengagement is one cause of its decline, it will be worth while asking why it has happened. The bias of the academic approach away from action is not a new thing, and it can hardly provide an adequate explanation by itself. An answer which goes a little deeper can be found, I think, again by a comparison with traditional political thought. The object of this was to arrive at the judgment that one form of political activity was better than another. Academic impartiality between what it believed to be good and bad it neither sought nor attained. Because its aim was to influence action, it had to consider the forces that move men, and these, as Hume knew, are not the products of abstract analysis but of the passions. And since not all passions could be regarded as conducive to a good end, it had to be the passions under the guidance of ethical motivation. In other words, politics was essentially a branch of morals or ethics. The conclusion might be drawn that the decline of political theory is a necessary result of the decline of moral philosophy. This merely pushes our problem one stage further back; but it is easier to see a possible explanation of the decline if it is true that the modern mind has fallen under the influence of two modes of thought which have had a fatal effect on its ethical content. These are history and science.

It may be thought at first sight that if this is true it is fatal to the whole argument of this book; for here is surely the influence of the Enlightenment, of which historical and scientific empiricism was the keynote. Such a view would be a complete misunderstanding, for there is another factor, which has been omitted in more recent thought, but which was an essential one in the Enlightenment, and that was the autonomy and primacy of ethics. The Enlightenment may sometimes have mistakenly derived its history and its science from its ethical ideas; at least it never made the mistake of trying to derive its ethics from its history and science. This is what its successors have done.

The historian naturally sees all ideas and ways of behaviour as historically conditioned and transient. Within itself, history has no standard of value but success, and no measure of success but the attainment of power, or survival for a little longer than rival individuals or institutions have survived. By itself, in political theory, history can produce only the crudest Machiavellianism. If all historians are not little Machiavellis, it is only because they take their political ideals from some other source and carry them into their history, which is, fortunately, almost unavoidable. It might sometimes be a good thing if they were a little more conscious of the ideals they are in fact applying and inculcating through their histories. This is a problem which cannot be discussed here. It is sufficient to say that at least there is a tendency among modern historians to regard the passing of ethical judgments as an illegitimate process against which historical discipline should be a safeguard. In so far as it is a successful safeguard it is also, indirectly, one against thinking about the problems of ethical and political theory at all.

The influence of historical thought did not stop at this. History acquires more positive, and more dangerous implications, when it is made into a philosophy of history. This was particularly the achievement of Hegel and Marx. The effect of both Hegelianism and Marxism was to associate ethics with the historical process – by which I do not mean the grand pattern of the universe, which I suspect was not revealed as a whole to either of them, but the little corner of the fabric which came under their immediate notice, the few strands which they took for the pattern of the whole. Unfortunately, it is possible that the universe is not devised like wallpaper; and if there is a pattern it may be constructed on a larger scale than could be encompassed in the gaze of a nineteenth-century prophet. Nor were they content merely to be prophets. Whether Hegel and Marx themselves intended this result or not, in those who followed them there was an uneasy slip from saying, 'This is what will be', into saying, 'This is what ought to be.' The result was to base moral judgments on temporary and limited historical phenomena. Hegelian and Marxist politics, therefore, have had the ultimate effect of setting up a politics devoid of ethical foundations. In this way they played an important part in creating a breach between modern political practice and the traditions of political thinking in the West.

The influence of history over the modern mind is, however, challenged by that of science. Particularly in the shape of mathematics and psychology, science has influenced political thinking from the beginning; though it is only in recent times that a general belief has grown up in the possibility and desirability of studying politics by the methods that have achieved such remarkable results in the natural sciences. The object of science is to show how things happen, and why, in the nexus of cause and effect, they *do* happen. There is no reason why political phenomena, as well as any other phenomena, should not be treated in this way, so long as we do not mistake the result for political theory and expect it to answer questions which in the nature of things it cannot answer. What I mean is simply that it is not the function of science to pass ethical judgments. The political theorist, on the other hand, is essentially concerned with the discussion of what ought to be. His judgments are at bottom value judgments. The kind of opinion he has to offer in the last resort is that one kind of political action is ethically preferable to another, not merely that it is more efficient, whatever that may mean; and we have seen enough in our day to know that the difference between political systems is not merely a difference between relative degrees of efficiency.

In case I am thought to be unjust to the political scientist, let me give what seems a fair description of the way in which he envisages his task. It is fallacious, says one writer, to suggest that the only way of understanding politics is to participate in it: we do not teach the principles of geometry by a manual training course in carpentry. Political science is a body of knowledge, which must be taught and learned like any other body of knowledge. This is what Hobbes held – that 'the skill of making, and maintaining commonwealths, consisteth in certain rules, as doth arithmetic and geometry; not, as tennis-play, on practice only'.[1] The political scientist, in so far as he wishes to remain a scientist, is limited to the study of techniques. A good deal of what is called political science, I must confess, seems

[1] *Leviathan*, Part II, ch. xx.

to me a device, invented by academic persons, for avoiding that
dangerous subject politics, without achieving science. Taking it at
the highest valuation, political science can give us guidance of
great importance in achieving the objects we want to achieve; it
cannot help us to decide what those objects should be, or even what
they are. And to believe that we are all agreed on them and therefore
do not need to discuss them is surely, in the light of contemporary
events, the wildest utopianism. In the last resort science, like history,
leaves us, as Ortega y Gasset put it, to drift:[1] we have a magnificent
technical equipment for going somewhere, without anywhere to go.
This is the meaning of political thought based on the modes of
inquiry of science and history and alienated from ethics.

The image of political life which emerges from the prevailing
tendencies in political thought is not a pleasing one. The State has
been compared to a ship in the sea of politics, with no port of embar-
kation or destination inscribed on its papers, manned by a pressed
crew, whose whole endeavour is devoted to the task of keeping the
vessel afloat in uncharted waters, with little to help them save their
own traditional seamanship and the records of earlier captains and
crews who have for all time tossed on the seas in the same endless,
meaningless motion. A depressing picture, I think, perhaps dreamed
up by some remote philosopher who has seen the ships scudding by
from the lantern-room of a dead lighthouse, dead because he has
carefully extinguished the light.

Luckily we need not take the picture too seriously: it is only an
analogy, and analogies are the camouflage of loose thinking. The
sea is, of course, the sea of politics, and the ship is the State, the
community as a political organization. But the bond that holds the
State together, the life it lives, is also politics. And how is the ship
distinguishable from the crew? The State is no mere wooden artifact
inhabited by men; it *is* men as political animals. And sea, ship and
crew move on together, for they are the same. How can we envisage
outselves as inhabiting the ship of State in the sea of politics when the
ship is ourselves and the element it moves in our own political being,
and *we* rouse the storms and *we* still the waters?

One thing is missing from the picture. It is missing from contemporary politics also. This, as I have said, is the idea that the ship is
going anywhere. A sense of direction is lacking, a feeling of purpose.
That, I think, is what the decay of political theory means in simple

[1] Ortega y Gasset, *The Revolt of the Masses*, p. 47.

terms. Does it matter? If we were all of us, all our time, porkers not even from the sty of Epicurus, perhaps it would not: our purpose would be set by something outside ourselves, and it would be just as well that it should not be revealed to us in disturbing detail. Such, of course, may be the facts of the case; but rightly or wrongly the human mind demands something more than living from trough to snout. In the absence of a more or less rational theory to justify its sense of political obligation and the rightful powers of government, it will fall victim to an irrational one. If it cannot have, say, Locke on *Toleration*, it will have, say, Hitler on *Mein Kampf*. That is what the decline of political theory means in practice.

The analysis I have made is perhaps moderately pessimistic; but it is not intended to lead to the conclusion that in political thinking we have reached the terminus, the end of the line. The reasons that I have given for its decline are in themselves encouraging, since there are signs that they may be only temporary aberrations. Historians are in revolt against philosophies of history: ethics is sapping the lack of morals of professors of history. Hegelian politics is already dead. Marxist politics is increasingly revealed as a dialectical apologia for the pursuit of power for its own sake. The inadequacy, in relation to the broader issues of political society, of the scientific study of administrative methods, constitutional devices, electoral statistics and the like – I hope it will not be thought that within their own field I am attempting to deny the value of the techniques of political science – is becoming apparent.

For a century and a half the Western democracies have been living on the achievements of the Enlightenment, and on the stock of basic political ideas that were last restated towards the end of the eighteenth century. That is a long time. The nineteenth century did pretty well on them but provided no major restatement for its successors. The gap thus formed between political facts and ideas has steadily widened. It has taken a long time for the results to become evident; but now that we have seen what politics devoid of moral and political theory means, it is possible that something may be done about it. After a generation's experience of drifting directionless on a stormy sea the need of recovering a sense of direction, and therefore control, is beginning to be felt. And if political theory revives, if the idea of purpose is reintroduced into political thinking, we may take up again the tradition of Western political thought, and in doing so resume that 'continuous transformation of morals into politics, which still remains politics', in which, according to Croce, lies 'the real ethical progress of mankind'.

It is possible to return now to the problem with which this inquiry began, that of the increasing re-brutalization of contemporary life, particularly, though by no means exclusively, manifested in its politics. In international relations, it may be said, an assertion of moral standards that the twentieth century has deserted is necessary not only for the survival of civilized life but for the survival of human life itself. This is the practical issue, and the first and simplest solution is obviously inadequate. Regimes which violently conflict with the ethical standards we have inherited can be, and have been, resisted and overthrown by force; but recent history shows that force by itself is not enough. Those who begin by opposing mere force to force, are liable to end by finding themselves copying the methods of their enemies.

It is evident, secondly, that an appeal to the conscience of the individual is also not an adequate solution, for this evidently varies from individual to individual and even more from society to society. It is a mistake to suppose that the followers of Hitler, like those of Stalin, had — or have — no moral principles. In a sense they had more than their enemies, for they were prepared to kill and torture millions to uphold them. Similarly, the dropping of two atomic bombs on Japan, and in fact all the bombing of civilian populations, might be presented as a profoundly moral decision. It was one of which Western Europe in the eighteenth century would hardly have been capable. The point is not that some individuals or societies are moral and others are not, but that different ones have different moral principles, and the problem is to choose between them.

Thirdly, the easiest solution is to refuse to see that there is a problem at all. There are traditional standards, it may be said, which were good enough for our fathers and are all the stronger for having religious convictions behind them: all we need to do is to return to them. It would be foolish to disregard the sanction that religion can add to a social ethic. The trouble is that any system that depends on the unquestioned acceptance of the decrees of a superhuman authority — apart from objections on philosophical grounds — can only function successfully so long as the authority does in fact remain unquestioned. Moreover, it has been shown that it is remarkably easy to replace one absolute authority by another, and the habit of accepting ethical standards because they are laid down by authority is easily transferred. An examination of the recent history of, say, Italy, Spain, Germany and Russia, countries in which religious authority appeared to be particularly strong, must lead to some doubts whether the religious sanction is an adequate barrier against the rise of ideologies which promote, justify and institutionalize systems of terror and torture. A further difficulty is that traditional systems of ethics are apt to include features which were perhaps appropriate to earlier social situations, but which in a new situation may have lost their ethical content and have sometimes even become repulsive to contemporary morality.

A fourth alternative, which has already been mentioned, is the appeal to science. There are intimate connections between the rise of science and moral progress. The scientific and empirical spirit of the seventeenth and eighteenth centuries provided an essential element in the ethical achievements of enlightened thought. One might have supposed that the further progress of the scientific outlook, and in particular its application in the field of social and political life, would have promoted, for example, a progressive decline in irrational cruelties. This has not proved so, and the reason, as has been suggested above, is that science by itself is a form of knowledge, not a stimulus to action. It can help us to adapt the means we employ to the ends we wish to achieve, it cannot choose those ends for us. This is why the great growth in scientific knowledge has proved no barrier to the decay of ethical thought. Indeed, the social sciences, as they have grown in stature, have endeavoured to assimilate the ethical indifference of the physical sciences.

This series of negative answers seems to leave us with only one recourse. The effective stimulus to social morality, I suggest, can only come directly from developments of the ethical judgment, such as took place in the Enlightenment of the eighteenth century. Fifth-century Greece witnessed a comparable wave of ethical thought, which continued in some respects up to the first century of the Christian era. In both these ages the process was set off by a great increase of interest in the problems of ethics. Correspondingly, the decline in standards in recent times was preceded and accompanied by a decline in the discussion of public and political behaviour in ethical terms.

In the absence of rational and ethical discussion of the ends of society, political theory has tended to turn into either the analysis of mere power relations, with no attempt at judgment on them, or else the repetition of shibboleths, words like 'peace' and 'democracy' which may mean anything or nothing, but which because of their former ethical connotation can be employed as substitutes for the discussion of practical ethical issues. They have become at best mere classificatory symbols like the old school tie, which can be used alike by those who are and by those who are not entitled to them. Their hollowness is the measure of the problem before us.

The apparent inadequacy of other solutions, however, does not mean that we are thrown back on a simple recapitulation of the ideas of the Enlightenment. It would be a mistake to suppose that they would necessarily mean to us what they did to their creators. The principles of the Enlightenment, to which we now cling largely out of sheer force of habit when we condemn the things in the contemporary world that we generally do condemn, may or may not be capable of resuscitation in the form in which they were originally stated. Codes of moral behaviour and ideals are necessarily related to circumstances; they may become irrelevant not only because of moral progress or regression, but also as a result of changes in the facts to which they are related. The Enlightenment can only be a starting-point. It represents the achievements of the last stage of vigorous ethical discussion in the history of Western civilization; and it is not difficult to see that we can profitably take up the argument where it was dropped then. Though we may hope to reach a minimum of ethical agreement, such as is needed to restore some sense of purpose to civilization and has always been necessary for the survival of a community, the actual discussion is more important than arriving at particular conclusions, which will, as always, have their limitations and their transient features. A genuine and widespread discussion of the problems of society and government, considered as moral issues, has the virtue that whatever conclusions are reached will not be arbitrary ones, created to fit the terms of an hypothesis: they will be framed by positive conditions and dictated by the needs of the age. The twentieth century is belatedly becoming aware that something is missing, though it hardly as yet knows what that is. The more 'advanced' the country, the more this gap is felt. It is the price that is paid for the creation of a technological society, which devotes endless energy to the problem of how to do things, but little thought to whether they are worth doing. Serious ethical and political discussion was the first victim; there are signs, where the devotion to technology has reached its height, that science may be the next. This is more or less speculative, but the results of the decline of moral and political theory have been patent in the world at large. They have naturally been most pronounced in countries where the ethical influence of the Enlightenment was most superficial, but it would be simple self-deceit to suppose that they are confined to them. Even if we condemn, for example, the monstrous cruelties of the contemporary world, the conflict between the behaviour which we condemn, and the moral consciousness which leads us to condemn it, is an unequal struggle so long as, while the behaviour is concrete enough, the moral consciousness remains merely an historical memory, a repetition of clichés with no active thought behind it. The object of this study has been to raise questions rather than to provide answers. But the thing we perhaps most need to learn is the importance of asking these questions. We have in-herited everything else from the Enlightenment and only forgotten the thing that was essential.

INDEX

INDEX

Rousseau (*cont.*)
  Contrat social, 25, 152-3, 168
  Discours sur l'origine de l'inégalité, 25, 150, 152-3, 168
  Discours sur les Sciences et les Arts, 149
  Economie politique, 156
  Emile, 154, 156-7
  Lettre à d'Alembert, 153-4
  Lettre sur la Providence, 154
  Nouvelle Héloïse, 154-6, 168
  Profession de foi d'un vicaire savoyard, 157
  Rêveries d'un promeneur solitaire, 159
Russell, Bertrand, 24
Rutherford, Thomas, 172

SADE, MARQUIS DE, 13
Sainte-Beuve, 146
Saint-Pierre, 127-8, 130
scepticism, 47-55, 64, 134-7
Schliermacher, 213
Schopenhauer, 217-19
sensational psychology, 68-72, 85-6, 113-17
separation of powers, 97, 103, 213
Shaftesbury, 48, 77-8, 82-3, 85-6, 141, 145, 155
  A letter concerning Enthusiasm, 77
Shakespeare, 31, 154
Sieyes, 189, 194, 203, 208, 211
  Qu'est-ce que le Tiers Etat, 211
Simon, Richard, 52-4
  Histoire critique du vieux testament, 54
Sirven, 124
slavery, 14, 131, 152
Smith, Adam, 87, 132, 173, 215
  Theory of Moral Sentiments, 87
  Wealth of Nations, 132
Smith, John, 55
Socinius, Socinians, 54-5, 58
Socrates, 227
Sorel, A., 188
sovereignty, 90-1, 97-8, 162-3, 170-1, 178, 189-94, 202-3, 209-11, 224
Spallanzani, 139
Spengler, 218
Spinoza, 52-4, 57, 133, 140, 237

Stalin, 183, 242
Stephen, Leslie, 81, 86
Stillingfleet, *Letter to a Deist*, 60
Strachey, Lytton, 159
Suarez, 91
Swift, Jonathan, 50, 79
Swinburne, 218

TAINE, *L'ancien régime*, 7, 182
Talmon, J. L., *Origins of Totalitarian Democracy*, 7, 182-5
Toland, John, *Christianity not Mysterious*, 62-3
toleration, 16-17, 57-60, 214, 225, 227
Tolstoy, 218
torture, 16, 231-3
totalitarianism, 182-5, 192-3, 223
Toussaint, 126
Toynbee, Arnold, 26, 218
Troeltsch, 221
Turgot, 183

UTILITARIANISM, utilitarians, 73, 86, 88-9, 118, 126-32, 165, 170, 174-9, 225, 234

VATTEL, 163, 200
Verlaine, 218
Vesalius, *De Humani Corporis Fabrica*, 37
Vico, 133
Vindiciae contra tyrannos, 91
Voltaire, 66, 79, 83-5, 109-11, 115-16, 119-26, 128, 130-1, 139-40, 144, 154-5, 157-9, 163-4, 170, 183-4, 215, 225
  Candide, 83-4, 121
  Charles XII, 109
  Dictionnaire philosophique, 85, 121
  Essai sur les moeurs, 110, 121
  Lettres philosophiques, 84, 119
  Le Mondain, 131
  Œdipe, 119
  Poème sur la Loi naturelle, 84

WARENS, MME DE, 147-8
Wassermann, 218